POSSESSIONS

Judith Richardson

POSSESSIONS

THE HISTORY AND USES OF HAUNTING
IN THE HUDSON VALLEY

HARVARD UNIVERSITY PRESS

Cambridge, Massachusetts, and London, England

2003

Library of Congress Cataloging-in-Publication Data
Richardson, Judith.
Possessions : the history and uses of haunting in the Hudson Valley / Judith
Richardson.
  p. cm.
Includes index.
ISBN 0-674-01161-9 (alk. paper)
  1. Ghosts–Hudson River Valley (N.Y. and N.J.) 2. Haunted places–Hudson
River Valley (N.Y. and N.J.) 3. Ghosts in literature. 4. Hudson River Valley (N.Y.
and N.J.)–Social life and customs. I. Title.
BF1472.U6R54 2003
133.1'09747'7–dc21   2003049950

TO THE RICHARDSONS AND THE JONESES

ACKNOWLEDGMENTS

Along the winding road to completing this project, I have accrued a number of debts. The book has benefited immeasurably from the interest and guidance of Lawrence Buell, who kept it from careening out of control, as I'm sure he felt it might on more than one occasion. I am grateful to Werner Sollors for his enthusiasm and encouragement throughout the project. I also wish to thank David Hall, Alan Taylor, and Wayne Franklin for their thoughtful readings of the manuscript, and Nina Cannizzaro, Katrina Olds, Eva Sheppard-Wolf, and Woden Teachout support and distractions. This project owes a debt as well to the late Alan Heimert, and to Elaine Forman Crane and Joyce Rowe for lessons in interdisciplinarity and votes of confidence.

Much of the research for this book went on at a local level, and I am grateful to staff and volunteers at archives, historical societies, and libraries up and down the Hudson and elsewhere in New York; in particular, I would like to thank those at the Greene County Historical Society, the Historical Society of Rockland County, the Westchester County Historical Society, and the New York State Historical Association Library, who sometimes had to dig pretty deep to help me find what I needed. Materials quoted from the Louis C. Jones Folklore Archives are reproduced, with thanks, courtesy of the New York State Historical Association Library, Cooperstown, New York. Also deserving credit here are the "local folk" of my own corner of the Hudson Valley, especially the girls of Birch Drive, who continue to share an unhealthy interest in ghostly things.

My parents, Ann and Roger, and siblings Susan, Ruth, Sarah, Roger, and Matthew can never be properly thanked. They have not only served as willing, unpaid research assistants but also, and more importantly, have sustained me over all my years with their humor and love. About Gavin

Jones—I can only say that he is my hero, reading countless parts of the manuscript countless times (without once sugarcoating his response), and looking after me in so many other ways. Finally, thanks to Eli Jones, who arrived just as this book was in its final throes, and who gave me other things to think about.

CONTENTS

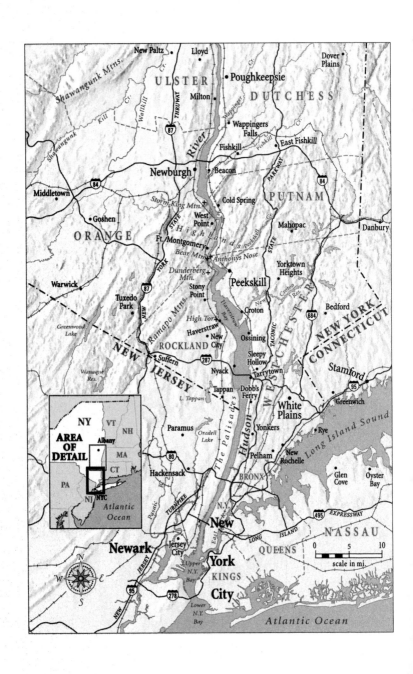

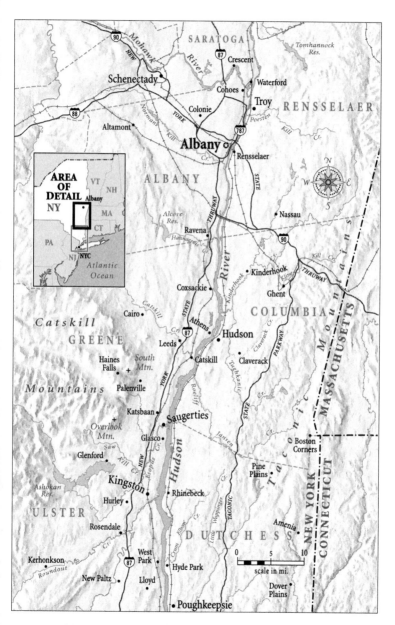

Map of the Hudson Valley, by David Deis, Dreamline Cartography, 2002.

he United States should be the country of the world least hospitable to ghosts, writes the landscape scholar Yi Fu Tuan: "It does not believe in the sanctity of the past. . . . The nation has its face to the future."[1] Nonetheless, Tuan tells us, ghosts can be found here—if we turn off the highways into the "backwoods" of Kentucky or Tennessee, to places where long-secluded populations retain old traditions. Really, though, we might look just about anywhere. As writers from Cotton Mather to Toni Morrison testify, American landscapes and imaginations have always been profusely haunted. And these hauntings are by no means limited to "isolated hollows"; in defiance of conventional wisdom, they often appear in places where social change threatens to obliterate any sense of historical continuity. One of the nation's most haunted regions, in fact, is physically and culturally linked to what is arguably the most cosmopolitan and diverse of American cities.

Over at least the last two centuries, the Hudson River Valley between Manhattan and Albany has developed a reputation as an uncommonly haunted place. Washington Irving described this area as abounding "with local tales, haunted spots, and twilight superstitions." Henry James, disoriented by the overwhelming newness of most things in *The American Scene* (1907), sensed in this region an "iridescence," a "shimmer of association [that] refuses to be reduced to terms; some sense of legend, of aboriginal mystery, with a still earlier past for its dim background." Throughout the nineteenth and twentieth centuries, guidebooks, travelogues, histories, and popular accounts were rife with claims of exceptional ghostliness, claims like that advanced by historian Maud Wilder Goodwin in 1919: the Hudson is "endowed [with] more of the supernatural . . . than haunts any other waterway in America." This reputation endures to the present day. According to the 1995 *Atlas of the Mysterious in North America,* "This area north of New York City has been famous for years for its breathtaking scenery and its spooky stories and sightings."[2]

Such claims are by no means hollow assertions. Underlying the Hudson Valley's reputation as a place given to hauntedness are hosts of individual hauntings recounted in literary offerings, newspapers, local histories, and folklore. There are ghosts of Indians and Dutchmen, ghosts of Revolutionary War soldiers and spies, ghosts of presidents, slaves, priests, and laborers. There are neighborhood ghosts and family ghosts, and ghosts whose identities are unknown. There are haunted cemeteries, houses, mountains, bridges, and factories. There are Spook Rocks, Spook Hollows, and Spook Fields. There are places haunted by famous ghosts; there are numerous places like the "Haunted Brook" in Westchester, which according to one late-nineteenth-century annalist "bore so bad a reputation for spirits that it was carefully avoided after dark by neighboring inhabitants."[3]

Why should this region, historically a place of rapid change and development, be so haunted? The answer lies in the fact that ghosts, those apparently insubstantial emanations from the past, are produced by the cultural and social life of the communities in which they appear. Ghosts operate as a particular, and peculiar, kind of social memory, an alternate form of history-making in which things usually forgotten, discarded, or repressed become foregrounded, whether as items of fear, regret, explanation, or desire. Always the subject of tremendous popular interest, hauntings demand deeper investigation because of what they reveal about how senses of the past and of place are apprehended and created, what they suggest about the marginal and invisible things that, for many recent scholars, texture and define identity, politics, and social life.[4]

Indeed, as scholarly attention has turned to the constructed quality of history and memory, ghosts have enjoyed a renaissance in recent years. Kathleen Brogan's *Cultural Haunting: Ghosts and Ethnicity in Recent American Literature* (1998) explores how ghosts feature in late-twentieth-century American writing about race and ethnicity. Renée Bergland's *The National Uncanny: Indian Ghosts and American Subjects* (2000) tackles the curiously understudied proliferation of Native American hauntings in American literature and culture. And Avery Gordon's far-ranging *Ghostly Matters: Haunting and the Sociological Imagination* (1997) pursues a sociology animated by the recognition that things apparently absent may be "seething presences."[5] Whereas earlier studies of ghosts in literature focused on psychological or aesthetic implications, these recent works share an emphasis on the social, historical, and political implications of haunting. Tracing how recent writers use the supernatural "to examine the troubled transmission of immigrant, slave, or native cultures," Brogan argues that hauntings illuminate "the hidden passageways not only of the individual psyche but also of a people's historical consciousness."[6] Avery Gordon writes, "If we want to study social life well . . . we must learn how to identify hauntings and reckon with ghosts."[7]

Although these studies begin to approach the real-life implications of haunting as social memory, and of ghosts as social artifacts and tools, their findings still tend to hover in rarified literary and theoretical spheres. They connect ghosts to issues of broad social significance—nationhood, ethnicity, gender. But they rarely touch ground.[8] By contrast, this book explores how hauntings rise from and operate in particular, everyday worlds; it builds arguments, quite literally, from the ground up, cordoning off a territory and a stretch of time, and examining hauntings as they work *in place*.

Possessions concentrates geographically on a rough oblong of land, approximately one hundred and fifty miles north to south, encompassing the New York counties bordering the Hudson River between New York City and Albany, bounded by New England states on the east, and generally keeping within twenty-five miles of the river on the west.[9] Chronologically, the study covers ground from the early nineteenth century to the late twentieth, with concentrations on the 1810s and 1820s, the turn of the century, and the 1930s and 1940s. These focal points reflect patterns dictated by the available material and represent moments in which hauntings seem most prolific or potent—the literary discovery of regional hauntedness in the early national period, a Gilded Age outpouring of regional writings and local histories, and the apotheosis of regional haunting in the mid-twentieth century, a period when hauntings intersected with conservation and preservation movements. Not surprisingly, my primary concern is with stories of ghosts attached to locations in the region. But a sense of hauntedness is not necessarily reliant on actual apparitions. I also investigate a variety of "ghostless" hauntings—simple claims of ghostliness, or assertions of eerie imaginative and emotional connection to the past at specific sites. I do not mean to use *haunting* simply as a synonym for social or cultural memory, although I certainly intend a connection between them.

Within these boundaries, I hunt for hauntings wherever and however they appear. Some of this pursuit takes place in the broad daylight of recognized literary sources, such as Washington Irving's stories from the early nineteenth century and Maxwell Anderson's 1937 play, *High Tor.* But I also chase down ghosts in less brightly lit corners of cultural production, resurrecting a vibrant yet largely unstudied regional corpus of guidebooks, travelogues, local and county histories, personal reminiscences, and collections of legends.[10] Digging even deeper, I unearth more ephemeral local stories from newspaper articles, folklore collections, letters, and manuscripts housed in local and state archives. To explore the diversity within Hudson Valley hauntings, I examine stories written by Anglo-American authors for regional, national, or even international audiences while also working to trace less broadcast instances and minority narratives told by racial and ethnic groups, immigrants, workers, and a more esoteric category of regional inhabitants for whom it is difficult to find a better term than "locals."

With this accumulation of sources, the book explores why, how, and to what ends the Hudson Valley has been haunted. It investigates how hauntings intersect with cultural history, public memory, economics, and land issues. The haunting of the Hudson Valley is by no means an anomalous eruption of vestigial superstition or superfluous tradition, but instead is intimately tied to the growth of the region. The area's hauntings emanate from social and historical tensions created by a rapid pace of development and obsolescence; they are related to social, cultural, political, and physical layerings that the restlessness of history bestows on the region, and are driven in part by ambivalent relationships between region and metropolis (and, by extension, the world beyond). Historian Raymond O'Brien argues in *American Sublime* that there are no outsiders in this region; one might as soon argue there are no insiders, or rather, that the question of whose place this is has always been unsettled.[11] In this sense, the Hudson Valley demonstrates what may be a particularly American form of haunting—one that draws on wide bases of culture and psychology, but is fundamentally predicated on social and historical discontinuities that imbue the past with a sense of mystery and strange possibility. Moreover, even as they seem to draw power from the past, the hauntings of the Hudson Valley are very much products of present need and desire. Varied and ambivalent, hauntings represent problems, foregrounded in this region, regarding possession and dispossession, rootedness and restlessness.

To draw out the relationship between a seemingly backward-looking hauntedness and the sustained progress of regional change in the Hudson Valley, the book pursues three overlapping areas of inquiry. The first two chapters are concerned primarily with understanding why hauntings congregate here, Chapter 1 teasing out a series of geographical, historical, and cultural influences, Chapter 2 focusing on the exemplary and influential case of Washington Irving, whose stylistics of vagueness both articulated regional instability and primed the ground for further haunting. Chapters 3 and 4 dive into the broader body of writing and folklore to see who and what haunt regional stories, examining storytellers and contexts as well as ghosts. Chapter 3 traces the career of a single local ghost as she evolves over two centuries of retellings, and highlights how ghostliness—a peculiarly malleable phenomenon—responds to shifting social contexts and concerns. Chapter 4 sifts through narratives of haunting from the late nineteenth and early twentieth centuries to uncover how preoccupations with Indian, Dutch, Revolutionary, and worker ghosts took shape from contemporary battles over local character. Ghosts may carry protests; they may also be used to legitimize specific territorial claims. And they can have material effects on the landscape. A case study of Maxwell Anderson's *High Tor*—a 1937 play about a haunted mountain in Rockland County, which anchored a conservation effort at this site—the fifth and final chapter investigates how and when hauntings have been successfully used as social and political tools, while also exposing an underlying cultural politics of possession in which very different ideas of the regional past contend for recognition and territory. There is substance in these shadows.

From beginning to end, *Possessions* is driven by questions of locality; it explores how haunting relates to the construction of localness in a region where social and historical connections seem particularly fragile. Yet this pursuit has implications beyond what Alan Taylor characterizes as the "relentlessly local."[12] Paradoxically, the broader significance of the project derives in part from its narrow focus. "To be sure," writes Raymond O'Brien, the Hudson "has its own history, patterns, and character; but there is absolutely nothing parochial about this river."[13] The site of key battles in the Revolutionary War, this stretch of territory is also linked to early American cultural emergence through such figures as Washington Irving, James Fenimore Cooper, Herman Melville, and the painters of the Hudson River School. It has been home to Roosevelts and Rockefellers and has been visited by millions of tourists from the United States and abroad. It has also been home to Native American tribes, Dutch farmers, African slaves, and Italian laborers. An area of enduring stature and importance in national historical consciousness and cultural iconography, the Hudson Valley also represents in microcosm conditions and problems—of territorial possession, of cultural conflict, of community formation—that have affected the country as a whole. Local hauntings transcend regional limits by signifying pervasive dilemmas of inclusion and marginalization, while also exposing instabilities at the foundation of social and historical understandings. With all their indeterminacy, ghosts have an unsettling capacity to switch sides, blur lines, and change meaning.

Possessions is about haunting, and about the history and culture of a particular region. But along the way it is also about historical consciousness, and about ethnic, class, and rural-urban tensions. It is about the ways in which people read and imagine, and how internationally relevant cultures and aesthetics infuse everyday life and landscapes—how narratives rise from and affect places. It is about visions of the past in a region that tends consistently toward change and discontinuity. And it is about belonging and possessing—issues that perennially trouble American minds.

> What a time of intense delight was that first sail
> through the Highlands! I sat on the deck as we
> slowly tided along at the foot of those stern
> mountains, and gazed with wonder and admira-
> tion at cliffs impending far above me. . . . And
> then how solemn and thrilling the scene as we
> anchored at night at the foot of these moun-
> tains, clothed with overhanging forests; and ev-
> erything grew dark and mysterious.
>
> —Washington Irving, unfinished article, 1851

1

"HOW COMES THE HUDSON TO THIS UNIQUE HERITAGE?"

*C*harles Gilbert Hine, an insurance magazine editor from Newark, New Jersey, who in the early twentieth century wrote a series of books on travels in the New York area, was by his own account a largely rational man, "not much given to see-ing things at night." Nonetheless, in writing of an extended walk he took down the west side of the Hudson River in 1906, Hine admits that he experienced some moments of uncertainty. As darkness overtook him in Ulster County between Katsbaan and Saugerties, he discovered that he was having trouble keeping his mind clear of strange apprehensions. "Even he who is not in all things too superstitious," he explains, "can hardly help peering curiously into the dark places as he pushes through the shades of night along a strange and quiet country road." The situation was exacerbated, Hine realizes, by "certain lines of reading indulged in while preparing for this trip and certain conversations held along the way," which caused his pulse to quicken "once or twice at some strange rustle in the nearby bushes."[1] The truth was that C. G. Hine, like thousands of others, had come to the Hudson Valley expecting to see a ghost or two.

"How comes the Hudson to this unique heritage of myth, ghosts, goblins and other lore?" asks Paul Wilstach in his 1933 historical guidebook *Hudson River Landings*. It was a question that elicited no small amount of speculation in the nineteenth and twentieth centuries. Perhaps the most common explanation—that to which Wilstach defers—was articulated by Maud Wilder Goodwin in *Dutch and English on the Hudson* (1919):

> Does the explanation perhaps lie in the fact that the Dutch colonists, coming from a small country situated on a level plain where the landscape was open as far as the eye could see, and left no room for mystery, were suddenly transplanted to a region shut in between overhanging cliffs where lightning flashed and thunder rolled from mountain wall to mountain wall, where thick forests obscured the view, and strange aboriginal savages hid in the underbrush? Was it not the sense of wonder springing from this change in their accustomed surroundings that peopled the dim depths of the *hinterland* with shapes of elf and goblin, of demons and superhuman presences?[2]

A synopsis of prevailing opinion on the matter, one widely repeated in the twentieth century by those who sought to understand the Hudson's "unique heritage," Goodwin's assessment rests none-theless on shaky ground, not least in her disproportionate empha-sis on the Dutch influence and in the reductive topographical determinism into which she falls. Still, Goodwin is not entirely without merit in positing a productive collusion of landscape, en-counter, and worldview. The reputation for hauntedness that gave C. G. Hine and many others pause, a reputation that was firmly en-trenched by the time Wilstach was writing in 1933, arose from an al-chemy of physical, historical, and cultural factors, ranging from the local to the international: a terrain amenable to readings of inher-ent spookiness; a history troubled by restless change and conten-tiousness, which yielded haunting uncertainties; and a diverse set of cultural influences, from Native American spirit beliefs to trans-atlantic romantic aesthetics, which encouraged visions of ghost-liness.

BROODING MOUNTAINS, SPOOKY WOODS

Lige Bayliss, a fisherman from Croton, had been at a dance in town one night and was walking back to Teller's Point, alone, at mid-night. And, according to the Croton fishermen who told Lige's tale to a folklore collector in 1920, he was getting "kind of nervous": "The big trees on either side made the road awful dark and spooky like, and how lonesome! There were funny kinds of noises; creak-ing and rustling of tree limbs; the stirring of reeds over in the swamp; and once in a while the croak of a frog, or the hoot of an owl or some such night bird." The atmosphere is ripe with hair-rais-ing potentialities. We all suspect that something strange is about to happen, and so does Lige: "what with the gloom of the big trees overhead and the dark mass of Money Hill before him . . . no doubt about that, Lige was scared."[3]

"Fear is in the mind," writes Yi Fu Tuan, "but, except in patho-logical cases, [it] has its origins in external circumstances that are truly threatening."[4] Landscape features, as they attach to both psy-

chological and cultural associations, are evocative entities, and
Maud Wilder Goodwin is right to point to something in the physi-
ognomy of the landscapes bordering the Hudson, the conditions
of topography, weather, flora, and fauna, as contributing to the
potential for hauntedness here. From the seventeenth century to
the present, in guidebooks and fiction, painting and histories, the
physical landscape of the Hudson Valley has time and again elicited description as provocative, mysterious, fearsome, mystical.[5]

Much of what has impressed observers over the centuries seems
to be the diverse, highly variegated character of the terrain.[6] As
one starts upriver from Manhattan toward Albany, the sheer cliffs
of the Palisades tower up to heights of five hundred feet along the
west bank for the first thirty miles. From there, the river widens
to more than three miles at the Tappan Zee and Haverstraw Bay,
bordered on the east by low hills, and on the west by the precipi-
tous faces of Hook Mountain and High Tor, which, though less
than a thousand feet high, rise abruptly and steeply from the water.
After Haverstraw Bay, the river winds more tightly between Stony
Point and Verplanck's Point, and the Highlands loom up, larger
and closer on both sides—Dunderberg, Bear Mountain, Anthony's
Nose, Breakneck, Storm King, the Beacons, each rising between a
thousand and seventeen hundred feet from the river's surface. Past
Newburgh Bay, the adjacent landscape flattens out somewhat, only
to rise again after Kingston, where the Catskills ascend along the
west side, and then subside into lower rolling hills and banks near
Albany. Back from the river are other sets of mountains: the
Ramapos on the border between Rockland County and New Jersey, the Shawangunks in Ulster and Orange Counties, the Taconics
in Dutchess and Columbia. The landscape surrounding the river is
also crossed by creeks and rivers: the Sparkill, the Croton River, the
Esopus, the Wallkill, Murderers Creek, the Kaaterskill, to name
only a handful. The region is dotted with lakes and swamps—the
"Great Vly" north of Saugerties, the "Great Swamp" west of

Newburgh, another "Great Swamp" in northwest Putnam County. Adding to the texture are caves, ravines, waterfalls, islands. Even during periods of heavy development, much of this terrain has been covered by trees and brush. Indeed, although the region's physical character has undergone significant change since early set-tlement, it has retained something of what Wilstach calls its "pri-meval impressiveness," both because conditions hindered devel-opment in some areas and because other sites have been left to revert to a more "wild" state.[7]

The shapes and contents of this landscape have proven fertile ground for hauntedness in several ways. Not only have individual features provided landmarks to which stories become attached—that is, not only has the terrain served as stage—but the landscape itself has resonated with fears and associations rooted deep in both human psychology and cultural history. Human beings have an "ingrained habit of anthropomorphizing nature," writes Tuan. "The forces of nature" have been seen throughout the world "as animate beings, as deities and demons, good and evil spirits."[8] Throughout much of human history and society, mountains have been perceived as active and ominous powers, while forests seemed terrifying and bewildering places.[9] In belief systems as far-flung as premodern Scandinavia and the twentieth-century West Indies, trees have had souls or have held the ghosts of dead ancestors.[10] Swampy regions, too, have traditionally inspired dread, not least because of the terrible creatures they might conceal in their depths, as John Stilgoe notes in his discussion of early modern Britain.[11]

Such beliefs and sensibilities are not irrelevant to a discussion of American landscape attitudes. In his study of Hudson Valley scen-ery, Raymond O'Brien argues that "concepts of mountain gloom, Old World superstitions of the forest . . . dissipated more slowly" in America.[12] And descriptions of the Hudson Valley often evince perceptions of an eerie sentience in the landscape. Mountains loom and brood.[13] Trees appear in regional accounts as ghostly,

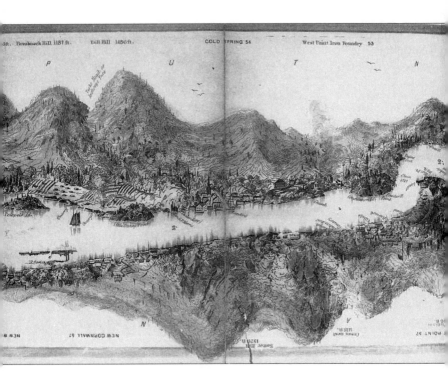

and as things mistaken for ghosts. One late-nineteenth-century Tarrytown historian describes the "gaunt, ghost-like arms" of an old tulip tree in the moonlight, while another suggests that reports of a headless ghost near Yonkers derived from "the gnarled and fantastic cedars."[14] In describing the Catskills, a Greene County historian notes that white birches added an air of "ghostliness" to the scene.[15] Forests more broadly, along with swamps, have been construed as dark and foreboding places where things might lurk, as places

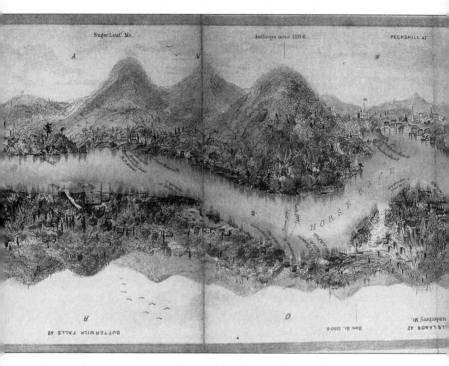

Panorama of the Hudson River from New York to Albany, by William Wade (New York: J. Disturnell, 1846), section showing the Highlands, downriver left to right. Courtesy of the Desmond-Fish Library, Garrison, New York.

containing a bewildering power of their own—something suggested in the numerous designations of "spook woods" and "spook hollows" in the region. According to an account given by folklorist Harold Thompson regarding one "Spook Woods" in the western Catskills, "It was commonly believed that cattle, driven through these woods, would scatter and run wild before the spooks. The road was quite likely to close in upon a traveller."[16] Similarly, speaking of "a dismal and fearsome swamp" in Dutchess County, which "almost swallows" the Albany Post Road, local residents told "stories of hideous and supernatural animals [hiding] deep in the dense thickets and among the stunted and twisted trees of the marsh."[17] In the words of a Rockland County historian, describing sightings of "weird wraiths" in Suffern around the turn of the century: "The bosky dells and gloomy glens that then bordered the Pascack [creek] were a stimulus to the imagination even of a midnight wayfarer not otherwise stimulant laden."[18]

Along with more permanent landforms, ephemeral aspects of nature in the Hudson Valley have fostered apprehensions of strangeness. The thunderstorms mentioned by Maud Wilder Goodwin have long been attributed to supernatural origins.[19] Atmospheric effects in the Catskills have been noted for adding a mystical quality to that region—something most vividly described by Washington Irving, but which resonates through numerous accounts of the area.[20] The everyday landscape was made uncanny, the possibility of ghosts increased, by the dark of night (as C. G. Hine asserted), by wind through dry leaves in the fall (as Lige Bayliss discovered), or by the mists which for Henry James added "luminous mystery" to the river's face, and which other writers have found particularly conducive to ghostly imaginings.[21] Animals, too, helped engender a sense of eeriness in the landscape, from the "plaintive note of a whippoorwill" and sudden startling splash of a sturgeon, which made the Highlands at night seem all the more strange and mysterious to Washington Irving, to the rustlings of animals in the thickets on Dunderberg, which gave a late-twentieth-century writer for *Hudson Valley* magazine an "uncanny" feeling.[22] A fine line between the natural and the supernatural is suggested by the numerous tales in which animals are mistaken for ghosts.[23]

On their own, and especially in collusion with one another, the region's natural features and phenomena—the overhanging cliffs and dark hollows and tangled forests, the thunder and rustling reeds and crying loons—lent themselves to a variety of reactions and emotional responses, from a sense of mystical immanence to one of pleasurable mystery or of outright fright. Altogether, the terrain was ripe for hauntedness, both in the psychological and cultural associations it evoked, and in what it might hold or hide—what might lurk "in the underbrush." Obviously, though, a perception of hauntedness also required a perceiver, and whatever diffuse potential lay in the natural landscape was intensified and given form by human experience and history in the region. Lige Bayliss was scared as he walked among the dark trees on Teller's Point at midnight, with Money Hill looming, and strange noises all around; but when he remembered that there had once been an Indian camp ground there, and that the Van Cortlandt family graveyard bordered the path, and when he began to recall rumors that pirates had once frequented the area—then his fears took on ghostly shapes.[24]

A HISTORY OF UNREST

The character of Hudson Valley history goes another long step toward explaining how the region came by its strange heritage of hauntedness. Despite tourbook images of the region as sleepy and timeless, the history of the Hudson Valley has largely been one of unrest, colored by territorial conflicts, social diversity and dissensus, and multiple, contending colonizations; it has taken shape from the movements of various populations through the region, from the rapid rate of change, and from an ambivalent hinterland relationship to what became in the early nineteenth century the nation's most populous city. This was a perpetually uncertain ground, a crossroads where no clear lines could be drawn between insiders and outsiders. Rather than dispelling ghosts, this history of unrest has been crucial in the production of hauntings.

The germinal moment of Hudson Valley history to which, like most, Maud Wilder Goodwin points is that of Dutch exploration and settlement. And there *is* something to this focus on the Dutch. Although settlement of New Netherland, beginning in 1624, was slow compared with contemporary growth of English colonies, the Dutch maintained a presence and influence in regional society and culture long after the English made New Netherland into New York, without battle, in 1664.[25] The Dutch presence set New York apart in its colonial milieu, and afterward gave the region a unique social and historical layer. The Dutch, though, were never alone in New York, nor was their possession of the territory ever secure. To begin with, there were those "strange aboriginal savages."[26] At the time of Dutch settlement, the river valley was inhabited by Lenape (Delaware), Wappinger, and Mahican tribes, with the Mohawks just to the northeast.[27] Although Dutch-Indian relations were not always violent, numerous incidents of misunderstanding, as well as a more broadcast uneasiness, are reflected in colonial accounts, and tension did on several occasions turn to outright warfare involving atrocities on both sides, as in the Indian Wars of 1643–1645 and the Esopus Wars of 1659–60 and 1663–64.[28] The Dutch colony also had to contend with other colonial powers—the French to the north, and especially the English to the east and south. A state of perpetual border warfare existed between New Netherland and the New England colonies, which continued even after the English took over New York (and indeed into the nineteenth and twentieth centuries).[29]

A sense of instability in colonial New Netherland/New York was further exacerbated by the extraordinary diversity and discord *within* the colony. Because the colony had difficulty attracting settlers from the Netherlands, it was forced to have an open-door policy, and almost half of the traceable immigrants to New Netherland during the seventeenth century came from places outside the Netherlands. The early colonial population included Germans, French Huguenots, Danes, Swedes, Belgians, and Norwegians, as well a significant number of African slaves; and when the region passed under English control, Scottish, English, and Irish elements and an increasing number of New Englanders joined the already uneasy mix.[30] The tensions and animosities caused by this ethnic heterogeneity constitute a major theme in contemporary and historical accounts of the region.[31] There were also unique class antagonisms created in New York by the manorial land system, begun by the Dutch and expanded by the English—antagonisms that led to armed uprisings by tenant farmers in the eighteenth and nineteenth centuries. "In a colony as complex as this one," writes historian Patricia Bonomi, "the materials for contention, of all sorts, were everywhere at hand."[32] A broad lack of social cohesion in the colonial period is evidenced by the fact that colonial New York had a significantly higher rate of crime and violence than the more homogeneous colonies of New England.[33]

From these shaky foundations, regional unrest and instability carried forward into the postcolonial period and beyond. First there was the Revolutionary War, which made the Hudson Valley the site of a disproportionate number of battles and produced intense in-fighting with long-lasting resonances in regional memory.[34] By removing most of the Native American population of upstate New York and a number of landholding loyalists, the war also paved the way for a massive in-migration of New Englanders in the late eighteenth and early nineteenth centuries.[35] The nineteenth century brought transportation developments that vastly increased accessibility and traffic along the river. With the invention of the steamboat, which made its debut run from New York to Albany in 1807, and the opening in 1825 of the Erie Canal, which linked the Hudson to the country's interior, the river became one of the busiest thoroughfares in the country.[36] By the 1850s the Hudson River Railroad was running the length of the east shore from New York to Rensselaer, and by the mid-1880s railroads flanked both sides of the river and crisscrossed the adjacent counties.[37]

These developments fostered tremendous social and economic

changes. Agriculture, the most prevalent activity in the Hudson Valley into the nineteenth century, was increasingly conducted with an eye to markets, and ultimately lost ground to western competition.[38] More strikingly, the region underwent a rapid and prolonged industrialization, peaking in the late nineteenth century, which added quarries, brickworks, tanneries, ironworks, and factories to the landscape.[39] Adjacent to the immigrant gateway of New York City, this industrial development also promoted demographic transformations in the region. At midcentury there was what one historian, speaking of Albany, has called the "Irish invasion," along with a large German immigration;[40] later in the century, the region's workforce and population drew in southern and eastern European immigrants, as well as African-American migrants from the South. These movements and migrations affected all the riverside counties, especially areas close to New York City: by the mid-1890s one-third of the population of Yonkers was foreign born, and another third was first-generation American, while the state census of 1925 reported that railroad workers living in Croton came from fifteen different countries.[41]

Improvements in transportation also aligned with the spread of romantic sentiment and aesthetics to produce another type of "invasion" in the nineteenth century: an enormous tourist interest in the river, which gave rise to a burgeoning number of resort hotels and recreational facilities along the Palisades, in the Highlands, and in the Catskills.[42] In the 1880s, with six trains a day arriving from New York City alone, between 60,000 and 70,000 tourists and summer boarders traveled to the Catskills every summer; by 1907 the number of annual visitors climbed to about 300,000.[43] The region was subject to more permanent urban extrusions as well. Wealthy New Yorkers and industrialists—including Rockefellers, Goulds, Vanderbilts, and Morgans—as well as artists and writers, lined the river's shores with summer homes and estates, and suburbs began growing up along rail lines, while the needs of the growing metropolis further encroached on the landscape in the form of massive reservoir projects.[44] The placid image these reservoirs now present masks the often bitter resentments that accompanied their development, as whole towns had to be moved or abandoned for their creation.

In the twentieth century, the social, economic, and physical character of the region continued to undergo radical transformations, and contests over territory and place continued to be predominant features of regional life. Suffering from southern and western competition, and in many cases terminally damaged by the Great Depression, a good deal of Hudson Valley industry fell to ruin in the early twentieth century.[45] As industry ebbed, automobile travel and spates of highway and bridge construction accelerated suburbanization, sometimes in explosive proportions: for instance, from 1955, when the Tappan Zee Bridge opened, to 1970, the population of Rockland County went from 89,000 to 230,000.[46] Such suburban development both paralleled and contended with a rise in conservation and park movements in the region, championed by such agencies as the Palisades Interstate Park Commission (created in 1900), which secured large parcels of land in the valley as recreational and scenic preserves. None of these changes came without battles. The construction of new highways, both because they displaced older routes, bypassing older towns, and because they were perceived to threaten local character and quality of life, often caused heated arguments.[47] Whereas industrial growth or reservoir building had caused outrage in the nineteenth century, in the twentieth century the erection of power plants became a perennial issue.[48] Not even the creation of parks has gone without opposition. These issues, the internal dividing lines they expose within the regional population, and the fact that some of the staunchest despoilers and defenders of the region were often far from "local,"

"The Hudson at 'Cozzens's.'" From William Cullen Bryant, ed., *Picturesque America; or, The Land We Live In* (New York: D. Appleton, 1872–1874). Courtesy of Department of Special Collections, Stanford University Libraries.

show how difficult it is, and has always been, to designate insiders and outsiders, how the ground is, and has always been, layered with contending desires and claims.

This restless and contentious history, replete with acts of dispossession, marginalization, and violence, was ripe for the development of regional haunting, not least because it left a considerable supply of potential ghosts. Along "no other river," the author of the 1868 *Legends and Poetry of the Hudson* asserts, have the "waves of different civilizations . . . left so many *waifs* upon the banks."[49] The rapid rate of development, and thus of obsolescence, and the frequent social shifts bestowed on the region a large number of "pasts" in a relatively brief period, providing a plethora of raw materials from which hauntings could emerge, while also effectively foreshortening historical time, so that even recent events seemed remote. As James Fenimore Cooper theorizes in the opening to *The Deerslayer* (1841), "On the human imagination, events produce the effects of time," and thus the shallow histories of America and of New York could seem ancient simply as a result of "an accumulation of changes."[50] Along with bolstering supply, historical developments in the region created a variety of social, economic, and cultural demands for ghosts, whether as emblems of guilt and protest or as icons of nostalgia and tradition. Hauntings proliferated, for instance, in conjunction with the nineteenth-century tourist industry's need to attract romantic-minded travelers, or from efforts to establish moorings in times of upheaval, as was clearly the case in Westchester in the late nineteenth century.

The specifics of historical supply and demand are important, and I return to them throughout subsequent chapters. But there is a particular underlying factor, deriving from the overarching tendencies of Hudson Valley history, which I want to explore in greater depth here. Most significant in the restless history of the region is that it created a sense of social and historical tenuousness that was crucial to producing ghosts. The uncanny, writes Renée

Bergland, is literally "the unsettled, the not-yet-colonized, the unsuccessfully colonized, or the decolonized."[51] Despite some long-standing settlements, and inhabitants who could trace their lineage back to the early colonists, the Hudson Valley has been, by and large, a place inhabited and crossed by strangers. The convergences of unfamiliar people, the uncertainty of place created by frequent influxes and movements, created a sense of troubling uncanniness and unfathomable otherness that could lend itself to a sense of hauntedness—something suggested by the frequent conflation or confusion of ostensibly living others with ghosts. Early descriptions and place-names suggest that the Dutch found Native Americans spooky; the Dutch in turn were cast as ghostly in the nineteenth and twentieth centuries.[52] One late-twentieth-century writer has attributed the proliferation of hauntings in the region to the fact that the later-arriving English "found the indigenous culture [of the Dutch and Germans] uncomfortably alien and thus inscrutable."[53] Ghostliness in part served to articulate and contain anxieties about strange places and people. Wondering why a cave in Dutchess County was called the "Spook Hole," a newspaper reporter in 1870 was told that it had once been occupied "by an old man of foreign aspect [with] a negress and their son."[54] In another instance, a man from Milton, in Ulster County, told the following story to a folklore student in 1945: "One night when I was a young man, I was walking home along the river road toward the station, when I suddenly heard footsteps following me. . . . I glanced back and saw a big black figure following me. I thought maybe it was a tramp or a nigger, so I pulled out my knife and snapped it like a gun. I turned around fast to scare whoever it was, but it was gone." Unable to identify this apparition, the man conjectures: "maybe it was the Black Lady," a ghost said to haunt the town.[55]

This uncertainty about who or what was out there had a historical correlative—an uncertainty about what had gone on here. In a country that, as Tuan writes, had "its face to the future," historical amnesia and a sense of pastlessness were common maladies.[56] In the Hudson Valley the disintegration of connection to the past could seem a chronic condition. From Irving's recurrent allusions to the history-erasing Yankee flood of the post-Revolutionary period, through the nineteenth and twentieth centuries, a troubled perception that history was being washed away under the myriad "waves of civilization" repeats as a leitmotif in regional writings. "We are drifting along with scarcely an effort to preserve from fast approaching oblivion the thousands of interesting facts, recollections, and reminiscences of the past, relating to our county," writes the editor of an 1874 Dutchess County book, *Local Tales and Historical Sketches*.[57] In the mind of Catskill historian Henry Brace, writing in 1884, it was already far too late. Had his work been undertaken seventy years earlier, he argues, "the annalist could have drawn a lively picture" from the reminiscences of now-dead townsmen. "Now . . . all that one, even with the utmost diligence of research and inquiry, can do is to sketch in meager and almost colorless outline the history of a secluded community."[58] Such laments over the lost past abound in local accounts. And if relatively long-settled residents were shaky on the historical facts, new arrivals and visitors sometimes sensed an unbridgeable gap between themselves and local history. In *The Old Mine Road,* even the inveterately curious C. G. Hine writes of passing "several stone houses . . . that suggest a possibility of stories and things, but if there are such they are a sealed book."[59]

This much-bemoaned sense of historical loss or obscurity has been central to the haunting of the region. While particular events, figures, and circumstances provided the potential substance for hauntings, and while historical demands made ghosts useful and desirable, it was ironically the *lack* of historical continuity and understanding that made the past mysterious and ghostly. This is a key point, one that goes to the very heart of my argument. Before discussing the historical reference points contained in various hauntings, as I do in later chapters, it is worth pausing here to notice how thoroughly regional ghostlore reflects disorientation, uncertainty, discontinuity, and unrootedness.

Recent scholarship has emphasized relationships between ghosts and language, ghosts and memory, ghosts and history. Renée Bergland writes explicitly: "Like ghosts, words are disembodied presences."[60] Although Bergland correctly suggests an expressive affinity between words and ghosts, the parity is not absolute. Rather, ghosts often represent the things that words have not expressed or cannot express. They emanate from and embody the blank spaces between words in historical narratives, the erasures and oversights—the "noisy silences and seething absences" described by sociologist Avery Gordon.[61] It is worth noting the correspondence between Henry Brace's lament at being able to present only a "meager and almost colorless outline" of local history, and the description offered when a folklore student in the 1940s asked her grandfather what ghosts looked like: "a ghost . . . has [the] shape and outline of the person . . . but they are not colored— merely a black and white outline. The whole figure looks light and wispy as if it could blow away any minute."[62] The common understanding of ghostliness articulated in this description is the very image of historical insubstantiality and fragmentariness.

Throughout the literature and folklore of the valley, ghosts are habitually discerned and described in terms of vagueness, colorlessness, wispiness, incompleteness; they are most often recognized and defined precisely by their lack of definition or identifiers. A "formless gray shadow" is reported to "whisk by in the neighborhood of the swamp," in Edgar Mayhew Bacon's *Chronicles of Tarrytown and Sleepy Hollow* (1897).[63] A "dark shapeless object . . . [a] mysterious mass" is seen to move "silently across the road," in Charles Pryer's *Reminiscences of an Old Westchester Homestead* (1897).[64] In folklore collected in the mid-twentieth century, vague ghosts are everywhere: a "figure in black" at a Rensselaer house; "a white figure" at a Kerhonkson house; "something white" that appeared "around a tree" in Cohoes, "first on one side . . . then on the other . . . [then] a gust of wind" and it was gone; a figure "visible though transparent," with a "white cloudy appearance" in a Mount Airy home; a "white form" in an abandoned house in Middletown.[65] There are hosts of shadowy, unidentifiable women; there are numerous ghosts without heads.[66]

These types and images are not unique to the Hudson Valley: they echo larger traditions and iconographies. Yet the fact that so many of the ghosts of the region are so inchoate or faded, so incapable of being identified, has aesthetic and historical implications. Embedded in these depictions of ghosts is a problem of communication, a loss of essential information, an inability to articulate—something reflected further in the general silence of the Hudson Valley's ghostly population. European ghosts often speak; New York area ghosts rarely do.[67] Like the ghosts that Rip Van Winkle encounters in the Catskill recesses, who disturb him most by the fact that "they maintained the gravest faces, the most mysterious silence," Hudson Valley ghosts are often either dead silent or, when they do try to communicate, are heard as muffled or otherwise incomprehensible.[68] And in many cases ghosts rob witnesses of the power of speech as well, defying description and eroding verbal expression.[69] The undescribable, unspeakable aspects of ghosts may simply stem from crises of abysmal horror or mourning. Yet the inarticulacy that defines so many instances of haunting in the Hudson Valley also shadows problems of historical continuity, of perennial change as repeatedly and cumulatively obscuring the regional past and undermining historical understanding. It is telling that whereas Irving describes the ghostly crew of "The Storm-Ship" as chanting, a late-nineteenth-century retelling says they chant "words devoid of meaning to the listeners."[70] The fault, of course, lies not with the ghosts, but with the observers. That is, if traces of the past presented themselves, if waves of settlers and visitors suspected that things had happened here, they were largely at a loss to identify them or to understand their implications.

Although my suggestion here—that the vagueness and incommunicativeness endemic to regional ghostliness is intertwined with a sense of historical uncertainty—is speculative, more concrete evidence of a link between regional ghostliness and a sense of rootlessness lies in the multiple ways that regional hauntings make reference to transience itself. There are, first of all, the wandering, transgressive habits of ghosts themselves, which seem to relate to senses of vulnerability, trespass, homelessness, and alienation. In the story of "The Spirit Lady," in *Reminiscences of an Old Westchester Homestead,* Charles Pryer writes that she "seemed to mind fences no more than grass-blades, and instead of climbing over seemed to glide through them."[71] Describing a ghost that passed her along the road, a Dutchess County woman said that he "seemed to come toward us out of nowhere. He seemed to glide past us like a streak."[72] That the author of *Legends and Poetry of the Hudson* chose to write of "so many *waifs*" along the river's bank is revealing in this regard, as the word *waif* connotes both fleeting wispiness and homelessness or abandonment.[73] Other accounts point to the transience of the living as the cause of ghostly restlessness; for instance, in *Myths and Legends of Our Own Land* (1896), Charles Skinner writes that "the walking sachems of Teller's Point" were awakened by "the tramping of white men over their graves."[74]

A link between regional haunting and a concern with transience is perhaps more profoundly reflected in the frequent haunting of sites of transition, such as roads, bridges, and taverns; and in the significant presence in regional lore of the ghosts of *transients*—hitchhikers, gypsies, tramps, itinerant musicians, pirates, and most prominently peddlers.[75] Peddlers tend to be coded as Yankee in American imaginations, and indeed such codings color early-nineteenth-century references to peddler ghosts in the region—something that in itself reflects a link between the Yankee invasion and the production of hauntings.[76] However, later stories of peddler ghosts seem to lose entirely such regionally or historically specific characteristics, as these ghosts come to epitomize more generally the intersection of shaky historical knowledge, transiency, and ghostliness. In *Local Tales and Historical Sketches* (1874), for instance, Henry D. B. Bailey presents a long tale about "The Haunted Tavern" in East Fishkill, which "was located some distance from the nearest settler, remote from any village, surrounded with forests dark and dense." At length, "startling stories . . . were circulated throughout the settlement . . . that [a] peddler never left the tavern," and the tavern gets a reputation for being haunted.[77] An entirely possible, yet fleeting and identityless presence, the peddler makes for an easy ghost story. Notably, the tale itself invokes historical vagueness, as Bailey leaves the reader to judge the truth of the reported events, while the book's editor cannot contain his concern that "those who are not well acquainted with the early history of the County may take fiction for fact, and so be unconsciously led astray."[78]

This trend toward vagueness continues in folklore collected in the twentieth century, where peddlers frequently feature as default explanations for otherwise unexplained hauntings and unidentified remains. Perhaps the most revealing of these instances is a reference from Ulster County, in which the collector writes:

Up the pond road on the way to Glenford, there is a small bridge, crossing a little mountain stream. This little bridge in the Vly [swamp] is called the Spook Bridge. I've always wondered why it was called the Spook Bridge. . . . This is how one of the neighbors living on this road told it to me:

"That bridge you see there now is not the original Spook Bridge. The old bridge was a little below the bridge now standing. It seems that there were some workmen up near that stream and they had a little cabin there where they stayed.

They were building the bridge at this time. One day, the workmen left and they had not finished the bridge. Someone went
in the cabin and there they found a pack-peddler's pack and
belongings behind an old trunk. I don't know jest [*sic*] why
they did this, but they looked under the old Spook Bridge
and there they found the body of the peddler. Well, they buried him there, and they say that when you go over that bridge
at night, you can see ghosts and spooks moving around there,
and they are all dressed in white. Yes, I reckon that old pack
peddler must have been murdered. It's funny how those men
disappeared so sudden like."79

Everything here is vagueness and transiency: a "spook" place whose
name suggests but does not specify some sort of haunting; the presence not only of a wandering peddler but also of unfamiliar and
nonlocal workmen (who also disappear like ghosts); ghosts and
spooks "moving around" and "all dressed in white"; a historically
uninformed interviewer; and, finally, language that emphasizes the
speculative nature of the whole account.

Louis Jones argues that peddlers recur so frequently in regional
folklore "because so many of them were murdered for the money
they carried with them."80 Jones's rationale, although it may have
basis in fact, seems to miss something. Peddlers, along with gypsies
and other transient figures, historically represented what might be
referred to as common strangers. They were both historical facts
and abstract symbols of community disruption.81 An American
version of the "Wandering Jew," they were uncanny presences, unsettling and unsettled, and in this held a certain kinship with
ghosts.82 Peddler ghosts served as a two-sided symbol of a troubled rootlessness, representing mysterious and disruptive presences
within the familiar landscape of more-settled communities, while
also emblematizing the potential perilousness of unfamiliar territories to strangers of all sorts. Along with the wider group of vague,

incommunicative, and transient ghosts in regional lore, these peddlers were closely intertwined with anxieties over transiency, mutability, and historical uncertainty, and the proliferation of their
ghosts suggests recourse to speculation and stereotype where historical substance was lacking.

The horror writer Stephen King has written that the basis of all
human fear is not an entirely closed door, but a door slightly ajar.[83]
Ultimately, Hudson Valley history was propitious for haunting
in both its accretion of pasts and its tenuousness of historical
continuity—a dual accumulation of substances and absences. History became, in essence, a matter of suspicion and conjecture. Of
course, the historical crises represented in ghostly vagueness presented opportunities as well—something suggested in the worries of
the editor of *Local Tales and Historical Sketches* that "those not so
well acquainted" with local history could be "led astray" by ghost
tales. As Hine writes of a mysterious house in Orange County,
which was presented to him "with the vague statement that many
historic memories cling about it": "Possibly the literary lights prefer
it so, as each can then clothe it with his own imagination."[84]

"Between Certain Lines of Reading"

Along with auspicious environmental and historical factors, what
must be considered in any speculation on the Hudson Valley's propensity for hauntings are the interpretive cultural frameworks and
animating mindsets, the myriad folk, religious, and aesthetic traditions that various "waves of civilization" brought to bear on the
scene. Primary among these were folklores and popular beliefs of
various groups who came to inhabit the region. These, however, are
also hardest to trace and verify because they are usually orally transmitted. Matters are further complicated by the fact that there has
been no end of offhand speculation, distortion, and invention regarding regional folk traditions, whether in attempts to demean or
to extol, by literary figures and historians alike. Invectives of partic-

ular superstitiousness, as we have seen, fall heavily on the Dutch; they also land on Native and African Americans.[85] Others single out Germans as the primary sources of regional ghostlore.[86] Still others have pointed at the invading New Englanders as the most prone to superstition, while similar credit or blame has fallen on later arriving immigrants.[87]

Certainly much of this finger-pointing goes unsubstantiated, and is in some cases simply derisive. Yet it also reveals how numerous folk traditions of haunting circulated in the region, traditions whose real presences and influences are discernible both by inference—by the presence of motifs analogous to those of other regions and countries—and by direct statements.[88] Although "any Indian lore that was here shows traces of having been improved upon by others," according to one historian, historical and anthropological data establish a regional background of Native American animistic beliefs, which envisioned the natural world as infused with spirits.[89] And the influence of these beliefs can be detected in regional hauntings through the twentieth century, both in stories of supernatural animals and spirits told by people of Native American ancestry still living in the area, and in the story culture of non-Native inhabitants.[90] In addition to explicit accounts in which non-Native individuals record hearing tales from Native American storytellers, there are elements in local lore that have striking parallels in Native American mythology.[91] More pervasively, the influence of Native American spirit beliefs can be detected in the sort of "Indian legends" that appeared in literary and popular works in the nineteenth century. A tale about a supernatural woman in the Catskills, for instance, who makes the sun, moon, and stars—a tale that Washington Irving appended to "Rip Van Winkle," and that became a mainstay of legend books at the end of the nineteenth century—resonates with a belief common to New York area tribes.[92] Likewise, a reference in A. E. P. Searing's *The Land of Rip Van Winkle* (1884) to a Native American water demon in a Catskill lake may seem fabricated, but in fact it corresponds closely to a malevolent water spirit often found in Lenape stories.[93] This is not to say that such legends are "authentic." Yet, similar to the relationship Eric Lott has identified between apparently derogatory blackface minstrelsy and African-American cultural practices, even the "counterfeit" legends purveyed by white writers reveal that Native American spirit stories infiltrated non-Native culture at some level and influenced regional hauntings.[94]

Similarly, although the Dutchness of regional ghostlore has been subject to distortion and fabrication, there *is* evidence to suggest that the Dutch imported and adapted a folklore of the supernatural to the Hudson Valley landscape. Comparative research has demonstrated that manifestations in the region correspond to Dutch lores of water, earth, and fire spirits, demons, and ghosts.[95] More directly, a "Low Dutch" story collected in the Hudson Valley area in the early twentieth century reveals the existence of a Dutch ghost-story-telling tradition in the region, and points specifically to a sense of locally situated spirits within that tradition. The story, which tells of a female spirit along the Normans Kill creek (near Albany), is interesting not least because of the diffuse but enduring background of belief and lore it points to. After a Dutch boy tells his parents of encountering the apparition, his mother says to him, "Promise me, [my] boy, that you will never again go there. . . . We can't explain it so well. . . . [We] have a whole row of things hiding in [our] thoughts that [we] know aren't good, and the reason is not always clear. We only know that it is not good there."[96] Further evidence that the Dutch liberally applied a supernatural sensibility to the regional landscape is manifest simply in the existence of numerous "spook" places (Spook Woods, Spook Rocks, Spook Hollows)—the word *spook* being a Dutch word for spirit or ghost.[97]

Assertions of African-American influence and participation in shaping and perpetuating an atmosphere of ghostliness also find basis. For instance, an Orange County historian writing in 1908 recollected a local slave woman who "had the gift of telling marvellously fascinating stories about fairies, witches and spirits . . . many a deliciously awful one was surreptitiously told the youngsters when [parents] were absent, during her visits."[98] Accounts given by three separate folklore collectors in the 1930s and 1940s similarly suggest that the maintenance and proliferation of ghostlore in the town of Kinderhook were largely the work of the long-standing African-American community there.[99]

Folklore collections undertaken in the twentieth century provide strong evidence of the persistence of such ghostlores and storytelling practices, as well as of a tangled interweave of folkloric traditions from other parts of the world and country, following the various waves of immigration into the region. In fact, one-fifth of the ghost stories collected in Louis Jones's New York State folklore archives in the early 1940s were explicitly European stories.[100] More importantly, this collection shows that stories set in the Hudson Valley were told by people from a broad range of backgrounds, from people of Native American ancestry and descendants of older settlers, to newer European immigrants and recently migrated southern blacks.[101] Polish children told of ghosts in a Rensselaer graveyard; African-American workers from the South told stories of a ghost at Crescent; a woman of Italian Catholic background revealed that she had been taught to say "Jesus, Mary, and Joseph, let no harm come to me," to keep a ghost from appearing at a murder site in Ulster County.[102]

In addition to suggesting that diverse folklores were applied to regional landscape and experience, a number of accounts point to moments of unsolicited transmission. Writing memoirs in the 1920s, an Ulster County woman recalled having tales of "banshees" told to her as a child by an Irish laundress.[103] One of Jones's students from Albany reported that her family's housekeeper, an African-American woman from Georgia, told her never to look back if she heard a twig snapping, because "that's the spirits cracking that wood."[104] Another student was warned by her grandfather, who had immigrated from Germany in the 1880s (and who seemed particularly prone to seeing ghosts around his Dutchess County farm), that "bad ghosts never have heads."[105] Certainly such traditions and beliefs were received and deployed with different degrees of conviction, and there are accounts that point to the disintegration rather than the maintenance of ethnocultural traditions of haunting.[106] But two things become apparent: first, that a large number of vernacular traditions of haunting have been available within the Hudson Valley region; second, that although regional historical knowledge may have been dim and obscure, there were thriving, multifaceted cultures of storytelling at work that, whether discretely or in combination, served to encourage supernatural and ghostly sensibilities, both within and across social and ethnic boundaries.

Yet folkloric backgrounds and local storytelling practices do not entirely explain the endurance and notoriety of the region's hauntedness; rather, while these strata of folklore and tales clearly fueled local instances, they have also been supplemented and amplified by a series of religious, cultural, and aesthetic movements in the nineteenth and twentieth centuries. Spiritualism, for instance, which found its largest number of adherents in New York State, made significant inroads into Hudson Valley culture; one of the movement's major proponents was Andrew Jackson Davis, the "Poughkeepsie Seer." The movement also apparently made its influence felt in some of the best houses along the river. In written memoirs, Mrs. Pierre Van Cortlandt, of Van Cortlandt Manor in Croton, recalled that in 1848—a crucial year for spiritualism—one of her brothers-in-law had been visiting the manor house, and "the conversation turned on visitations from spirits, etc." That very night he "woke from a sound sleep with the consciousness of some one near him and distinctly heard the steps and the rustle of a dress coming through the adjacent parlour." Mrs. Van Cortlandt also remembered that when a medium visited the house in the 1860s, a spirit again announced its presence.[107] Though not focused on site-specific hauntings, spiritualism in the mid-nineteenth century, as well as subsequent parapsychological movements at the turn of the century and later in the twentieth century, aroused popular interest in the supernatural and fertilized the imaginative ground from which tales of hauntings might spring.[108]

More crucially important in the development of a regional proclivity for haunting were two interrelated, European-born movements, rising in the late eighteenth and early nineteenth centuries, which had profound influence on American tastes and culture: a wave of gothic literature that presented supernatural apparitions and emphasized irrational terrors; and a multifaceted romantic movement, which featured a historical localism—the latter reflected in such different entities as Wordsworth's poetry of peasant life, Scott's balladry and historical romances, and the Grimms' folklore collections. Hauntedness could not but have been encouraged by a variety of impulses commonly associated with romanticism: an emphasis on imagination and emotion over reason; a belief in inspired genius, as well as *genii loci;* a sensitivity to the supernatural or transcendent within the physical, and especially the natural, world; an intense interest in the folk past; and a yearning for the marvelous and mysterious.[109]

Despite the frequent and insistent claims that American culture was (and should be) rational and pragmatic, gothic and romantic tastes began infiltrating American culture even before the end of the eighteenth century, and swelled in influence as the nineteenth century unfolded. "[A] flood of books from Europe reached these shores each year," writes literary scholar Donald A. Ringe, citing works by Ann Radcliffe, Friedrich von Schiller, Walter Scott, and E. T. A. Hoffmann; "the reading public devoured them, and the writers read them as well."[110] The effects of such infusions and influences were myriad. Not only did supernatural lore become part of the common "imaginative furniture" of the popular and literary mind, but romantic influences also led writers, artists, and the population at large to turn a new eye to the landscape, and to the various historical associations and "folk" dispensations available in it, in a search for spiritual, emotional, or imaginative connection, and for grounding traditions of place.[111] As David Hall writes with regard to the proliferation of local history writing in nineteenth-century New England, what eighteenth-century historians had generally dismissed as "unfortunate 'superstitions'" came to be seen in the nineteenth century as containing "something of value—something peculiarly 'native' and also very 'old.' As the Enlightenment gave way to Romanticism, so did 'superstitions' give way to the categories of 'folklore' and 'legend.'"[112] And despite the common complaint of American authors that the United States lacked everything necessary for romances, by the mid-nineteenth century even the loudest of these plaintiffs found usable materials in American conditions and landscapes.[113]

As romanticism infused American culture more broadly, it also became attached to the Hudson Valley in somewhat unique ways. Located adjacent to a burgeoning, increasingly cosmopolitan center of commerce and culture, the river valley delivered a landscape well suited to romantic tastes. Its attributes drew the attentions not only of a rising number of tourists, but also of influential American artists and writers, whose works in turn fortified a sense of the region as peculiarly romantic. Beginning in the 1820s, the artists of the Hudson River School—Thomas Cole, Frederick Church, Asher Durand—profusely depicted Hudson Valley landscapes as imbued with a sort of epic immanence, in images that were widely echoed in popular illustrations. American writers also made explicit reference to the Hudson Valley, rendering its landscape and history in a variety of romantic shades. Most prominent in this regard was Washington Irving. But there were also Edgar Allan Poe, William Cullen Bryant, Herman Melville, and James Fenimore Cooper,

View of Round-Top in the Catskill Mountains (1827), by Thomas Cole (1801–1848). Oil on panel, 47.31 × 64.45 cm. Gift of Martha C. Karolik for the M. and M. Karolik Collection of American Paintings, 1815–1865; 47.1200.
© 2002 Museum of Fine Arts, Boston.

not to mention writers like Joseph Rodman Drake, James Kirke Paulding, and N. P. Willis, whose names have weathered time less well.[114]

Although such writers and artists did not treat ghosts per se in the way folkloric treatments often did, their depictions of the region reflected and engendered a broad sense of hauntedness in the regional landscape and history. And while there would have been hauntings in the Hudson Valley without romanticism, the romantic movement, by making such things eminently valuable, fueled the elevation of hauntedness to a regional aesthetic and encouraged the proliferation of local tales. (That New York became a center of publishing, as well as a center of literature and art, further nurtured these trends, as such local books as *Chronicles of Tarrytown and Sleepy Hollow, The Land of Rip Van Winkle,* and *Reminiscences of an Old Westchester Homestead* were harvested by national publishing firms like G. P. Putnam's.)[115] Romantic influences in the formative moments of regional and national culture intertwined with the rise of a cultural establishment in the New York area. Superadded to the region's evocative landscape and shadowy history, this confluence ultimately helped affix in the Hudson Valley a penchant for hauntedness that continued to thrive alongside a more enduring popular interest in ghosts and the supernatural, and that would only swell in periods of heightened value on tradition, as it did in the late nineteenth and early twentieth centuries, and again in the 1930s and 1940s.[116]

To tell the truth, the Squire confesses that he used to take a pleasure in his younger days in setting marvellous stories afloat, and connecting them with the lonely and peculiar places of the neighborhood. Whenever he read any legend of a striking nature, he endeavored to transplant it, and give it a local habitation among the scenes of his boyhood. Many of these stories took root, and he says he is often amused with the odd shapes in which they have come back to him in some old woman's narrative, after they have been circulating for years among the peasantry, and undergoing rustic additions and amendments.

—Washington Irving, *Bracebridge Hall* (1822)

IRVING'S WEB

2

iscussion of Washington Irving's work has been marked by recurrent debate about Irving's sources. In 1930, for instance, when Henry A. Pochmann demonstrated through careful textual comparisons that both "Rip Van Winkle" and "The Legend of Sleepy Hollow," Irving's two most popular tales of the Hudson, were based on identifiable German folktales, he ruffled some feathers.[1] True, in a note appended to "Rip Van Winkle," Irving had more than hinted as much, and mention of German sources had cropped up periodically in nine-teenth-century commentary.[2] In fact, even late-nineteenth-century Rand McNally guidebooks had admonished: "No intelligent person, probably, believes that [Rip Van Winkle] ever really existed. . . . Irving did nothing more . . . than to rewrite . . . a superstition which has reappeared in every European land and nation since earliest times." However, during the century following the publication of *The Sketch Book* (1819–1820), the presence of non-American antecedents for Irving's Hudson Valley tales had been shrouded over. As the protesting Rand McNally guide admitted: "it is not surprising that many believe the story to be derived from a tradition in circulation among the Dutch pioneers, and handed down to Irving's time."[3] This belief was well entrenched in the Hudson Valley itself. By 1920 a Westchester man who was collecting "legends that had been handed down from father to son in Westchester County" could state without hesitation that "Washington Irving undoubtedly founded his Legend of Sleepy Hollow from just such a source."[4]

Thus, while literary scholarship accepted Pochmann's revelation—thirty years later Daniel Hoffman saw it as the reason Irving's debt to "native folklore has scarcely been acknowledged"—protesting rumbles were heard over the years from other quarters.[5] In 1939 pioneer New York folklorist Harold Thompson wrote, with Pochmann clearly in mind:

> Frequently I am asked whether the supernatural element in the stories of Washington Irving was obtained from the folk in America or was borrowed from European legend. There is never time for a proper answer—the subject deserves a doctoral dissertation or two, but I can suggest to the laymen a few facts. You have to remember that Irving was the son of a Scot, and that in childhood he was privileged to hear the ballads and tales of a Scotch maid. . . . You must remember also

that the scenery of the Hudson obviously demands a phantom ship and a headless horseman. . . . No German folktale fully explains *The Legend of Sleepy Hollow;* you must see Kinderhook as it is and imagine Tarrytown as it was. We can show you the Van Tassel House, built in 1736; if you are not convinced by the iron figures in a brick wall, you can fall asleep in the afternoon sunshine while the fair prospect dims, and you will hear in dream the thundering hooves of Irving's horseman. . . . Irving did not need to visit Germany—which he did two years after writing the *Sketch Book*—nor must we suppose that he was just introduced to German legends in Sir Walter Scott's library. He could have heard plenty of German as well as Dutch legends along the Hudson.[6]

The last line became a refrain for local historians, who similarly worked to suggest that, if Irving's Hudson Valley tales owed something to German folklore, that folklore might nonetheless be of a domestic rather than imported variety. In 1958, for instance, Walter V. Miller, a Columbia County historian who often wrote for the local newspapers, acknowledged ancestors in German lore for the headless horseman and for Rip Van Winkle, but strove to imply that these tales made it to Irving's ears during a stay in Kinderhook in 1809. Nearby communities, Miller explained, were settled by Germans who "possessed a culture and background that was rich in tales of folk lore and legend." These legends, Miller argued, had been transmitted and adapted to fit into "the changed scheme of things," and "thus have become basis for some of the legends and superstitions ofttimes attributed to other sources."[7]

Questions about Irving's locations also sparked debates, both in and beyond the region. "Which town owns the improbable, if well-known ghost, the Headless Horseman?" asked the Halloween 1982 edition of a North Carolina newspaper. Does he ride "through the copses and thickets near Tarrytown, across the old log bridge which is now paved? Or more than 100 miles farther up the Hudson Valley, in Kinderhook, N.Y., where his appearance is said to be accompanied by a blast of wind that can be heard all over Columbia County. Where is Sleepy Hollow?"[8]

In part, these persistent battles to locate Irving's sources and places derive from Irving's own wiliness in simultaneously revealing and covering his tracks. Throughout his work, Irving gives with one hand and takes away with the other. He raises the possibility of outside influence at the end of "Rip Van Winkle"—giving, Pochmann points out, not quite the right reference for the German folktale—only to have his narratorial persona, Geoffrey Crayon, aver that Diedrich Knickerbocker (Irving's fictitious historian and the narrator of "Rip Van Winkle") found the legend current among Catskill folk.[9] In "The Legend of Sleepy Hollow," which makes no direct mention of German folk literature, Knickerbocker says he heard the tale from "a pleasant, shabby, gentlemanly old fellow" in Manhattan.[10] Yet in "Sleepy Hollow," a sketch published in *The Knickerbocker* twenty years after *The Sketch Book*, Irving has Crayon assert that it is to Knickerbocker's consultations with Dutch housewives and with an "old negro" in Tarrytown that "we are indebted for the surprising though true history of Ichabod Crane and the headless horseman."[11] "I am an old traveller," Crayon begs in *Tales of a Traveller*. "I have read somewhat, heard and seen more, and dreamt more than all . . . and I am always at a loss to know how much to believe of my own stories."[12]

Irving's baiting of readers, however, does not entirely account for the endurance and, at times, the vigor of source debates. Clearly, there are issues in this hunt that go beyond an intellectual game of hide-and-seek. The perennial concern with Irving's sources has to do with underlying questions of authenticity—something that Irving himself seems to have realized. If he was at the outset surprised at the scrutiny his tales received—responding in an irritated footnote in *Bracebridge Hall* to the "divers writers in magazines" who had "discovered" Rip Van Winkle "to have been founded on a little German tradition" and who had "revealed [the matter] to the world as if it were a foul instance of plagiarism"—he seems to have grasped by the time he wrote *Tales of a Traveller* (in which he offered a preemptive though vague reference statement) that "the public is apt to be curious about the sources whence an author draws his stories, doubtless that it may know how far to put faith in them."[13] This concern with authenticity, which broadly reflects efforts to locate *American* roots of a literature of which Irving is seen as progenitor, is more specifically a reflection of the degree to which Irving's stories have become enmeshed with sense of place in the Hudson Valley, as seen in the defensiveness of local and regional accountings. At stake in questions of Irving's sources, in other words, were the very foundations of regional image and identity.

Understanding how the Hudson Valley gained its particular reputation for hauntings requires paying special attention to Irving, both as an instance—exemplifying in his own experience and tales how a web of geographical, historical, and cultural factors produced ghosts in a place that ostensibly lacked the historical depth for them—and as major influence in the subsequent development of regional hauntedness. Certainly there were local hauntings in the Hudson Valley before Irving, but Irving's literary renderings set in place a reputation for haunting, as well as a troop of ghosts that have been invoked and absorbed in the region to the point that questions of their authenticity have been largely rendered moot.

LIFE

Growing up in a country where "the works of man gave no ideas but those of young existence" and in a city with, as yet, no developed literary establishment, Washington Irving was surprisingly well positioned, personally and historically, both to see and to communicate a certain ghostliness in the regions adjacent to Manhattan.[14] Like New York itself, a small but growing port city poised between worlds, Irving stood, in the years leading up to *The Sketch Book,* double-faced in an uncertain borderland—a nebulous middle ground that on one hand threatened to quash literary aspiration but on the other hand might serve as the type of "neutral territory" which Nathaniel Hawthorne wrote of as being especially propitious for fostering romantic imaginings.[15]

Born in 1783 at the very close of the American Revolution, Irving was the American child of immigrant parents—his father, a hardware merchant and Presbyterian deacon, strict and pragmatic, born in Scotland, and his mother, more disposed to support her youngest son's artistic leanings, born in England.[16] He dabbled halfheartedly or unsuccessfully in a number of professions and activities: law, his brothers' business, politics, the military. Interspersed with these other ventures were fits of writing: letters from "Jonathan Oldstyle, Gent." in the *Morning Chronicle* in 1802; and *Salmagundi,* a series of sketches and satires, written along with his brother William and James Kirke Paulding in 1807 and 1808. In 1809 Irving published *A History of New York by Diedrich Knickerbocker,* a book that began as a parody of a popular travel guide to New York but turned into a comic history of the Dutch colonial era and a satire of contemporary American politics. The book was a great success; the fact that it elevated Irving's status to that of the best writer in New York, however, suggests the meagerness of literary production there, and explains, in part, Irving's hesitation to devote himself to authorship. Despite the success of the Knickerbocker *History,* it would be ten years before Irving found the inclination to write anything worthwhile again.

Much of what might be called Irving's dilemma of identity—a sense of alienation, dividedness, and uncertainty—can be traced to the more general condition of being an American and a New Yorker in the post-Revolutionary era, a time when the country was still largely dependent, economically and culturally, on England.[17] He was "born and brought up in a new country"—to borrow from

Crayon—"yet educated from infancy in the literature of an old one."[18] Irving read Shakespeare, Chaucer, Burns, Milton, Goldsmith, Addison, Scott, Defoe. He made forays into Scottish Common Sense philosophy; he also devoured travel books and romances. In all, this reading left him disposed to find the Old World more real than the New, even before he made his first overseas tour in 1804–1806.

At the same time, New York had another face turned inward toward the upriver frontiers, which still contained Native Americans in Irving's younger days, as well as Dutch populations. A delicate, cosmopolitan Anglophile on one hand, Irving nonetheless came to know something of the hinterlands near his native city. In his boyhood he had engaged in rural pursuits in the upper parts of Manhattan and in Westchester, frequently visiting at the home of a friend in New Rochelle, and going squirrel hunting at Tarrytown in 1798.[19] A more extensive acquaintance with the river began in 1800, when he sailed to Albany on the way to visit a sister in Johnstown. Between then and 1815 Irving made the trek up and down the river a half-dozen times and also spent time in regions along the river's shores during extended visits at the country houses of various friends: retreating to Lindenwald, the Columbia County home of his friend William Van Ness, after his fiancée's death in 1809; exploring the Hudson Highlands, accompanied by Walter Scott's *Lady of the Lake,* in 1810; staying at Clermont, the Dutchess County home of the Livingstons, in 1812.[20]

It is not hard to picture a young Irving enchanted, romantically musing over the striking scenery and "peculiar" characters of the Hudson of his youth, mainly because he said so much in later years to foster pictures of his own bewitchment. His squirrel-hunting venture in Tarrytown is reconjured in an 1839 sketch, in which Geoffrey Crayon recalls "twisted roots and sunken logs . . . towering oaks, and clambering grape-vines" along the Pocantico, where, he confesses, "my boyish fancy clothed all nature around me with ideal charms, and peopled it with the fairy beings I had read of in poetry and fable."[21] His first view of the Catskills from the river in 1800 is similarly recollected in a selection written for *The Home Book of the Picturesque* in 1852: "As I beheld them thus shifting continually before my eye, and listened to the marvellous legends of [an Indian] trader, a host of fanciful notions concerning them was conjured into my brain, which have haunted it ever since."[22]

There is, of course, great danger in relying too much on Crayon and on the recollections of an older Irving to reconstruct Irving's sense of place in his pre–*Sketch Book* days, especially given that Irving's main literary and intellectual models in his younger years were neoclassical writers like Goldsmith and Addison, skeptics, and satirists.[23] Even in Irving's later, more romantic writings he maintains a level of irony that makes such effusions suspicious. This is not to say, though, that the reactions Irving later records regarding the Hudson Valley scene are completely retrospective fictions. Rather, Irving's pre–*Sketch Book* writings and journals reveal that he was beginning to attempt a fusion between the raw materials in the Hudson environment and a developing romantic awareness, informed by a self-conscious philosophical interest in questions of perception. Irving had included in *A History of New York* evocative images of the Highlands at twilight, when the "mellow dubious light that prevailed, just served to tinge with illusive colours," so that "the mountains seemed peopled with a thousand shadowy beings."[24] In his journal of 1810, Irving can be seen experimenting with the river scenery around the Highlands, thinking about aesthetics in language imbibed from European theorists (he mentions Burke at one point), and testing the ideas on the surroundings: "The Idea of a broad & at the same time deep & unobstructed river fills the mind–Possesses Sublimity." He compares the dilapidated buildings at West Point to "the ruins of some feudal castle." In another entry he describes a waterfall near Highland Grange: "Mountain brook splashing & dashing along among mossy rocks–trees half fallen whose foliage over hang the water . . . weeds & nameless vagrant vines hanging in festoons."[25] Other notes in Irving's 1810 journal evidence an eclectically developing interest in the supernatural and the psychological: references to philosophical studies of superstition; mentions of Rosicrucian mysticism; discussions of memory, perception, dreams; quotations from Milton on ghosts and spirits, as well as from Scott's *Lay of the Last Minstrel;* and references to his own attraction to the supernatural, his recollections of "delicious horror . . . on hearing the stories of faris [*sic*] ghosts & goblins."[26]

These instances suggest elements that would coalesce in Irving's tales of haunting, while the aesthetic language, emotional responses, and subject matter reveal his developing romantic inclinations. Still, besides a reference to a dream of a ghostly Indian and a brief sketch of a conversation with the incarnated mountain Anthony's Nose, one looks in vain in the early journals for the type of local ghost story that would make Irving a household name.[27] And although Irving had incorporated references to supernatural lore in the region in *Salmagundi* and *A History of New York,* these were curtailed.[28] While Irving apparently glimpsed potentials in the Hudson Valley scene before going abroad in 1815, he was ill disposed to argue, at least publicly, with the contemporary cultural assessments he later parodies through Geoffrey Crayon: the American nation was one "where history was, in a manner, anticipation, where every thing in art was new and progressive, and pointed to the future rather than to the past"; it was a country to which "historical and poetical associations . . . could rarely be applied."[29] If romance and history were to be found in the world—if, as Crayon states his own motives in *The Sketch Book,* one wanted to lose oneself in the "shadowy grandeurs of the past"—one had to go abroad.[30]

Irving himself had left for England in 1815 on a trip that would ultimately keep him in Europe until 1832. It was in England, ironically, that Irving discovered how the Hudson Valley might be haunted, or rather that he was able to synthesize his Hudson Valley experiences and his literary and philosophical sensibilities in such a way that they not only achieved for him international acclaim but would haunt the Hudson Valley for centuries to come. He had amassed scenic and historical backgrounds; he had apparently given some thought to the particular problems of historical consciousness in the United States. What Irving gained during his time in Britain, which allowed him to think further about, and, even more, to *write* about the Hudson Valley scene as full of "haunted spots," was a more thoroughgoing immersion in the romanticism of the English literary scene; an introduction to usable models in European writings, as well as models of successful authorship; and, finally, a nostalgia-conducive distance from his domestic scene.

Compelled to write for a living by the failure of his family business, Irving had to decide what to write. In this he took cues from his environment, both physical—writing about English landscape and customs—and literary. As Daniel Hoffman writes, "Washington Irving was fortunate . . . to be alive and in England at that moment in the history of literature."[31] He visited Coleridge in 1817. More important, he went to Scotland to seek out Walter Scott. Scott's novels were wildly popular in the United States, and Irving was clearly among his American fans. When Irving arrived, he found himself utterly embraced by Scott (who, in fact, had read the Knickerbocker *History*).[32]

Scott had found success by drawing on folklore, particularly legends of the supernatural, and by attaching these legends to Scottish scenes in his novels. "Tradition depends on locality," he had written in his preface to *Sir Tristrem*. Even "a race of strangers" living in a new place would welcome stories by which it could connect itself with local tradition, "as transplanted trees push forth every fibre that may connect them with the soil to which they are transferred."[33] In Scott's company Irving found affirmation for his interests in the supernatural and in legend, as well as encouragement to use them in his writing. Scott, it seems, may also have exercised a particular influence on the haunting of the Hudson Valley by pushing Irving to learn German and to read the German folktales that were to provide a framework of plots and character types for several of Irving's Hudson tales.[34]

Irving may never have fully developed a theoretical understanding of the romantic movement, nor did he ever quite give himself over to writing straightforward ghost stories; a degree of humor or skepticism was never entirely absent from his tales of the Hudson Valley, and this was important to both their success and their influence.[35] Nonetheless, he did have romantic inclinations that his situation in England clearly brought to the surface (and that were further elicited by his attention to developing American popular tastes).[36] If Irving was inspired by the English countryside and company to write more romantically, and if Scott pushed him to consider the importance of storied associations in the creation of place, perhaps the final factor that enabled Irving to turn a romantic eye to his home ground was that in England his perspective on America became informed by distance. Nostalgic and homesick, Irving could write about ghosts in the Hudson Valley, not simply because the Hudson was haunted, but because *he* was haunted by the Hudson—by a sense of estrangement from it, and by the certainty that it was being transformed in his absence.[37] "Those who have studied the history of their own hearts must be sensible what a powerful . . . dominion the local scenes of . . . childhood have," writes Irving in one of his English notebooks: "The remembrance of the Hudson, that noble river, which was the wonder and delight of my boyhood, remains with me as a kind of mental property."[38]

The force of the alchemy by which the hybrid elements came together—by which Irving's sense of place and history in New York interacted with his more developed romanticism—is indicated in an often-repeated anecdote about the writing of "Rip Van Winkle" in

June 1818. In the year leading up to this point, Irving had advanced little in the writing of the projected *Sketch Book*. Having been to see Scott, and reading German folklore, he was staying with his sister Sarah and her husband, Henry Van Wart, in Birmingham. One evening, trying to cheer Irving, Van Wart began reminiscing about days in Sleepy Hollow, and as Stanley Williams recounts, Irving fled to his room, where "thoughts came with a rush, faster than he could write them." Appearing at breakfast the next day with a manuscript, "he said it had all come back to him; Sleepy Hollow had awakened him from his long dull, desponding slumber; and then he read the first chapters of 'Rip Van Winkle.'"[39]

Anecdotes aside, Irving clearly had an epiphany in England. Geoffrey Crayon's stated wish in *The Sketch Book* is not to know the past, but to lose himself among its "shadowy grandeurs." He wants to feel and suspect history's weight, but he is more interested in its shadows than its substance. His romantic pleasure resides in the tempting impossibility, the sense of mysterious, deep meaning, and the longing that exist in the separation from history. In earlier writings, Irving had experimented with the literary, comic, and political potential that the obscurity of his region's past afforded.[40] What he realized more fully in England at the end of the 1810s was that the experience Crayon desired could be had along the Hudson as well as the Thames or Avon, that the feeling of shadowy grandeur that Crayon sought in the castles and abbeys of Europe might be found in the sublime scenery and perhaps even shadowier history of New York. "We live," Crayon tells us that Diedrich Knickerbocker used to say when speaking of New York, "in the midst of history, mystery, and romance."[41] Irving discovered a way to work not just the history but even more the elision of the past in the Hudson Valley. As Crayon-Knickerbocker, the consummate insider-outsider at home and abroad, he could conceive of the Hudson Valley as haunted, and configure a type of hauntedness suitable for the place. The result was a small but influential set of stories and sketches—"Rip Van Winkle" and "The Legend of Sleepy Hollow" in *The Sketch Book*," "Dolph Heyliger" in *Bracebridge Hall*, "The Money Diggers" section of *Tales of a Traveller,* and later sketches for *The Knickerbocker* magazine—in which elements of Hudson Valley scenery, history, and lore were transfigured into desired objects within an international romantic economy, and into usable traditions at home.

LEGEND

The convergence of scenic, historical, social, and aesthetic factors that worked to produce a regional tradition of hauntedness, and that are exemplified within Irving's own experience, can also be traced within his tales. Indeed, part of what makes Irving so useful for understanding the development of a Hudson Valley haunted-ness comes from his degree of self-consciousness. His attention to the subjective aspects of hauntings led him to include in his tales and sketches diagrams of their inner workings. Irving's tales are often as much about the making of ghost stories as about ghosts.

A somewhat skeletal exposition of this tendency is found in "The Haunted House" in *Bracebridge Hall* (1822), which is itself not so much a tale as a recipe for a local haunting. Geoffrey Crayon, having been asked by his English hosts to tell a story (but lacking the wherewithal to come up with one on his own), defers, as usual, to a selection from Diedrich Knickerbocker, who prefaces his main tale, "Dolph Heyliger," with a reference to a haunted house in a then more rural Manhattan. The base for the haunting is set forth in the physical conditions of the structure and environs:

The house stood remote from the road, in the centre of a large field, with an avenue of old locust trees leading up to it, several of which had been shivered by lightning, and two or three blown down. A few apple-trees grew straggling about the field; there were traces also of what had been a kitchen-garden; but the fences were broken down, the vegetables had disappeared . . . with here and there a ragged rosebush, or a tall sunflower shooting up from among the brambles, and hanging its head sorrowfully, as if contemplating the surrounding desolation. Part of the roof of the old house had fallen in, the windows were shattered, the panels of the doors broken. . . . The appearance of the whole place was forlorn and desolate, at the best of times; but, in unruly weather, the howling of the wind about the crazy old mansion, the screeching of the weathercocks, the slamming and banging of a few loose window-shutters, had altogether so wild and dreary an effect, that the neighborhood stood perfectly in awe of the place.[42]

The ghostly potential of the place is not simply a result of its physical attributes, however; it derives from the way these conditions are linked to a problem of historical continuity and causality. This "old mansion" in "the ancient city of the Manhattoes," Knickerbocker tells us, is "one of the very few remains of the architecture of the early Dutch settlers, and must have been a house of some consequence at the time when it was built" (248). The prior Dutch presence here, reflected in the structure, provides the grounding for the haunting; what is also key, though, is the lack of neighborhood knowledge by which to explain the abandonment. Knickerbocker's statement, like the house, is full of holes resulting from the pace and character of change in the neighborhood, and a concomitant historical nearsightedness. The house, which Knickerbocker knew as a boy to be haunted, is a ruin whose history and significance can be apprehended only dimly: "The origin of this house was lost in the obscurity that covers the early period of the province," and "the reason of its having fallen to decay, was likewise a matter of dispute." Because the reasons for its state are not known, "the most current, and of course, the most probable account"—the default explanation—"was that it was haunted, and that nobody could live quietly in it" (249). Not only does the decay of the house make it an apt scene for haunting after the fact, but the decay is explained by preexisting haunting. Hauntedness serves as both consequence and cause.

The scene, which might otherwise be read simply as one of mundane failure (Knickerbocker provides vague suggestions to this end) or as the evidence of social change, is allowed to take on mythic dimensions through the fertile imaginations of current neighbors. A local perspective is provided by neighborhood boys (including the young Knickerbocker) who have, in turn, imbibed influential tales from the usual, marginal suspects: "not an old woman in the neighborhood but could furnish at least a score [of corroborating ghost tales]. There was a gray-headed curmudgeon of a negro who lived hard by, who had a whole budget of them to tell, many of which had happened to himself." The boys—who know next to nothing about the true history of the house—are deeply predisposed by stories they have heard to think it haunted. Knickerbocker says, "the place was so charmed by frightful stories that we dreaded to approach it." And so, each half-heard noise and half-glimpsed shadow yields new tales of ghosts: "there were sure to be a host of fearful anecdotes told of strange cries and groans, or of some hideous face suddenly seen staring out of one of the windows" (249).

The process of haunting and rehaunting occurs in the larger narrative, too, as Knickerbocker goes on to tell how, after the old negro "Pompey" died, and "the plough . . . passed over his grave, and levelled it with the rest of the field," and "nobody thought any more of the gray-headed negro," his skull was discovered on the property, giving rise to a new generation of rumors and tales: "a knot of gossips speculating on [the] skull . . . determined it to be the remains of some one that had been murdered, and they had raked up with it some of the traditionary tales of the haunted house" (250). Again, we see how the presence and remains of marginal others in the region lend themselves to the production of ghosts, the obscurity of the African-American past redoubling that of the Dutch.

In adding this further iteration, though, Irving does more than underline the fruitful interaction of local story culture and unintelligible historical residues. Notice what the knowledgeable Knickerbocker does: "too considerate of other people's enjoyment ever to mar a story of a ghost or a murder" (250), he declines to dispel the ghost stories and quietly reburies the skull. Thus, while on one hand the tale lays bare the bones of the haunting—identifying, at least for the reader, the source of the mysterious skull, and suggesting the process by which ghostliness gathers around inscrutable historical remnants—in the same instant the historian Knickerbocker, both in reburying the skull and in writing up the anecdote, plants seeds for new generations. In this, Irving points to another layer at work in perpetuating tales of haunting: the overarching desires and expectations of narrator, author, and audience. The haunting is produced from the materials the American traveler has handy, as they suit the narrator's and the author's romantic leanings, plus their gauging of audience. Indeed, the resurrection of "The Haunted House" has been occasioned by a request from Crayon's English hosts, whom he knows to be fond of ghost stories, just as the writing of *Bracebridge Hall* was predicated on the success of *The Sketch Book*, whose formulas it clearly emulated.

The elements more starkly laid out in "The Haunted House" had received a meatier, more regionally central, and historically contemporaneous treatment in "The Legend of Sleepy Hollow." In this story, Irving can be observed similarly interweaving bits of landscape, history, "superstition," and aesthetics. The reader is drawn in at the outset—through a combination of locational mapping and evocative landscape description—from the broad expanse of the Tappan Zee, through a spacious cove, through the market town of Tarrytown, and into a "lap of land among high hills."[43] Revealing that this "sequestered glen" is named "Sleepy Hollow," partly as a result of the "peculiar character of its inhabitants" (272), Irving refers to the uncanny potential in the special historical conditions of the area. As in "The Haunted House," he points particularly to early settlement by the Dutch, whose descendants in this case still predominate in the location. He also draws attention to the period of Native American inhabitance (a wizard chieftain, he says, cast a spell here) and to local incidents of the Revolutionary War, including the capture of the British spy André and a "nameless battle" that is said to have left the neighborhood its most notable ghost: a headless Hessian trooper on horseback. Along with geographical and historical landmarks, the narrator describes the local cultural atmosphere: the people are "given to all kinds of marvellous beliefs," and "the whole neighborhood abounds with local tales, haunted spots, and twilight superstitions" (273).

These things standing, the scene awaits an animating bolt. This comes in the lanky form of the itinerant Yankee schoolmaster, Ichabod Crane. Ichabod represents a contemporary historical phenomenon, what Irving calls here "the great torrent of migration and improvement" spearheaded by New Englanders, "which is making such incessant changes in other parts of this restless country" (274). New Englanders were pouring into New York during the first two decades of the nineteenth century, impressing their stamp on regional commerce, politics, and culture with alarming speed.[44] Irving jokes about the foreshortened historical memory that he implicitly associates with this torrent of Yankee "progress," writing that his protagonist came to Sleepy Hollow "in a remote period of American history, that is to say, some thirty years since" (274). Still, Ichabod is a less-than-benign interloper: he beats his lessons into his pupils and courts the belle of the neighborhood, Katrina Van Tassel, while rolling his eyes greedily over the potentially profitable land of her father. The surprise, however, is that Ichabod—the representative of the race of pioneers to whom Irving attributes both brevity of memory and a capacity to drown out existing local custom—is essential in activating the neighborhood's latent capacities for hauntedness. Through Ichabod, Irving highlights productive potential in both the minglings and the rifts that occur at the shifting social and cultural frontiers of the Hudson Valley.

Ichabod Crane strides into Sleepy Hollow having been raised on a steady diet of Cotton Mather and witch lore, "in which, by the way, he most firmly and potently believed" (276), and has "an appetite for the marvellous" as extraordinary as "his powers of digesting it." Once in Sleepy Hollow, Ichabod further feeds his habit on the gossip of Dutch housewives, who "as they sat spinning by the fire" told of "haunted fields and haunted brooks, and haunted bridges and haunted houses, and particularly of the headless horseman." As we see in scenes forecasting the tale's climax, these indulgences induce dire effects in Ichabod's perception of his surroundings. "As he wended his way [home]," Irving writes of one instance, "by swamp and stream and awful woodland . . . every sound of nature, at that witching hour, fluttered his excited imagination"; and more than once he is "appalled by some shrub covered with snow, which like a sheeted spectre beset his very path!" (277, 278).

The traps have all been set, then, for Ichabod, who, by courting the only daughter of the wealthiest man in the neighborhood, has roused the ire of rival suitor Brom Bones. Having had his imagination topped off at Van Tassel's party, where the men told tales in a "drowsy under tone" that "sunk deep" in his mind (290), Ichabod finds himself out in the suggestive gloom of Sleepy Hollow at night, where duskier elements of place, history, and mind gather themselves together with increasing potency:

The night grew darker and darker; the stars seemed to sink deeper in the sky, and driving clouds occasionally hid them from his sight. . . . He was, moreover, approaching the very place where many of the scenes of the ghost stories had been laid. In the centre of the road stood an enormous tulip tree, which towered like a giant above all the other trees. . . . Its limbs were gnarled, and fantastic . . . twisting down almost to the earth, and rising again into the air. It was connected with the tragical story of the unfortunate André, who had been taken prisoner hard by. . . . The common people regarded it with a mixture of respect and superstition, partly out of sympathy for the fate of its ill starred namesake, and partly from the tales of strange sights, and doleful lamentations, told concerning it. (291–292)

The scene is calculated to put Ichabod at the mercy of the images that have been implanted in his mind: "All the stories of ghosts and goblins . . . now came crowding upon his recollection" (291). Thus, when "in the dark shadow of the grove, on the margin of the brook, he beheld something huge, misshapen, black and towering" (292), and when he is joined by a dark rider whom he is horrified "on perceiving" to be headless (293), Ichabod takes it for the famous ghost.

It is important to pause here to highlight the psychological elements and language in Irving's tales. Clearly, Irving is concerned with the power of perception and imagination at work in the evocation of hauntedness. He is intrigued by the involuntariness with which stories come to the mind, and by the degree to which they suggest outside correspondence and cause. Irving's phrasing in describing Ichabod in the dark woods—the stories "now came crowding upon his recollection"—reappears in various forms throughout his work. In *Bracebridge Hall,* for instance, Crayon speaks of poets' minds as having "been impregnated" by "popular fancies" and of the parson as having "become infected" by superstitious tales. Crayon himself admits that when alone he finds "these themes have taken hold of my imagination," so that as he looks out over the moonlight-streaked grounds his mind is "crowded by 'thick

Headless Horseman of Sleepy Hollow (1840–1865, New York
City), by George Washington Allston Jenkins. Oil on canvas, 26 × 36⅛ inches. Gift of Benjamin
G. Jenkins. Courtesy of Historic Hudson Valley, Tarrytown, New York.

coming fancies.'"[45] In *Tales of a Traveller,* Irving experiments further; the whole book, in fact, centers on scenes of storytelling and result-ing misperceptions in the auditors' external experiences. Such im-ages and scenes in Irving's tales, as in contemporary gothic and ghost tales more generally, denote a prefiguring awareness of the unconscious mind: tales that were told to Ichabod in a "drowsy un-der tone" in the dark and have "sunk deep" into his mind be-come the "visionary propensity" that the narrator claims is "uncon-sciously imbibed by every one who resides" in Sleepy Hollow for a time (273). Critics G. R. Thompson and Donald Ringe have argued that Irving maintained a suspicion of the imagination.[46] Although Irving's tales were in part effusions of romanticism, they may also be seen as investigations of the romantic mindset, whose emphases on genius, inspiration, and overwhelming emotion paralleled the surrender to imaginative excess that opened the way for hauntings.

But "The Legend of Sleepy Hollow" is not purely psychologi-cal or aesthetic exegesis. Irving instead attaches the outbreak of ghostliness to decisive historical and social conditions. That is, Ichabod's apprehension of the ghostly Hessian is the product both of what he knows by heart and of what, as an outsider in the com-munity, he does not know. The Dutch in the story may tell ghost tales, but Irving presents them as more or less aboriginal, and com-fortable with the ghosts, tales, and neighborhood, in a way that Ichabod—even as he begins to add local stories to his "budget" of tales—is not. Quite specifically, the neighbors might have reason to think the midnight rider something other than a ghostly manifesta-tion, as they have heard Brom Bones and his crew on many occa-sions "dashing along past the farm houses at midnight, with a whoop and halloo" so that "the old dames, startled out of their sleep, would listen for a moment . . . and then exclaim, 'aye, there goes Brom Bones and his gang!'" (281). Ichabod simply does not have the local knowledge to suspect that the ghost might be Brom Bones in disguise. The source of the haunting resides in the fact that neither Ichabod nor the reader can be sure of the identity of the mysterious Other that Ichabod encounters in Sleepy Hollow. Meanwhile, a reciprocal haunting is effected by the uncanny once-presence and now-absence of the interloping Yankee, as the ruins of the schoolhouse—Irving's often-used symbol for the Yankee imposition in New York—are said by the Dutch locals to be haunted by the vanished schoolmaster (who they do not know has simply moved on).

At a basic level, there is no story here without Ichabod, and not only because his presence and disappearance leave material for further local tales. The neighborhood might abound with "local tales, haunted spots, and twilight superstitions," but the telling of the tales and the reincarnation of the ghost are occasioned by Ichabod's appearance on the scene and his taste for ghost stories (as well as his eyebrow-raising ambitions with regard to the neighborhood heiress). Ichabod raises old ghosts anew. Moreover, through Ichabod, the intruding, transient New Englander, the local legends are given new life. Not only might one imagine this chatty, superstitious Yankee, this "travelling gazette," as Irving calls him (276), peddling his supernatural encounters in new venues, but, as Irving indicates in the closing frame, the legend is being told at the corporation meeting in New York City (despite the protest of a member that it has no moral). It also earns a place in Geoffrey Crayon's *Sketch Book* (which would be an international hit).

The idea that the Yankee "torrent" helped yield a certain ghostliness in the Hudson Valley appears in other places and forms in Irving's work. For instance, in "Conspiracy of the Cocked Hats," a piece for *The Knickerbocker* magazine, Irving's Roloff Van Ripper writes: "Poetry and romance received a fatal blow at the overthrow of the ancient Dutch dynasty, and have ever since been gradually withering under the growing domination of the Yankees." His next statement not only half-contradicts the previous one, but also suggests the ways in which the maligned Yankee invasion has helped create the romance: "But poetry and romance still live unseen among us, or seen only by the enlightened few, who are able to contemplate this city and its environs through the medium of tradition, and clothed with the associations of foregone ages."[47] The past becomes ghostly, and thereby more valuable, *because* it has been forced by the glaring light of Yankee progress into the shadows.

Van Ripper means to suggest that the "enlightened few" who bring romance to light are descended from early Dutch settlers. But what Irving suggests here and demonstrates in his tales is that production of hauntings derives largely from the acts of intruding others, who both find and make more alien the residues of the regional past, and who read local scenes through perspectives conducive to seeing ghosts. Both the interloping Ichabod and the narrator of "The Legend of Sleepy Hollow" are implicated here.[48] That Irving intends to conjoin these two is suggested in parallel scenes early in the narrative. In the opening, the narrator recollects breaking the peculiar quiet of Sleepy Hollow—represented by the "murmur" of the brook—with the report of his gun while squirrel hunting there in his boyhood (272); a page or two later, we are told that "the low murmur" of Ichabod's pupils is "interrupted now and then by the authoritative voice of the master, in the tone of menace or command" (274–275). Both Ichabod and the narrator are intruders with an eye for the supernatural, who find themselves for moments of time amid the suggestive landscapes, hazy history, and somewhat "peculiar" people along the Hudson. And although the locals may have their ghost stories, these intruders figure prominently in the creation of haunted-place legends in that they draw these images out of the "sequestered glens" and run them into a main stream, fashioning and reproducing them for nonlocal audiences.

As in "The Haunted House," "The Legend of Sleepy Hollow" finally reflects back on the author himself as a factor in the creation of regional hauntedness: Irving, too, is an intruder, through whom productive cross-breedings yield ghosts. He is a savvier and more worldly Ichabod, bringing along in his imaginative strides through the Hudson Valley a romantic tendency and a mind "infected" by reading and foreign travel. Refitting the ghost types found in German tales, he is able to communicate his apprehensions of local conditions while also bolstering the development of domestic lore. Transforming the German legend of "Peter Klaus" into "Rip Van Winkle," Irving expresses a sense of mutability in the rapidly changing Hudson Valley scene. The ghosts, returning at intervals, are the measure of historical change and jolting dislocation, as indeed is Rip, who can be said to be haunted as much by the future as by the past; he is himself a ghost in the new order, exclaiming, "every thing's changed—and I'm changed—and I can't tell what's my name, or who I am!"[49] In "The Legend of Sleepy Hollow," meanwhile, the particular ghost designation applied to the type of phantom horseman, which Irving has borrowed from the German, is doubly, perhaps even triply, fitted to haunt the region. The Hessian, who may be seen as a nod to the ghost's ancestry in German folklore, simultaneously corresponds to facts of regional history: Hessian soldiers fought for the British in Revolutionary War battles nearby. Also, though, the ghost represents the problems of historical amnesia in the region. In essence, a Hessian killed in the Revolutionary War seems to have little to do with either the Dutch or the Yankee protagonist in Sleepy Hollow, and is thus all the more strange and frightening as something whose relevancy cannot be gauged. The headless, identityless Hessian killed in a "nameless battle" is thus both a historical possibility and a convenient device, the ghost of a mercenary and a mercenary ghost.

Neither "pure" local folklore nor heavy-handed impositions of European romanticism, Irving's tales are at every level the products of hybridity, and we see in them how a surprise eruption of ghosts in the Hudson Valley in the early nineteenth century emerged from concatenations of personal, local, national, and international elements. The tales derived from Irving's own sensibilities and insecurities and from the transatlantic ascendance of romantic literary and popular tastes. They were linked to contingencies of local geography and experience and to a problem of historical memory amid progress, which had peculiar salience in the Hudson Valley, but which resonated with American cultural anxieties and desires more broadly. "We have . . . lost sight of just how central a figure he was to Americans in the early decades of the nineteenth century," Jeffrey Rubin-Dorsky writes. "In many respects his story was theirs."[50] Irving's tales, like Irving's own story, offered remarkable images of the conditions that made the Hudson haunted in the early nineteenth century.

What makes these tales even more remarkable is that they predicted, and moreover prompted, the further development of hauntedness in the Hudson Valley. As regional geography continued to support new commercial, social, and cultural interpositions, scenes of encounter and interpretation like those depicted in Irving's stories were replayed throughout the nineteenth and twentieth centuries. Instead of Cotton Mather, Walter Scott, or "Peter Klaus," however, what generations of Hudson Valley visitors and settlers had in mind was Washington Irving.

AFTERLIFE

The Sketch Book of Geoffrey Crayon, Gent. was a great success in its moment, selling out and garnering praise both in the United States and—unprecedented for an American author—in England. The book was reprinted throughout the nineteenth and twentieth centuries with notable frequency, while individual sketches and tales from *The Sketch Book,* as well as *A History of New York, Bracebridge Hall, Tales of a Traveller,* and other works were extracted for collection or individual publication. According to Rubin-Dorsky, not only can *The Sketch Book* be placed on the "all-time American 'bestseller' list," but "'Rip Van Winkle' was probably the most popular and reprinted piece of the nineteenth century."[51] Of "Rip Van Winkle" and "The Legend of Sleepy Hollow," William Cullen Bryant wrote in 1860: "In our country they have been read, I believe, by nearly everybody who can read at all."[52] In 1901 Henry W. Boynton wrote that "a great many editions of Irving, cheap and costly, complete and incomplete, have been issued from many sources. . . . his original publishers are now selling year by year, more of his books than ever before."[53] Tales have been translated into Dutch, French, German, Catalan, Polish, Yiddish, Chinese, and other languages. They have also been dramatized, most famously in Joseph Jefferson and Dion Boucicault's long-running nineteenth-century staging of "Rip Van Winkle"; interpreted into musical forms; depicted by Thomas Cole, John Quidor, Asher B. Durand, F. O. C. Darley, N. C. Wyeth, and Maxfield Parrish, among many others; and made into films and cartoons.[54] Even though literary critics became disenthralled with Irving in the early twentieth century, Irving's Hudson Valley tales clearly had long-lasting appeal and resonance in the wider world, and an impact on the development of American literature.

Nowhere, though, did the tales have more effect or enduring influence, nowhere were they more often read and repeated, than in the Hudson Valley. If Irving had been "the most fashionable fellow of the day" in London, in the Hudson Valley he became the "regional patron saint."[55] Irving had a tremendous influence in the Hudson Valley, not only because prereadings of Irving colored the view of generations of outside visitors to the region, but also because Irving's spirits were embraced and reiterated within the region in multifarious ways in the nineteenth and twentieth centuries, leaving traces in regional writing, landscape, and experience. As early as 1828, an anonymous visitor to the Catskills was warning readers of *The Atlantic Souvenir* that the host at "Rip's Cottage" was not a descendant of Rip Van Winkle.[56] As late as 1996, North Tarrytown officially changed its name to Sleepy Hollow. The incorporation of Irving's tales into the cultural landscapes of the Hudson Valley was immediate, multifaceted, and enduring, rising at times, especially the late nineteenth century, to feverish pitch, and remaining as a touchstone of regional image and identity into the present.

The processes by which Irving's tales were incorporated in the Hudson Valley illustrate various social, political, and commercial uses of haunted-place legends to which I return in subsequent chapters. Gauging the extent of Irving's influence, however, is no easy task. One might first point macroscopically to proliferations of and references to Irving's tales in regional writing. Raymond O'Brien writes in *American Sublime* that "the legends of Sleepy Hollow, the Dunderberg, and the Catskills were taken so seriously [in the Hudson Valley] that they became a part of almost every historical account thereafter."[57] Explicit traces of Irving and his tales appear time and time again in regional writings: in tourbooks such as *The Tourist, or Pocket Manual for Travellers* (first edition, 1830), *Sketches of the North River* (1838), *The Hudson by Daylight* (various editions, 1873–1912), and *Hudson River Landings* (1933); in travel narratives such as *The Hudson: From Wilderness to Sea* (1866), *Summer Days on the Hudson* (1876), and *The New York and Albany Post Road* (1905); in local histories and folklore collections, including *Historical Collections of the State of New York* (1842), *Legends and Poetry of the Hudson* (1868), *Picturesque Catskills* (1894), *Chronicles of Tarrytown and Sleepy Hollow* (1897), *The Hudson* (1939), and *Hudson Valley Tales and Trails* (1987); in memoirs such as *Reminiscences of an Old Westchester Homestead* (1897) and *When Granny Was a Little Girl* (1926); in children's books like *Spooks of the Valley* (1948); in other regionally focused literary productions like Maxwell Anderson's play *High Tor* (1937) and T. Coraghessan Boyle's *World's End* (1987); as well as in hotel brochures, railroad and steamboat publications, and newspaper articles. This catalogue is by no means exhaustive. One finds reference after reference not only to the most prominent ghosts from the most famous tales—Henry Hudson's ghost crew or the Headless Horseman—but also to subsidiary legends from the major tales, as well as ghosts and goblins from less-well-known tales: the white woman of Raven Rock, the wizard Indian chieftain, and hauntings at André's tree from "The Legend of Sleepy Hollow"; the Indian woman who cuts the old moon into stars from "Rip Van Winkle"; the ghost ship and the Dunderberg imps from "Dolph Heyliger"; the rowing ghost of Rumbout Van Dam from "A Chronicle of Wolfert's Roost."

Looking more microscopically, one may also trace Irving's influence in individual acts of writing, reading, and rehearsal through which his ghosts were imaginatively reconjured in the landscape. Indeed, many of the references to and reiterations of Irving's tales were intended to be read *in situ*. For instance, noting the "solicitude evinced by travellers" to learn about the river, while lamenting that "the guidebooks in general use deal more in dull statistics" than in "those storied reminiscences that so often throw a charm around natural scenery," the writers of the 1838 *Sketches of the North River* instructed visitors to read Irving while touring the Catskills:

> It is among those wild mountains, a fitting stage for scenes of diablerie and wonder, that Irving has laid his inimitable tale of Rip Van Winkle; and it is only in such a region, with the grand and terrible around you, that it can be read with the most zest: seated upon a lonely rock in some dark dell, you become imbued with the spirit of its conceptions, and at every rustling sound turn round in expectation of meeting the little Dutchman with his wonderful keg of liquor, or of seeing the silent group bowling away at their ninepins.[58]

Such scenes of reading Irving in place, and into place, were not just guidebook chestnuts. Commenting on the legends of the Highlands through which his party was passing on a river tour, the author of an 1876 travel narrative notes: "Of course [our] interest in these legends had been rendered keen, and even intense, by reading Irving's matchless stories."[59]

That residents as well as tourists indulged in Irving-induced visions is evidenced in an extended and animated account found in A. E. P. Searing's *When Granny Was a Little Girl,* a "narrative of a childhood along the Hudson River" in the 1860s. Searing tells how each year her family had a "Rip Van Winkle Day," a holiday that involved a retelling of the story of Rip Van Winkle in the mountain setting where the tale was reputed to have taken place. In this memoir, Searing provides a palpable sense of the depth and the endurance with which these evocations impressed themselves in her imagination, thereby taking life in the scene. Speaking of herself in the third person, as Anne, she writes:

> at the entrance to Palenville Clove was the ruin of an old house that used to be pointed out as the one where had lived Rip Van Winkle. . . . It was silvered with the weather of years long ago. Stooped and haggard, it brooded like an old, old man over the tangle of what must have been once a garden. Or, no—it was like the ghost of a house, the ghost of a garden. Anne felt all at once that she must . . . go to it.
>   . . . An overflowing stillness came out of the old ruin. . . . Anne had never known such silence . . . this silence seemed breathless with meanings that one could feel but not quite understand. . . . Her mind struggled with the time that separated her from the bygone life of this old house and she longed unspeakably to see it all as it had been when dear kind lazy old Rip lived in it. Then, suddenly, as if doors unfolded and opened, back there she was! She was looking into mist, or was it savory smoke spirals that wreathed from an iron pot?
>   . . . The pot seemed to bubble—but as silently and soundlessly as crackled the dancing flames. A lank figure sat cross-legged by the hearth.[60]

Searing drives home the power in her father's rehearsal of the tale in suggestive surroundings: "the ravine, after Father's story, was ghostly. None of them would have been greatly surprised to see a squat little Dutchman, puffing under the barrel strapped to his back, toil up the rocky ascent." That these images made an enduring impression on Searing is reflected in her later recollections. When as an adult she goes to see the play *Rip Van Winkle,* featuring actor Joe Jefferson, she says, "even he, great though he was, did not fill her fancy as her father did that afternoon. She was thinking all the time of what she had 'seen' at the old house."[61]

Irving's influence is a composite of such instances of personal and local investment. In the 1880s a man who believed "Rip Van Winkle" had taken place on his property refused to sell to a hotel, claiming that the land was "too sacred to be profaned" by tourists.[62] In the 1970s a town history included the story of a ghost ship that "may have started with Washington Irving . . . but we will claim it as part of our lore since the vessel sailed past the town of Lloyd."[63] Of course, references to Irving could be grudging and dismissive as well as embracing: when a pair of *Yankee* magazine reporters went looking for Irving's ghosts in the 1950s, they met with a bored shrug from an "old boy" in Catskill, who pointed them out of town.[64] Nonetheless, what emerges from the accretion of individual accounts is a sense that Irving's presence looms large. Like Ichabod Crane, who, fed on a steady diet of neighborhood tales, could not help seeing ghosts in the Sleepy Hollow night, countless Hudson Valley visitors and residents found themselves, albeit usually willingly, under the spell of Irving's tales as they looked out on the surrounding scene.

Yet from the few examples mentioned here, it becomes evident that Irving's stories are not his alone. His imaginative territory has been colonized. Although Searing does mention Irving once, the tale in her memory is "Father's," and as she writes of her experience in Palenville Clove, it becomes hers. In considering Irving's influence, what must be discussed, finally, is how the afterlife of Irving's tales was achieved and maintained both through reinvocations of Irving and through acts of appropriation that sought to affix the ghosts while removing the writer from the picture.

"There is . . . a 'magic in the web' of all his works," insists Wallace Bruce in *The Hudson: Three Centuries of History, Romance and Invention* (1907). "We somehow feel the reality of every legend he has given us."[65] A lecturer, poet, diplomat, and guidebook writer, Bruce was perhaps Irving's and the Hudson's most fervent devotee at the turn of the century. He cited Irving in his guidebooks and histories; "lovingly dedicated" his 1881 poem, *The Hudson,* to Irving; and compiled a travel companion of Irving's tales, *Along the Hudson with Washington Irving* (1913).[66] Bruce's statement, in part, epitomizes the emotional and imaginative acts by which Irving's tales were repeatedly reenlivened in regional imagings, and also represents one mode—what might be called "invocation"—by which Irving's influence was maintained in regional culture. This mode—which involved calling Irving by name and directing readers to his writings—can be seen in the passage from the 1838 *Sketches of the North River* imploring visitors to the Catskills to read "Rip Van Winkle" and, more simply, in the conclusion of an 1868 book, *Legends and Poetry of the Hudson:* "How the literature of our country and particularly our river is indebted to his genius!"[67] However, Bruce reveals the power of another mode at work in the incorporation of Irving's tales into the region, one involving a subtle but significant twist of causality. "As long as the Mahicanituk, the ever-flowing Hudson, pours its waters to the sea," he continues, "as long as Rip Van Winkle sleeps in the blue Catskills, or the 'Headless Horseman' rides at midnight along the Old Post Road *en route* for Teller's Point, so long will the writings of Washington Irving be remembered and cherished."[68] Bruce's wording, even as he is reaffirming Irving, marks a shift in Irving's position with regard to his tales.

Bruce does not write that as long as Irving is read his creations will survive. He writes, rather, that Irving will be remembered as long as the ghosts he described inhabit the scene. The language here moves away from presenting Irving as the *creator* of tales and toward describing him as *chronicler* of them—as historian or folklorist who has only presented findings, albeit in a convincing and entertaining fashion.

Similar characterizations can be found in other turn-of-the-century allusions to Irving. Take, for instance, C. G. Hine's travelogue, *The New York and Albany Post Road* (1905). In his chapter "Irvington to Tarrytown: The Land of the Midnight Hessian," he sets a scene that clearly owes something to Irving: "As we proceed toward the land of enchantment the surroundings seem to take on a more mysterious air. Sounds that awhile before meant nothing more than the wind in the trees now begin to make one think of the rush of galloping . . . Hessians on mischief bent." Now, having first evoked the ghosts, Hine alludes to Irving, but only obliquely, referring to the proximity of Sunnyside—"the abode wherein so many of these marvels were clothed in becoming language"—and then calling up "the artist" to describe the scene. Both the structure and the wording here serve to obscure Irving and to divorce the hauntedness of the place from Irving as author. The marvels exist; the artist only "clothed" them in "becoming language." Irving is mentioned once by name a few pages later, but then Hine slips into mystifying allusion, calling him "the grand sachem of all the wizards, who wove the romance of the headless horseman . . . so tightly about the spot that [it is] to-day part and parcel of it." Hine's next venture, *The West Bank of the Hudson River* (1906), continues in this vein. In telling a story from Coxsackie (Greene County) of romantic rivalry between a Yankee and a Dutchman, Hine refers to a similar instance "down the river," adding parenthetically, "for the facts in this case see the writings of Mr. W. Irving."[69]

Clearly, Hine has his tongue in his cheek at points here and is not denying a debt to Irving. He knows his Irving, and he expects that his readers do as well. That he takes Irving for granted is a point in itself worth emphasizing. Nevertheless his writing both derives from and contributes to a sense of the priority of the hauntings over the haunter. Such presentation of Irving as more historian than fiction writer runs throughout the twentieth century. For instance, Paul Wilstach claims in *Hudson River Landings* (1933) that Irving "confirms" the presence of supernatural creatures in the Highlands, and elsewhere cites "Irving's account of the legend of *Ichabod Crane and the Headless Horseman*" (not "The Legend of Sleepy Hollow").[70] At other times, as in *History of the Tarrytowns from Ancient Times to the Present* (1975), writers correct Irving: "Legend tells us, that three ghosts, not just Irving's lady in white, roam the area" of Raven Rock.[71] Such instances signal a naturalization of Irving's legends and suggest that the places Irving designated were subject to rehaunting as well. They also point to an eclipse of the writer in the long shadows of his creations.

These texts may be seen as partial heirs of much less subtle piratings of Irving's thunder that were particularly rampant in the second half of the nineteenth century. Long before writers like Bruce and Hine were evidencing an absorption of Irving's tales as folklore and history, there were more deliberate attempts to imbue the tales with an air of authenticity by throwing a veil over Irving. A notable example is found in the 1868 volume *Legends and Poetry of the Hudson.* The author, who appropriately remains anonymous, but who clearly asserts a degree of regional insidership, writes that in wandering along the river banks, "we have found a few strange stories and legends almost lost and forgotten in that most sad of burial places—the ashes of our father's fire-sides." Conceding that "others"—presumably meaning Irving—"may have already obtained the 'Golden Fleece,'" the writer contends, "there still remain beautiful legends to be narrated." The little volume is a hash of borrowed legends, quotations of poetry, verse versions of tales, and excerpts from stories. Rip Van Winkle and Henry Hudson's ghost crew, the Storm-Ship, the Heer of Dunderberg, the legend of Ontiora (which Irving mentions in "Rip Van Winkle"), and others make appearances. Diedrich Knickerbocker is mentioned, and, as noted above, the book pays homage to Irving in closing; but in the course of things, Irving is quite deliberately obscured. "How the old Legends and Traditions come thronging upon us mingled with recollections of fireside laughter and fireside tears!" the little volume overflows. "Here the story of the 'Storm Ship' was repeated over and over again." Claiming that this legend is "peculiarly and distinctively *the* legend of the early settlers," the writer says, "still, about the glowing fireplaces of olden dwellings scattered along our River, it is repeated in the long winter evenings somewhat as follows."[72] What follows is a passage lifted straight from *Bracebridge Hall*.

A similar, though more broadcast, act of incorporation and effacement occurs in Charles M. Skinner's *Myths and Legends of Our Own Land* (1896), a regionally arranged collection of American legends that begins at the Hudson River. Skinner's project is clear from the outset; he writes in his preface: "It is unthinkingly said and often, that America is not old enough to have developed a legendary era . . . and the Rhine and Hudson are frequently compared, to the prejudice of the latter." Skinner, hoping to bulk up the "slight" bibliography of "American legends," promises tales that "have been gathered from sources the most diverse: records, histories, newspapers, magazines, oral narrative." At least eight of the twenty-five Hudson Valley tales, plus two more in the "Manhattoes and Nearby" section, can be traced to Irving. Skinner mentions Irving occasionally—for instance, in introducing the tale of Rip Van Winkle—but the overall goal is obviously to pitch the stories as bona fide regional folktales; "Rip," Skinner writes, "was a real personage." Irving's position in Skinner's "The Galloping Hessian," meanwhile, is nearly metaphoric, as the tale begins "in the flower-gemmed cemetery of Tarrytown where gentle Irving sleeps."[73]

As might be guessed, tourist-dependent businesses were particularly watchful for opportunities to capture Irving's ghosts. Eager to turn tales into site-specific legends, they were not particularly concerned with precise literary history. For instance, as Catskills-area historian Alf Evers details, when the actor Joe Jefferson suggested that Rip had lived in Palenville and had slept in Kaaterskill Clove, rather than in Sleepy Hollow near the Catskill Mountain House, the owner of a rival hotel seized on this, reprinting the tale in his hotel publication "in so confident a manner that innocent guests assumed that Rip was an old retainer" of the establishment. Not wishing to discourage any potential travelers to either site, the New York, Buffalo and West Shore Railroad presented the claims of both hotels in their promotional booklets.[74] A. E. P. Searing (who married an Overlook Mountain House backer) let the others haggle about Rip Van Winkle, grabbing instead the prize of Henry Hudson's ghostly crew. She told readers of her 1884 book *The Land of Rip Van Winkle* that these ghosts were believed by early Dutch settlers to haunt Overlook Mountain.[75] According to one early-twentieth-century writer, who himself had come looking for Rip, "It is to Irving and not to the Great Spirit that the Catskill innkeepers should give thanks for their bank accounts. . . . Every summer half a million people visit these hills partly on account of that story."[76] Even in the late twentieth century, the Catskill tourist industry was still turning to Rip Van Winkle hunts to boost business.[77]

Irving, of course, set the groundwork for the proliferation and adaptation of these hauntings, not only by providing a set of usable ghosts and sites, but also by setting them up as independent of him. Beyond his shiftiness about sources and his efforts to suggest origins among the Hudson Valley folk, he worked to spin, within

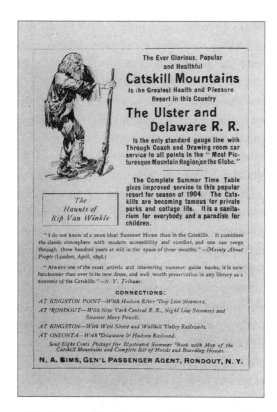

"The Haunts of Rip Van Winkle." Advertisement for
the Ulster and Delaware Railroad. From Wallace
Bruce, *The Hudson* (New York: Bryant Literary
Union, 1901).

and across texts, a whole web of cross-references to Hudson Valley places, ghosts, and personages that appeared in his own tales.
Diedrich Knickerbocker—Irving's dummy historian and the source
for "Rip Van Winkle," "The Legend of Sleepy Hollow," "Dolph
Heyliger," and other Hudson Valley ghost tales—is fleshed out as a
real entity by Geoffrey Crayon (himself a ghostwriter for Irving) in

prefaces, and particularly in Irving's contributions to *The Knicker-bocker* magazine in the late 1830s and early 1840s. Crayon is repeatedly called in to testify for Knickerbocker's dubious references, offering "a few particulars" regarding Sleepy Hollow, for instance, when he discovers that "the very existence of the place has been held in question by many; who, judging from its odd name, and from the odd stories current among the vulgar concerning it, have rashly deemed the whole to be a fanciful creation."[78] Characters in the stories take on added substance, as well, through Irving's cross-references. Dr. Knipperhausen, owner of the haunted house in "Dolph Heyliger," reappears in "The Adventure of the Black Fisherman" in *Tales of a Traveller,* where Irving goes to the trouble of providing a footnote denoting the doctor "the same, no doubt, of whom mention is made in the history of Dolph Heyliger."[79] Irving leans tale upon tale for mutual support, obliquely referring to "Rip Van Winkle" to prove claims made in "The Storm-Ship" in *Bracebridge Hall:* "for indeed it had already been reported," he writes, "that Hendrick Hudson and his crew haunted the Kaatskill Mountain."[80] He similarly provides retroactive support for "The Legend of Sleepy Hollow," explaining in "A Chronicle of Wolfert's Roost" "the origin of that potent and drowsy spell which still prevails" in Sleepy Hollow.[81] A glance over Irving's pieces for *The Knickerbocker,* in fact, reveals sweeping acts of self-referential atmospherics: here he speaks of "the wizard region of Sleepy Hollow," "the spell-bound recesses of Sleepy Hollow," "that spell bound region," "the wizard spell of ancient days [that] reigned over the place."[82] And so on. If readers could not be counted on to chase these leads down through various books, they might find many of them gathered in Irving's 1849 collection *A Book of the Hudson,* which, Irving himself wrote in the preface, "might form an agreeable and instructive handbook to all intelligent and inquiring travellers about to explore the wonders and beauties of the Hudson."[83] Such efforts to give his creations the semblance of truth helped secure their proliferation in regional imaginations.

The other crucial element undergirding the adoption of Irving-esque hauntings in the Hudson Valley was, paradoxically, Irving's vagueness. Irving has been credited with having initiated the "inconclusive ghost story."[84] His equivocal story endings, which leave room for supernatural, psychological, or rational explanations, resound as more than literary achievements. Irving may have been joking, philosophizing, or experimenting. Nevertheless, despite telltale pumpkin remains in Sleepy Hollow, despite inconsistencies in Rip's story, despite the fact that the final line of "Dolph Heyliger" hints that he made it all up (he was "the ablest drawer of the long bow in the province"), readers were not explicitly disabused of the possibility that ghosts, or simply ghost stories, had a place in the Hudson Valley.[85] Donald Ringe writes: "The key to Irving's success is his careful manipulation of point of view." *The Sketch Book, Bracebridge Hall,* and *Tales of a Traveller* "are presented as the work of Geoffrey Crayon, a persona with the kind of mental attitude which permits the use of Gothic materials in a rationalistic context."[86] Irving's ultimate shiftiness, linked as it was with a set of images and locations, allowed for graftings and affirmations, whether deadpan or humorous. Irving thus provided a set of usable hauntings, a more general way of seeing which valued ghostliness, and a fertile equivocation that served to prime the canvas for later generations.

Irving was aware that his tales had taken on a whole life of their own in the Hudson Valley landscape, and moreover, he seems to have sanctioned their escape. When in 1858 a boy from Catskill, having argued with an old man about where Rip Van Winkle lived, wrote seeking Irving's expertise, Irving's response was typical: "I can give you no other information concerning the localities of the story of Rip Van Winkle, than is to be gathered from the manuscript of Mr. Knickerbocker, published in the *Sketch Book*. Perhaps he left them purposely in doubt. I would advise you to defer to the opinion of the 'very old gentleman' with whom you say you had an argument on the subject. I think it probable he is as accurately informed as any one on the matter."[87]

Through proliferation and appropriation, invocation and erasure, Irving's tales yielded strange and multifarious progeny in the Hudson Valley. The epigraph to this chapter suggests that Irving would not have been at all dismayed to find the ghosts he set loose come back in "odd shapes" in "some old woman's narrative." Yet perhaps even he would have been surprised and perplexed by what Westchester historian Edgar Mayhew Bacon once experienced, as recalled in his *Chronicles of Tarrytown and Sleepy Hollow* (1897):

> About twenty years ago the writer was passing, one morning, through the little lane that borders the Pocantico, between Broadway and the site of the burned factory (Brombacher's), when he overheard an Irishwoman, who stood by her cottage gate, relate this marvellous tale to her neighbors:
>
> "It was n't late, mebby not mower than tin o'clock, an' me waitin' here be the gate for Dinny to come in . . . when upon me sowl, thrue as I'm standin' here, I see right out there in the road a big, black, shadder-like, *widout any head,* an' him on horseback at that."
>
> There was no doubting the sincerity of the tones. I looked at the ghost-seer. Honesty and ignorance shared the realm between them. Had she possibly had her imagination fired by reading Irving? It is easier to believe that she had actually seen the Headless Hessian.[88]

In presenting this profane eruption of what might be considered the neighborhood's most sacrosanct tale, a bemused Bacon clearly means to highlight incongruities. This is not quaint Sleepy Hollow: not only has the Industrial Revolution arrived in Tarrytown, but also, given Bacon's opening reference to the burned factory, it seems to be in distinctly unpicturesque decline. And the voice reciting the tale is not that of an old Dutch housewife; it is the brogue of an Irish immigrant, emphasized by Bacon's attempt at dialect writing. On top of this, Bacon implicitly distinguishes between his own more literary reading of Irving and this woman's more literal reincarnation of the ghost into the mundane environment. Is her headless horseman the same as his? If this woman, a presumably uneducated newcomer, had heard of the headless horseman, then how? The unstated possibility—that the tale is in circulation as local folklore—seems ultimately to be Bacon's point, although he does not comment on whether this folklore has trickled down from Irving or exists independently of him.

There is, of course, no knowing. Bacon's anecdote, which seems to indicate the thoroughness and diversity of Irving's influence, in the end presents a dilemma, raising to the surface questions that have run underneath this discussion of Irving. Are references to headless horsemen, ghost ships, and ghosts at Raven Rock all derived from Irving, are they independent, or have they been adapted and incorporated to the point that they no longer bear reference to Irving? The "web" of Irving's work has served to sustain and anchor generations of spinners; yet it can also seem a trap, making it difficult to know what predates Irving, and to isolate the not-Irving in what follows him.

Ultimately, though, two things seem true: first, that the specific hauntings, as well as the general atmosphere of hauntedness, that made a literary debut in Irving's writing became ingrained and valued ingredients of regional literary and vernacular culture; and second, that the absorption and perpetuation of images from Irving's tales were possible only because the images were adaptable to the

diverse social, political, and cultural conditions and needs of individuals and generations. Just as Irving's own tales cannot be read as
simple replays of German folklore, each reference to a headless
horseman or ghostly Dutch sailor, even if it borrows a strand from
Irving, must in the end be considered as a discrete instance that, like
all ghost legends afloat in the region, is motivated by particular
contexts, and carries unique valences and functions.

The legend of "Spooky Hollow" is too well known to repeat here beyond the fact that "a Mr. Salisbury" caused the death of a Negro woman slave. . . . On stormy nights she is supposed to appear there and scream. However, Miss Frances Mann . . . told me that her father had a friend . . . [who] said that the woman who was killed was not a Negro slave but a German girl, an indentured. She was a Hessian.

–Letter to the *Catskill Daily Mail*, August 7, 1942

"The Sutherlands" . . . is a romance founded on this story. . . . In filling out her tale [the author] varies from the commonly received statements of facts in the case, by making the murdered girl a colored slave, half Indian and half mulatto, instead of white.

–Rev. Charles Rockwell, *The Catskill Mountains and the Region Around* (1867)

Any way, it was a girl, and she ran away.

–C. G. Hine, *The West Bank of the Hudson River* (1906)

THE COLORFUL CAREER

OF A GHOST FROM LEEDS

*D*ead women roam the roads, streams, and woods of eastern Greene County. A woman in white has been reported wandering along the aptly named Murderer's Creek in the town of Athens. A woman in black, whose identity in life is not known, has been seen stalking the Green Lake Road in Leeds, according to the Catskill *Examiner* of December 1906. Another woman, this time in gray, meanders in the woods along the Leeds–Catskill Road near Cairo, "singing a melancholy song." "Who she is," wrote Charles Wilde in 1937, "no one knows."[1]

Each of these ghosts has a story, and occasionally hints about the history and meanings underlying these stories come to the surface. The woman in white, for instance, has been identified as Sally Hamilton, whose brutal unsolved murder in 1813 shocked the town of Athens. The same ghost has also been identified as Mary Johnson, killed in 1841.[2] Mostly, however, this ghost in white, like her counterparts in gray and black, goes unidentified. These ghosts seem to want to say something about the history and character of the place they haunt, but their stories have all but dissolved. Lacking traceable history, they exist only as suggestive, elusive shades of obscurity.

There is, however, another ghost who haunts the vicinity: the ghost of a female being dragged behind a ghostly horse, reported variously near Spook Rock and Spooky Hollow on the outskirts of what is now the village of Leeds.[3] This ghost is one of the most enduring and well-known ghosts of the region, as well as one of the most shifty—she may appear as white or black, Indian or Scottish, Spanish or German. Her story, which has its origins in an obscure eighteenth-century murder case involving the richest man in town and his servant, wends through generations of variations from the early nineteenth century to the present.[4] Although the case is full of holes, the story of this ghost is unusually traceable, presenting a remarkable opportunity to witness the evolution of a local haunting—to look closely at what haunts the towns of Greene County, at why this ghost story emerges in the first place, and also at how the ghost's identity changes according to the contexts of time and individual motive.

This chapter tracks the checkered career of the ghostly servant girl through four episodes. The first takes us back to the village (then called Catskill) in the eighteenth century, to reconstruct the original incident and legal case on whose facts—and gaps—the subsequent ghost stories are founded. From there we move to the 1820s to investigate the first print version of the ghost story, probing the conditions and motives that brought the story to the surface and that colored the details of this crucial telling. Next we confront a pair of later nineteenth-century writings based on the tale in order to consider the ghost's mutations of shade and meaning, its susceptibility to being drawn into various social, cultural, and political agendas. Finally, we return to Leeds to contemplate materials collected or written in the town in the mid-twentieth century, to show how the ghost links into contests over local history and identity, and how her variations operate with regard to both local issues and outside interpretations. Ultimately, the story of Leeds, intriguing in its own right, opens the way into a larger investigation of ghost types in the Hudson Valley, not only because it links into a series of prevailing motifs, but also because it reveals an underlying, productive ambivalence within ghostliness itself that undergirds the meanings and uses of regional hauntings more broadly.

THE MYSTERIOUS MANUSCRIPT

In the far from spooky library of the Greene County Historical Society, in Coxsackie, New York, there is a mysterious manuscript. This document, a bill of indictment from 1762, is mysterious not only because it eluded for many years those digging for hard facts about a ghost story they had heard, but also because, even as found, it confounds as much as it illuminates.[5] A single sheet with writing on two sides, it reads:

> The Jurors for our Lord the King, for the body of the County of Albany, upon their Oath do Present: That William Salisbury of Katskill in the County of Albany, Yeoman, on the twenty Sixth day of May in the twenty-Eighth year of the Reign of our late Soveraign Lord King George the Second, with force and Arms, &c, in and Upon Anna Dorothea

Swarts, then Serving the said William Salisbury and in his Service at the Katskill aforesaid retained, did make an Assault, and the Body of her the said Anna Dorothea Swarts then and there with a Certain Cord did bind about, and the Said Anna Dorothea Swarts so being bound, to the tail of a Certain Horse of him the said William Salisbury of the Value of three pounds, then and there with the same Cord did Bind and tye, and the said Horse then and there with force and Arms did beat and force and Compell the said horse So Swiftly to Run that the Horse aforesaid the aforesaid Anna Dorothea Swarts upon her Body did Strike, of Which the said Anna Dorothea Swarts then and there Instantly died. And so the Jurors aforesaid upon their oath aforesaid do say that the Said William Salisbury the said Anna Dorothea Swarts then and there in Manner and form aforesaid, feloniously, Wilfully and of his Malice aforethought did Kill and Murder against the peace of our Said Late Lord the King his Crown and Dignity.

[reverse side]

Ignoramus

Abraham Douw   foreman

1762

Albany 1762

[King?] vs Salisbury—Ignored.[6]

The William Salisbury named in the bill of indictment belonged to a prominent local family, one of the founding families of Catskill. The town in which he was born and lived out his life stood on a 35,500-acre tract that his grandfather, Silvester Salisbury, commander of the British fort at Albany, had purchased from local Indians in 1678, for which he was granted a patent in 1680.[7] The so-called Catskill Patent was the largest and most valuable patent granted for lands entirely within what would become Greene

County.[8] Silvester having died in 1680, his son, Francis, established his family on the patent, building a stone house on his division of the property in 1705, which, according to *The History of Greene County* (1884), "was once the largest and most costly house between Newburgh and Albany."[9] Born in this house, of this family, in 1714, William Salisbury had an auspicious start in the world; from these "yeoman" foundations, he went on to be a very prosperous man. According to tax records, by 1766 he was not only the richest man in Catskill, but also among the top one percent of those taxed in the enormous area then covered by Albany County, a territory whose inhabitants included Van Rensselaers, Livingstons, and Schuylers.[10]

Despite his ancestry, wealth, and position in the town, it seems that William Salisbury, who was later ambiguously described as "a man honorable alike in his descent and in his descendants," would have gone generally unremarked but for one event.[11] Sometime before 1755, William Salisbury acquired a servant named Anna Dorothea Swarts, and in that year, according to the bill of indictment, he dragged her to death by tying her to his horse. It is here that the mysteries begin.

First, who was Anna Dorothea Swarts? If William Salisbury remains elusive as a historical figure, Anna Dorothea Swarts occupies a historical void. Beyond the bill of indictment, there is nothing to indicate that she existed at all. Her name and the fact that she was a servant are all that are recorded, and these specifics turn out to be ambiguous identifiers.[12] She was probably indentured, yet since the term *servant* was a slippery one, used to denote a variety of labor arrangements from slavery to hired help, the conditions of her servitude are open to conjecture.[13] Like most of the early Catskill landholders, William Salisbury held slaves—twelve are mentioned in his will, not counting the children who were willed along with their mothers[14]—and the surname Swarts is clearly related to the Dutch and German words for "black." If she was indentured, how did she come to be so? Was she an orphan, an immigrant, the daughter of a poor local Dutch or possibly German family?[15] Not even her age at the time of her death is mentioned in the indictment, although the value of William Salisbury's horse is.

Beyond the questions raised in these omissions and empty spaces, the indictment presents more positive mysteries in the strange details of the case it delineates. Why, in the first place, would William Salisbury have tied his servant to his horse? Had she run away? Had she been mistreated, as one strain of later speculation asserted? Had untoward advances been made? Or, as another argument would counter, had she behaved badly? Had she, as some said later, been frequenting the house of a "low family" of which Salisbury disapproved? Had Salisbury tied her to his horse to retrieve her or to punish her?[16] More curious, why did it take seven years for the matter of her death to come to court?[17] Albany County, a large frontier territory with a diffuse population, had a woefully poor record in law enforcement; a much lower percentage of cases made it to a court decision there in the mid-eighteenth century than elsewhere in the colony.[18] But William Salisbury clearly did not disappear to escape prosecution, and the gap between event and bill of indictment is extraordinary beyond what can be explained by any slowness of county courts.[19] And why, if the case was important enough to dredge up after all that time, was it subsequently "ignored"?

We can, of course, speculate on what happened, with recourse to historical and legal contexts. The most salient starting point is the fact that Anna Dorothea Swarts was a servant at a time when ideas of social order—especially concerns over perceived threats from the subordinate populations—were reflected in laws curbing servant liberties, particularly after the so-called Negro Plot of 1741.[20] Catskill inhabitants would not have been immune to concerns over servants and slaves. Blacks, mostly enslaved, made up 15 percent of the population of Albany County and 20 percent of that of bordering

Ulster County in the mid-eighteenth century. Even as late as 1790, slaves constituted 15 percent of Catskill's population.[21] Although there were laws in place to protect servants from unduly harsh treatment, and although servants often successfully appealed to the courts, officers of the law were, as one historian put it, "emphatically instructed" to help chase down runaways, and law and custom allowed masters not just of slaves but of apprentices and indentured servants to inflict corporal punishment.[22]

Beyond the specifics of servant status, something of what occurred—and perhaps here something of the apparent waverings of justice—may be explained by the particular turbulence of the 1750s and 1760s in upriver New York, where real and perceived threats to social order were coming from both external and internal sources. The years between the incident and indictment coincide almost exactly with the years of fighting in the French and Indian War, and despite the pretensions of large stone houses and a population of 136 taxpayers by the 1760s, the town of Catskill lay near a still-vulnerable frontier. Indeed, well into the nineteenth century, maps record an "Indian Foot Path" running along what would have been Salisbury property, and one nineteenth-century source claimed that "Indians used to come every summer [and] encamp for a few weeks in a chestnut grove on William Salisbury's farm," asserting that the land had belonged to their ancestors.[23]

Uneasiness over external threats would have been matched in these years by deep concern on the part of local elites over internal order. Anna Dorothea Swarts had been killed, and the indictment had been brought and dismissed, during a decade when the antagonisms produced by New York's peculiar manorial land system were coming to a head. Tenant-farmer, antilandlord activism had begun to gather steam in the early 1750s, erupting on Livingston and Van Rensselaer manors, just across the river from Catskill, in 1753 and 1754 respectively, and reaching a series of violent climaxes from Albany to Westchester in 1766.[24]

It is possible that the intensified social antagonisms of these years churned what seemed a forgotten incident to the surface as part of an attack on privilege. It is also possible that a desire by the regional elite to maintain control caused the resulting indictment to be summarily quashed. Both the heightened anti-elite activity and the general leanings of the courts at the time are suggested by the fact that prosecutions for "violations of public order"—riots and breaches of the peace, generally considered crimes of the "lower orders"—were extraordinarily high in colonial New York at that time, especially in rural areas, where "violations of public order" were the most likely of all crimes to result in a guilty verdict.[25]

Although court records for Albany County are missing for 1762, something about the specific sympathies of the grand jury in the Salisbury case may be suggested by the fact that Abraham Douw—the foreman—had a tax assessment in 1766 of thirty pounds, an indication that he was a man of comfortable means.[26] More suggestive is the fact that in 1763 (when the county court records resume), Douw frequently appears on the panel of presiding justices, along with one Rensselaer Nichols—William Salisbury's brother-in-law, a man whose name speaks volumes.[27] Perhaps an even more precise hint of a privileged intervention in Salisbury's case lies in a peculiar claim, contained in *The History of Greene County,* that James Barker—the patroon of what is now the town of Cairo, a prominent lawyer, and a friend of Salisbury's—assisted in the defense, and that it was probably through his efforts that "Salisbury was saved from the gallows."[28] Taken together, such disparate facts and statements seem at least to indicate the possibility that strings were pulled in Salisbury's case.

So perhaps Anna Dorothea Swarts's death was an accident, or the threat of war delayed court attention. Perhaps the rise of anti-elite sentiment resurrected a poor girl's "murder" after seven years, or a desire for order colored the grand jury's view of William Salisbury's alleged actions. Perhaps it seemed, in a community in which slavery was legal, in which laws curtailed the potentially subversive activity of servants and apprentices, in which public whippings were common sentences, and in which theft could be punished by death, that William Salisbury was well within his rights and responsibilities in tying his servant to his horse, particularly at a moment when any signs of insubordination were keenly felt.

Ultimately, attempts to explain the strange events and turns of the case dissolve into speculation, as nothing else about the case seems to have survived from the period. We are left with the single mysterious sheet, which raises its grim details only to turn its back on them with its final judgment, or lack of judgment, contained in the word "Ignoramus," whose literal meaning ("we do no know") and legal meaning ("we take no notice of") waver between two equally unsatisfying options: a void of information or a deliberate act of denial.[29] If the case brought any particular notoriety or infamy to William Salisbury at the time, no evidence of it has survived. No newspaper would be printed in Catskill for thirty years to come; no written comment or disapproval seems to exist. A keen and romantic eye might detect a hint of remorse in William Salisbury's naming of a daughter baptized in 1756, "Annatje" (eerily, the only one of his eleven children who died young).[30] But there is nothing explicit to indicate that these incidents adversely affected William Salisbury, or any sign that Anna Dorothea Swarts was mourned. With the dismissal of the indictment in 1762, the matter appeared to be over. Even the bill of indictment vanished, and Anna Dorothea Swarts passed from public record and memory. Or so it seemed.

"A SKELETON HALF ENVELOPED IN A WINDING SHEET"

Years passed without a word about this incident appearing in the public record. But then in 1824, more than sixty years after the indictment had been dismissed, and more than twenty years after

William Salisbury's death, evidence arose suggesting that the incident had not entirely vanished from local memory, that the matter had not entirely been laid to rest. That year, Colonel William Leete Stone, editor of the influential New York City newspaper the *Commercial Advertiser,* had been invited to visit the newly opened Catskill Mountain House.[31] While in the vicinity, Stone heard a ghost story that he subsequently committed to print.[32]

Along the road from Leeds to Cairo, Stone's attention was directed to "an ancient and spacious stone house" standing amid an "extensive farm of about 1,000 acres . . . hardly anywhere to be equalled for the rich, picturesque, and beautiful."[33] More than the scenery, though, what caused Stone to "linger longer at this spot than our wonted manner" was "an interesting tale connected with it, which is no fiction": "During a part of the 17th and nearly the whole of the 18th century, [this land] belonged to a single owner! When young he was a man of violent passions. A servant girl having once run away, he pursued and overtook her, and, in his exasperation, tied her to his horse's tail to lead her home. By a fright, or some other cause, the horse ran off, and the unfortunate girl was dashed to pieces against some rocks and stones." In the story Stone tells, the matter is not dismissed outright by the court: "The unhappy master was arrested, tried, and convicted of murder!" However, as "he was rich, of a powerful family for the times," and "it being on all hands allowed to be a hard case," he is sentenced to be executed only if he should live to be ninety-nine years old; in the meantime, at least according to "Tradition," he is required, in Hawthornesque fashion, to wear a noose around his neck. Neither of these already more symbolic than severe sentences is particularly effective. Although the man lives to be one hundred, the deferred execution is never effected; "the revolution had intervened,–a new government bore rule." And although "a few years ago, there were those living, who pretended that they had seen a neat silken string worn in compliance to the sentence," they said it was worn "to appearance as ornament."

Still, the court's ineffectual judgment is to some degree overridden by another verdict, at once more ethereal and more enduring. The incident, writes Stone, had "almost become a forgotten tradition," but "the keen eyes of superstition had seen, and her tremulous tongue related, many tales of startling terror concerning the appearances at the fatal spot, pointed out to this day, where the poor girl had lost her life." Indeed, the "unhappy master" and anyone else who might pass by the fatal spot at night could find themselves confronted by a small mob of ghosts:

> Sometimes sighs and lamentations were heard in the air, like the plaintiveness of the soft whistling wind. At others, a white cow, which was said to have been a favorite when the deceased was alive, would stand lowing among the rocks, while again at others, a shagged white dog would stand pointing and howling toward the mansion. . . . A white horse of gigantic size, with fiery eyeballs and distended nostrils, was often seen to run past the fatal spot, with the fleetness of wind, dragging a female behind, with tattered garment and streaming hair, screaming for help. At other times the horse would appear to drag a hideous skeleton, clattering after him, half enveloped in a winding sheet, with cries and dismal howlings; while again a female figure would at times appear sitting up a huge fragment of rock with a lighted candle upon each finger, singing wildly, or uttering a piercing cry, or an hysterical laugh.

The first printed evidence that the case of William Salisbury's servant had been remarked upon and echoed in local memory, and the earliest printed version of what would be a long-running Hudson Valley ghost story, Stone's narration represents a crucial moment in the haunting of Leeds. To understand the import of the story, we must pay close attention to the historical contexts and conditions accompanying its transmission and giving shape to its details.

That William L. Stone came to hear and to tell this ghost story, as well as what he told, is intertwined with the economic, social, and cultural history of the village of Leeds and of the town of Catskill of which it is a part. In 1824 Stone passed close by the place where William Salisbury had died just over two decades earlier, but a historical gulf separated the two men. Although great changes had taken place during the second half of William Salisbury's life—in his last twenty-five years, Salisbury, without having moved from his stone house, found himself in a new town, county, state, and country—his death in the autumn of 1801 corresponded with almost symbolic precision to the arrival of the nineteenth century in Leeds, which brought with it an unprecedented acceleration of development. The Susquehanna Turnpike, incorporated in 1800 to connect Catskill Landing to the developing interior, and probably the road along which William L. Stone would later pass, had completed its first four-and-one-half miles by August 1801, running right by the dying man's house.[34] This and other turnpikes constructed within the next few years promised to make Catskill one of the main commercial hubs on the river, at least in the decades before railroads and before the Erie Canal. Although signs of growth could be detected in Catskill before the turn of the century—for instance, a newspaper had started printing at Catskill Landing in 1792—a sense of overnight transformation is apparent in early-nineteenth-century accounts. Writing in 1803, for instance, the Rev. Clark Brown was effusive about current and impending developments: Catskill Landing, which had only five dwellings in 1787, now had twelve warehouses; two hundred buildings, many "of brick mostly two stories high"; thirty-one mercantile stores; a court; a jail; and a printing office. More than $300,000 of produce was now being shipped from the Landing to New York annually; the mails came and went twice weekly from Hudson, across the river; and in October 1803 semiweekly stagecoach service to Albany and New York would start. Catskill now had fifteen schools and a library. Most dramatic of all, "land which sold for ten dollars an acre in 1786 now sells for $400."[35] The population of the town had doubled between 1790 and 1810, and by 1813 it was being predicted that Catskill would become "the third if not the second city on the Hudson in wealth, population and commercial importance."[36]

William Leete Stone, on his arrival in Catskill in 1824, would comment: "Her enterprise is genuine New England—her capital commanding—her industry indefatigable—and her activity unrivalled in that section of the state."[37] As Stone recognized, the rapid development of the Catskill area was linked to the movement of a tidal wave of New Englanders into northern, central, and western New York in the years between the Revolution and the 1820s—a movement that caused New York's population to quadruple between 1790 and 1820, propelling the state from fifth to first in population, and giving it top rank in manufacturing, banking, and commercial exports.[38] On the southern edge of the territory most affected by this migration, Catskill was drawn into the current, both in its connections to the fast-developing interior of the state and in alterations of local character.

Something of the social and cultural shift from the Catskill of the eighteenth century to that of the early nineteenth century may be read from the reaction to the aforementioned murder of Sally Hamilton in Athens, the town just north of Catskill. This incident has sometimes been paired with the Leeds ghost story in gazettes and histories.[39] Although the cases are certainly different, the great ado surrounding the murder of the genteel Hamilton in the more "enlightened" decades of the early nineteenth century both emphasizes the lack of ado over a poor servant girl's death in the mid-eighteenth century and suggests how the developing cultural atmosphere might have nurtured recollection of the servant girl's tragic story.[40] Hamilton, the daughter of Samuel Hamilton, Esq., was returning home one night in 1813, when, within twenty rods of the house, she was beaten and killed. Her body was found several days later in Murderer's Creek. The murder and its aftermath were widely reported in a manner both sentimental and sensationalistic. A Hudson newspaper, proclaiming the murder a *"most daring atrocity,"* detailed the signs of violence on Hamilton's body and reported that she had been *"wilfuly murdered by some person or persons unknown."* "No occurrence," the article commented, "has ever taken place in this vicinity, that has ever excited to an equal degree the sensibility of the community." Hamilton, the newspaper averred, "possessed to the full an equal share of the attractions and accomplishments of her sex [and] a most irreproachable character," and her funeral was attended by "a large concourse" from the towns on both sides of the river. Rewards were offered, and a number of trials were conducted and followed by the public over the next several years. Hamilton's parents erected a gravestone "Sacred to the memory of Sally Hamilton" and engraved with a poem.[41] If the unsolved mystery of the murder suggests an underside to local growth—a transient population, which might include murderous strangers (a falsely accused army deserter was among those tried)— the reaction to the murder suggests the rise of new cultural values, as well as the rise of communications, particularly newspaper coverage, which linked what had once been local enclaves into broader sensibilities, and drew outside attention to those enclaves.

William Stone in many ways embodied the changes being brought to bear on eastern Greene County. He was the child of New Englanders who had relocated to New York, and he was a newspaper man. In fact the Hudson newspaper that reported Sally Hamilton's murder was the *Northern Whig,* which Stone would own and operate from 1814 to 1816. More to the point, if Stone's comments, cited above, reflected the general economic and demographic shifts in the area, his very presence in 1824 was linked to new directions in the area's economy and cultural setting. Whereas turnpikes and tons of produce were portentous news in 1803, in 1824 it was the opening of the Catskill Mountain House, the first of the Catskill resorts, which indicated Greene County's future, especially as visions of commercial prominence were deflated with each mile dug on the Erie Canal. "The vicinity of the Catskill Mountain," Stone writes, "has now become one of the most popular places of fashionable resort in the United States."[42] The opening of the Mountain House, very visibly set on a mountainside ledge, signaled a developing interconnectedness to new, romantic values and aesthetics that would draw tourists, writers, and artists into the area.[43]

These developments, as we shall see, animate the ghost story Stone wrote of Leeds; but it is also important to understand that not everything in Catskill had changed. Indeed, this was in large part the basis of its romantic attractiveness. Alongside the signs of modernization in the Catskill area were still to be found holdovers from the eighteenth century. If maps had come to be dotted with New England names, they also indicated that many of the "old families" remained, particularly in more hinterland sections like Leeds. In fact Salisbury descendants were still living in the Salisbury house when Stone passed by. And old hierarchies, practices, and concerns also endured locally and regionally. The land problems that had brought some upriver tenant farmers to arms in the mid-eighteenth century had not dissipated. Slavery also continued to be legal in New York until 1827, and according to the *History of Greene County,* "Most of the old landed proprietors continued to hold slaves up to the time of the final act of manumission."[44]

It is from these overlapping histories that the ghost story of Leeds emerged in the early nineteenth century; and William L. Stone's story about an "unhappy master" and an "unfortunate servant" is clearly related both to what had changed and to what was

"View from the Mountain House, Catskill," by W. H. Bartlett. From *American Scenery; or Land, Lake, and River Illustrations of Transatlantic Nature* (London: G. Virtue, 1840). Courtesy of Department of Special Collections, Stanford University Libraries.

left in the neighborhood of Leeds. The story contains an intersection of old and new history; it reflects both local and external meanings and modes, and the ghosts who inhabit the tale operate on multiple planes of implication and intent.

As the earliest print version to appear, the tale captured by Stone is more likely than later versions to have been founded solely in local telling; and on one level the ghosts in the tale reveal roots in local culture, memory, and social dynamics. Stone never explicitly reveals his source for this story, but there are reasons to believe that it came from what might conventionally be called the local folk: small or tenant farmers, working townspeople, or perhaps slaves or their descendants. The folkloric underpinnings of the tale are suggested both by the indications of oral transmission that Stone incorporates into the story and by the types of ghosts that appear. In particular, the ghost cow, dog, and horse that appear in the Leeds ghost story have analogues in the folklore of northern Europe and Britain, as does the figure with candles for fingertips.[45] Ghostly animals recur in other area folklore as well, and ghost dogs in particular often appear as surrogate or companion ghosts who either defend or reveal something otherwise hidden.[46]

The story proves that the case of William Salisbury and Anna Dorothea Swarts did not pass without public comment in the neighborhood. Although the courts and official history turned a blind eye, as Stone puts it, "the keen eyes of superstition had seen, and her tremulous tongue related, many tales of startling terror." The story also acts as a medium for rendering an alternative local judgment, serving to affix blame and guilt where courts and official records had failed. This is apparent in the transformation made of the legal outcome of the case. Instead of the case's having been "ignored" at the grand jury stage, the legend holds that Salisbury was "tried, and convicted of murder!"—a shift that emphasizes a sense that status and wealth, not innocence, were the keys to Salisbury's escape from real punishment.

Within the story, the ghosts themselves serve to communicate the alternate judgment regarding the case of William Salisbury, to maintain recollection of the incident in the public mind, to indicate guilt, and to frighten and admonish the community that has allowed the injustice. The ghost cow, as it stands "lowing among the rocks," mourns; the dog, which stands "pointing and howling towards the mansion," accuses; the female figure, with candles for fingertips, as she screams wildly and laughs hysterically, seems to embody a tragic irrationality in the circumstances and outcome of the case. Perhaps the most suggestive and literally revealing of the ghosts in Stone's narration are the spectral forms assumed by the dead girl herself. In one instance, the female figure appears in tattered garments with streaming hair, a macabre sexualized image, especially as she is being dragged by "a white horse of gigantic size, with fiery eyeballs and distended nostrils." In the next instance, she is even more completely exposed, a skeleton "half enveloped in a winding sheet." She is a woman very visibly undone, and, beyond implications of actual sexual improprieties, the image conveys a sense of force and violation.

While clearly revealing an enduring sense of historical injustice, the retention of this obscure servant girl's case in local consciousness implies more than just memory of a past event. The distinct class line embedded in the story—in the types of ghosts, in the transformation of the verdict to emphasize wealth, and also in the exaggeration of Salisbury's hold over the land in the opening to the tale—suggests that the incident resonated with more contemporary local issues and tensions. The story hints at simmering resentments over local power disparities, which had erupted in the mid-eighteenth century and would erupt again in the 1830s and 1840s.

But this is not all there is to the story. Indeed, there is a certain duplicity detectable in the tale. While the tale and its ghosts may encode local culture, opinions, and tensions, they are at the same time colored by Stone's reading of the situation, his editing of and editorializing on the story as received. Although he was born in the Hudson Valley in 1792 and had done stints at newspapers in Hudson and Albany, Stone was hardly a "local."[47] And as a man of strong Federalist and then Whig affiliations, and a Mason to boot, he was, as he said, "no democrat." Speaking of universal suffrage, he said: "I hate the mob!"; elsewhere he called the farmers who participated in Shays' Rebellion "the deluded multitude."[48] Thus he would not, it seems, have been sympathetic to the democratic undertones of the ghost story from Leeds. At the same time, Stone was thoroughly devoted to the development of upstate New York, had sincere historical interests, and was a man of literary aspirations. Alongside his newspaper work, he had started literary journals, and he wrote numerous tales and sketches about New York and New England.[49] Something of Stone's political and cultural leanings at the time of his trip to Catskill may be gauged from the pages of the *Commercial Advertiser* from the late summer of 1824. Alongside coverage of the French general LaFayette's return tour, of Greeks fighting for independence, of the work of the American Colonization Society (Stone was antislavery), and of general political wranglings in Albany, the *Commercial Advertiser* contained long articles about Lord Byron; extracts from Walter Scott's latest, *Redgauntlet;* and a lengthy review of Irving's *Tales of a Traveller,* this last appearing in the same edition of the newspaper in which Stone described Catskill Landing as part of his series "Ten Days in the Country."[50] The review is suggestive of a qualified romanticism that is also evident in Stone's ghost story. Denouncing "that craving and unhealthy appetite which prevails so much now-a-days, after every thing new, marvellous, or ghostly," the review nonetheless praises Irving's latest ghost tales on the grounds that, as they tend to question their own substance, they simultaneously entertain and instruct.

In this light, the ghosts in Stone's story begin to reveal other aspects in their character, aspects not entirely compatible with the local meanings and motivations that the tale suggests on another level. The ghost types in the tale may have deep roots in vernacular religion and culture, representing images that had long been part of an "iconography of death."[51] Yet they are also, at the moment in which Stone is writing in the 1820s, very much contemporary and literary. Indeed, in certain characteristics—particularly their explicit whiteness (white cow, white dog, white horse) and the appearance of the ghost as a skeleton—Stone's ghosts of Leeds show a decided family resemblance to the types of ghostly creatures who inhabited gothic tales of the late eighteenth and early nineteenth centuries, with which both Stone and his readership would have been familiar. So common were such images in gothic literature that as early as 1798 an American magazine printed a tongue-in-cheek "Recipe for Modern Romance" calling for tales of "ghosts dressed in white" perambulating about, perhaps a "skeleton with a live face or a live body with a head of a skeleton," or again "a ghost all in white."[52] A more immediate and direct influence may be detected in the appearance of a "woman in white" in *Tales of a Traveller.*[53]

Hints that Stone manipulated the ghosts of Leeds to suit romantic tastes arise in another tale, set in neighboring Ulster County, that appears in his 1834 collection, *Tales and Sketches, Such as They Are.* In this story of the ghost of a murdered peddler, Stone first describes the ghost looking as he did in life except that he was "deadly pale." Later a more significant distinction surfaces concerning how the ghost is seen. While "for the most part, in these oft-repeated nightly visitations, the [peddler] appeared as when a regular and substantial inhabitant of this world"—that is, while most people described the ghost as recognizably life-like—Stone writes: "Sometimes, indeed, in the eyes of more excitable and poetical temperaments, the spectre was invested with more picturesque, if not more terrific characteristics. The eyes of the steed had been seen to glare like fire-balls, while flames and smoke were breathed from his distended nostrils, and instead of the [peddler], a skeleton sat upright upon the box—'Whose loose teeth in their sockets shook, and grinned terrific, a sardonic look—.'"[54] In the correspondence of characteristics and types, this later tale suggests that the characters of Stone's tale from Leeds are to some extent drawn from stock, or brought into line with what, for Stone's readership, might be expected of a ghost. An admission of sorts may also be seen in the attribution of the skeleton to "poetical" origins, while its literary lineages are immediately apparent in its attachment to quoted material.

It becomes clear that the ghosts from Leeds have been genericized to suit the tastes of readers and would-be tourists—an act that employs the ghosts in a political as well as aesthetic duplicity, a counteraction that is being effected in the tale. Stone to some degree abstracts the ghosts from their politicized local meanings and contexts. Indeed, although protesting voices are heard through the narrative, Stone consistently distances himself from the townsfolk's judgment. His version of the tale defuses the popular indictments suggested in the story, calling Salisbury the "unhappy master" and wavering in its assignation of blame. ("By a fright, or some other cause," the narrator explains, "the horse ran off.") The popular voice is characterized as a "superstition," itself personified as a shrewish gossip, and the veracity of those who claimed to witness the ghostly appearances is questioned. "It would be difficult," Stone writes teasingly, "to prove that the spectators approached very near." Later he writes, with what seems intentional ambivalence, that "there were those living, who pretended that they had seen a neat silken string" around the man's neck. Sympathy for the master is also evident in the closing strains of the passage: "For 75 years he had led a quiet and inoffensive life, and who would rudely break in upon his repose?. . . . Peace be to his ashes!"

Stone's version of the tale simultaneously suggests and obscures origins, meanings, and transmission. The figures are vague, half-revealed characters, seen or heard at unpredictable intervals, existing mainly at the level of speculation and rumor. And their modes of manifesting themselves, while linking them to existing lore and types, also serve to efface implications and identities. In an anecdote accompanying the ghost story from Leeds, Stone can be seen blanking out names, presenting the local tavern owner, the dupe of the tale, as M____g S____n (for Martin G. Shuneman).[55] In the case of Anna Dorothea Swarts, part of her blankness and loss of identity probably results from Stone's, and perhaps his informant's, ignorance of her name and background. Nonetheless, in presenting his version of the story he has heard, and in aligning it with recognizable, desirable stereotypes, Stone further blanks the ghosts that on another frequency suggest guilt or protest. The ghosts in their emphasized whiteness, shroudedness, and skeletal overexposure are both positive types and symptoms of distances and effacements, something that also renders them negatives.

The pale ghosts in the story told by William Leete Stone are thus thoroughly double-sided. On one hand drawn from folk culture, on the other from literary stock, these ghosts half reveal and half obscure local content and discontent. They seem to carry a critique of a locally infamous injustice and of a local power imbalance, yet in the plastic insubstantiality of ghostliness, they are susceptible to being tied to other agendas. Still, Stone cannot be blamed too much for his rendering. What he has essentially done is to draw out a latent vagueness and tenuousness within ghostliness itself. Moreover, the half-obfuscation that the ghosts themselves embody, their blankness, as it emphasizes their malleability, would paradoxically aid in their perpetuation. Stone's capture in print of this tale at what might be considered a critical moment of Hudson Valley haunted landscape formation, as well as his particular blank-slate rendering of it, helped fix the story in place while providing invitation for later adaptation. This was especially true as Stone's potentially ephemeral little tale gained a degree of permanence, appearing in Barber and Howe's *Historical Collections of the State of New York* (1842) and in Charles Rockwell's *The Catskill Mountains* (1867). Stone's tale, it turns out, was not simply duplicitous; it was also crucial to the extended haunting of Leeds.

"A Color of the Supernatural"

"Some characters," writes Charles M. Skinner in *Myths and Legends of Our Own Land* (1896), "prosaic enough, perhaps, in daily life, have impinged so lightly on society before and after perpetrating their one or two great deeds, that they have already become shadowy and their achievements have acquired a color of the supernatural."[56] Although it would be difficult to label Anna Dorothea Swarts's death a great deed, she had nonetheless acquired a "color of the supernatural" by the mid-1820s. At that time the color was undeniably white. But William L. Stone's version of the tale was by no means definitive or proscriptive; quite the opposite, it seems. As the century progressed, this ghost underwent a series of chameleonlike mutations as a string of writers and tellers developed shadings and highlights on the ghostly negative provided by Stone. The way in which the ghost's identity and, more specifically, her color shifted to suit changing contexts and needs can be traced in two later nineteenth-century stories—one a novel titled *The Sutherlands* (1862), the other Charles Skinner's version of the tale in *Myths and Legends of Our Own Land*.

The Sutherlands, written in the early 1860s by Miriam Coles Harris, wends its way through almost five hundred pages of romantic plots and subplots, ranging from England to Catskill. But it takes as its foundation the ghost story from Leeds. The geographical and chronological setting, the dragging death, the unusual court sentences, and stories of ghostly repercussions all reappear in Harris's book. "The country people would walk miles around to avoid passing within earshot of [Sutherland's house]," the narrator declares. "Ghosts, they believed, were its habitual tenants: [the] poor murdered [girl], chained to her ghastly horse, dashed nightly past the old man's window—the clatter of . . . hoofs upon the rocks reechoed there the whole night long."[57]

But here the girl who will curry the disfavor of her master, meet her death tied to a horse, and finally reappear as a ghost is not white but a slave of mixed African and Native American ancestry, with the Cooperesque name Nattee. Nattee is a favorite in the eighteenth-century household of Ralph Sutherland—a favorite with everyone but Sutherland, a mean-tempered, boorish slave-holder who, through will and violence, has carved a domain out of the wilderness along Catskill Creek. Having fallen under the influence of an antislavery Methodist preacher, and having been whipped by Sutherland for eavesdropping on a family conversation, Nattee runs away. For days she is relentlessly pursued by Sutherland and his neighbors, as well as by his slaves, who are too afraid of him not to comply. "A more diligent and thorough [search]," writes Harris, "had never scoured the Five-Mile Woods."[58] But it is Sutherland who ultimately finds her, and thus the story turns toward its recognizable conclusion.

In a note appended to the 1871 edition of *The Sutherlands*, Harris states: "The extraordinary sentence passed upon the murderer, his strangely extended life, and the manner of the victim's death are traditions fully credited and widely diffused in the locality described."[59] Although the statement seems to echo Stone's assertions, it is quite possible that Harris herself had been in Catskill prior to writing the novel and had acquired knowledge of the legend independently. In *The Catskill Mountains*, Rockwell states that Harris had "spent some time in the neighborhood where these events are said to have occurred [and] made herself familiar with the traditions related."[60] A cosmopolitan New Yorker, Harris probably stayed at some point at the Catskill Mountain House or one of the other Catskill hotels that sprang up after it, where she could have been exposed both to Stone's version of the story and to stories from more local sources. Details in the novel suggest at least some knowledge or investigation of local places (Kiskatom, Five-Mile Woods), history (local quarrying, religious history, slavery), and family names. The name Harris gives her fictionalized Salis-burys—Sutherland—which seems on one hand simply meant to suggest South Land, was also the name of a family that lived on Salisbury lands in the mid-nineteenth century, and thus perhaps reflects local research by Harris into the event.[61] Most telling may

be the name of the slave, which, although it seems intended to resonate with Cooper's noble near-savage, Natty Bumppo, may also be
a phonetic spelling of the Dutch name Annatje (related to Anna),
as the *je* in Dutch would be pronounced like *ie* in English.[62] This
correspondence would imply that Harris literally *heard* the story
from someone who knew something of the dead girl's name. It is
therefore possible that Harris's romanticized, fictionalized account
reveals aspects of the story unseen in Stone's whited-out edition.

Nonetheless, it is also apparent that Harris has seen in the ghost
story of Leeds both literary and political opportunity, and that she
colors the story to fit contemporary agendas and sensibilities. Her
opening, in fact, boasts of the potential for historical reimagination
made possible by the passage of time. Setting her tale one hundred
years earlier (almost precisely coincident with the year of the original indictment), she writes, "There can . . . be no one to contradict
the assertion that [the weather] was soft and sunny; it cannot possibly be proved that there was a cloud in the May sky . . . or that the
tall poplars by the roadside did not throw their long shadows over
greener fields than 1860 has seen, or is likely, with its drought and
heat, to see."[63]

Written on the verge of the Civil War, the novel employs the
ghosts of Leeds in an antislavery agenda, one that seems directed
against Northern complicity. When Nattee runs away, pursuing a
"dangerous experiment of liberty," Harris writes, at once excusingly
and accusingly, that "such was the sympathy among those early ad-
vocates of the peculiar institution, settled by the mother country
upon the colonies before they were old enough to choose for themselves, that one and all, for miles around, lent readily their influence against the fugitive."[64] Although the novel is outwardly
historical, these comments on local sympathy with the "peculiar
institution" would have had contemporary regional and local implications. Not only was slavery legal until quite late in New York,
but southerners were frequent guests at Catskill-area hotels, and the

men of Greene County had voted for Stephen Douglas over Abraham Lincoln in 1860 (they would also vote overwhelmingly against black suffrage in 1869).[65] Whether or not she has so specifically gauged the local political and social sensibilities, Harris's frequent use of the word "fugitive," her long and peril-filled account of Nattee's attempted escape, and the collusion of the Sutherland's neighbors in her recapture are surely meant to evoke the notorious Fugitive Slave Law of 1850 (which legally enmeshed the North in upholding slavery) in order to make northerners question and renounce their own complicity in such tragedies and in the system that produced them. Although the characterization of Ralph Sutherland as having a "native perversity" dilutes the message somewhat, Harris points to a systemic corruption underlying the awful results of the story. This is suggested, for instance, in the foreshadowing observations of Sutherland's English nephew: "It seemed . . . as if the household were all wrong—a good and prosperous edifice founded on shifting sands. . . . What was it but the reward of iniquity?"[66] The statement, especially when aligned with Harris's identification of the ghost, casts a wide net of blame and guilt, pointing to slavery and also to questionable acquisitions of Native American territory.[67]

Harris had clearly been influenced by Harriet Beecher Stowe's *Uncle Tom's Cabin* (1852); what she hit on in the ghost story of a servant girl from Leeds was an opportunity to create a northern "Uncle Tom"—a tragic figure who, more than the theoretical arguments echoing in Sutherland's nephew's silent musings, might operate as an emotional catalyst for antislavery sympathy. Renée Bergland, in her book on Indian ghosts in American literature, writes that America in the mid-nineteenth century was haunted by "African American slaves and Indians as well as disfranchised women and struggling workers."[68] Miriam Coles Harris's version of the servant girl's ghost is all of these. Given a ghost of ambiguous identity, who nonetheless points to a tragedy resulting from the inequalities of class and caste, and who echoes the problematic powerlessness of women which underscored nineteenth-century sentimentalism, Harris adds a specific weight and meaning: she taps into a contemporary romanticization of African Americans, evident in *Uncle Tom's Cabin,* together with an evocative profusion of Native American ghosts in that era, to produce a sentimental if uneven social critique of slavery and dispossession.[69]

It seems that, writing a generation later, this identification was precisely what Charles Skinner, a newspaper columnist and writer, wanted to avoid when he composed a version of the Leeds ghost story for his collection *Myths and Legends of Our Own Land* (1896). Skinner was almost certainly aware of both the Stone and Harris versions of the tale. His description of the various manifestations (including the secondary ghosts that had gone missing from *The Sutherlands*) undoubtedly owes something to Stone:

> After dark [the master's] house was avoided, for gossips said that a shrieking woman passed it nightly, tied at the tail of a giant horse with fiery eyes and smoking nostrils; that a skeleton in a winding sheet had been found there; that a curious thing, somewhat like a woman, had been known to sit on his garden wall, with lights shining from her finger-tips, uttering unearthly laughter; and that domestic animals reproached the man by groaning and howling beneath his windows.[70]

Skinner's debt to *The Sutherlands,* which went through eleven printings in nine years, is also evident as he begins, "Ralph Sutherland, who, early in the last century, occupied a stone house a mile from Leeds, in the Catskills, was a man of morose and violent disposition." Yet the ghost in Skinner's tale is not the anonymous servant of Stone's version, nor is she Indian or mulatto, nor even a slave. She is "a Scotch girl . . . virtually a slave . . . bound to work for [Sutherland] without pay until she had refunded to him her passage-money to this country."[71]

As in Harris's case, Skinner's identification may derive from local sources—particularly a Reverend Searle who was also cited in Rockwell's *The Catskill Mountains* (1867). Nonetheless, if Skinner did read Rockwell, he would have had several options available to him, including versions of the tale by Stone, by Harris, and by William Salisbury's own grandson, who thought that the girl was German.[72] Moreover, Skinner was not averse to taking liberties in his retellings (something most evident in his recreations of tales by more prominent authors).[73] What, then, accounts for Skinner's apparently deliberate choice to make the ghost a Scottish servant?

On one side, the identity and condition of the servant girl in Skinner's tale seem related to a concern with contemporary labor conditions, a prominent topic in Skinner's column for the *Brooklyn Daily Eagle*.[74] In particular, Skinner's version of the story suggests sympathy with the working and living conditions of European immigrants, a new kind of industrial slavery that was a central concern of this period, exposed in contemporary works such as Upton Sinclair's *The Jungle* (1906). On the other hand, the assignation of Scottish ethnicity, as opposed to African, for instance, seems to reflect both the desires and fears of Americans looking to forget the perceived fiascos of Reconstruction, while facing increasing immigration from southern and eastern Europe. As the titles of his books attest—notably *Myths and Legends of Our New Possessions* (1899) and *American Myths and Legends* (1903)—Skinner wrote with the nation in mind, both in the sense that he was writing for a national audience and in the sense that he saw himself contributing to an imaginative act of nation-building. Skinner's claim in his preface that his tales "have been gathered from sources the most diverse . . . in every case reconstructed," takes on particular valences in the context of the late nineteenth century.[75] Skinner's *Myths and Legends* collections and his ethnic reconstruction of the ghost from Leeds parallel other nationalistic endeavors from the period, such as historian Frederick Jackson Turner's influential 1893 essay, "The

Significance of the Frontier in American History," and the "White City" at the Chicago World's Columbian Exposition, whose expansive yet unified visions of American national achievement derived, in part, from the effacement or marginalization of potentially discordant ethnic or racial elements.[76] These efforts coincided with the dramatic rise in the South of Jim Crow laws in the 1890s, which were effecting wide-scale marginalization of African Americans through political disfranchisement and segregation. Indeed, *Myths and Legends of Our Own Land* was published in the same year that the Supreme Court delivered its famous, long-standing "separate but equal" ruling to uphold segregation in *Plessy v. Ferguson*.[77]

In this light, Skinner's decision not to cast the servant girl as a black slave seems part of a more endemic whitewashing that is evident within the wider scope of his collection. One has to look hard in *Myths and Legends of Our Own Land* to find an African-American character; of the few black characters in the New York stories, one is an "ill-disposed, ill-favored blackamoor," another a "dark-featured" man, perhaps "Egyptian."[78] The preface is more deliberate in its categorical eviscerations: "as to folk-lore, that of the Indian tribes and of the Southern negro is too copious to be recounted in this work."[79] And at least one of the stories in the southern section of the book explicitly reveals Skinner's awareness of fears of racial disorder during and after Reconstruction: every time the Republicans were about to win an election, the story goes, a spectral barge with "gigantic Negroes who danced on deck, showing horrible faces" would appear on a Virginia river.[80] In making his ghostly girl Scottish, Skinner is able to maintain a plausible yet evocative otherness in the story, which allows for sympathy and drama even as it satisfies a national wishful thinking for a whiter American past and present that was evident both in Jim Crow laws and in the rise of movements seeking to limit immigration from "darker" nations.[81] Even though Skinner's ghost is an immigrant, she is of the white, English-speaking variety.

Spooky Hollow

The accounts we have examined thus far demonstrate how the ghost from Leeds has been swayed by the broadest aesthetic, social, and political movements. Stone's white ghosts are painted with reference to a transatlantic romanticism and the rise of cosmopolitan tourism, Harris's ghost girl is colored to support an antislavery agenda, and Skinner's ghost is rewhitened in a nationalistic sweep. The vicissitudes of color and ethnicity in these accounts suggest the wide potential contained in this ghost's underlying indefiniteness—its susceptibility to abstraction and interpretation according to taste and need. Yet it is also true that these accounts were written by "outsiders." As each of these versions claims a local base while enlisting the ghost to serve larger purposes and audiences, the question inevitably arises whether these stories have any special reference or relevance to the town of Leeds. In other words, we are left wondering: What is the ghost's *local* color?

Charles Rockwell in 1867 characterized the Leeds ghost story as "so often repeated, and so religiously believed in all the country round." Visiting in 1906, C. G. Hine claimed, "Many are the ghost stories based on this legend."[82] But although these references bespeak a continued local proliferation of the story, the local sensibilities regarding the tale in the nineteenth century are largely irretrievable. Local lore tends to be ephemeral, often lost or inaccessible, and to a large extent the story from Leeds is no exception.

Yet for various reasons, among them the development of folklore courses at the New York State College at Albany under Louis Jones in the 1940s—an outgrowth of the tremendous interest in folk cultures that emerged during the Depression—a significant record remains of what was available and current in the Leeds area in the mid-twentieth century.[83] Materials collected by Jones's students, along with contemporary letters and articles, provide an opportunity to examine the legend as it existed locally: to see how the various versions and details were situated with regard to local sources and society, and to consider how and why the ghost of Anna Dorothea Swarts continued to exist and evolve in Leeds.

Perhaps the most compelling of the contributions to be entered on this story in the Jones Archives is a letter that appeared in the *Catskill Daily Mail* in August 1942, written by one Ella Rush Murray:

> The legend of "Spooky Hollow" is too well known to repeat here beyond the fact that "a Mr. Salisbury" caused the death of a Negro woman slave, who ran away, by catching her at the "Giant's Bowling Alley" on the Old King's Road and tying her with a rope to his horse. . . . On stormy nights she is supposed to appear there and scream. However, Miss Frances Mann, whose father, John T. Mann, was the owner of what is now Day & Holt Co., told me that her father had a friend, a Mr. Van Deusen, a lawyer, who lived in the old part of the house now the property of Mrs. Ely Parker Spalding on Spring Street. Mr. Van Deusen said that the woman who was killed was not a Negro slave but a German girl, an indentured. She was a Hessian, and when, during the Revolution, the Hessians were in camp at Saugerties with the English troops, she asked Mr. Salisbury for permission to go to see her fellow country-men. He quite naturally refused.
>
> The rest of the story is the same.[84]

The letter is telling in both its consistency with and its difference from treatments of the ghost story examined so far, and it deserves close attention for what it reveals about the place and implications of the ghost in Leeds.

To some extent, the details of Murray's letter might suggest the influence of outside narratives; for instance, the starting assumption that the ghost is a "Negro woman slave" may seem to derive from *The Sutherlands*. That such sources were available locally and might infuse local lore is evidenced by other entries in the Jones Archives, which refer to Stone, Harris, and others.[85] But what sets Murray's letter apart is its explicit localism. The letter reveals that the proliferation of ghost types in Leeds cannot simply be dismissed as a sort of contamination. In her references to local landscape and belief, and in her apparent spontaneity of purpose (unlike Jones's students, she is not deliberately collecting folklore), Murray proves that the ghost had a real presence in the local scene. This is evident, in part, in her offhand reference to Spooky Hollow, which, along with a Spook Rock, was related to the story of the ghostly servant girl. Murray simply takes it for granted as a known landmark; she begins her letter not by locating it but by using it to identify a "ridge on the Leeds road just back of 'Spooky Hollow,'" before getting to her main discussion.[86] Murray's letter shows that people in the town talked about the ghost (for instance, Miss Frances Mann). And she reveals that the legend—specifically the belief that the ghost was a black slave—had local currency; it was "too well known to be repeated." Her statement finds support in a Catskill *Daily Examiner* article from 1935 which called it "common knowledge" that Spooky Hollow was haunted by William Salisbury's "slave girl."[87]

What is ultimately most interesting in Murray's account, however, is that even as it shows the haunting to be a well-established part of local landscape and life, it also uncovers the existence of a meaningful contention over the ghost within the local community. Indeed, Murray's purpose in writing is not to reemphasize the common interpretation, but rather to bring up a counterclaim she has heard, specifically that the ghost is that of a German indentured servant, a Hessian killed during the Revolution, rather than a black slave. Although it is often much more difficult to apprehend local motives, as opposed to those of "outside" writers like Harris or Skinner, the fact that Murray situates the contesting claims over the ghost's identity with regard to local sources provides something of a key for unlocking the local implications of the contending racial assignments. Specifically, dimensions of the local battle over the ghost emerge when we know something about "Mr. Van Deusen."

The Van Deusen who stands at the end of Murray's somewhat tortuous path of names most likely either was, or was related to, Dr. Claudius Van Deusen, described by C. G. Hine in 1906 as "a typical, old-style country doctor, with all the best that the word implies; a finely educated man."[88] More than this, Van Deusen, who in the late nineteenth century lived in one of the Salisbury houses, was related to the Salisburys. His step-grandfather was William Salisbury's son.[89] First prompted by a magazine article (probably one appearing in *Harper's*), Van Deusen had begun trying, as Hine writes, "forever to lay the ghost" in an article for the *Catskill Recorder* in 1883.[90] He was still trying in the early 1890s, contributing an account to R. Lionel DeLisser's *Picturesque Catskills* of 1894, and still working to redeem the historical Salisbury from the legendary one when Hine spoke to him more than a decade later. The substance of Van Deusen's version, as it appeared in DeLisser's and Hine's books, was that the girl was the daughter of "poor whites," that her services had been purchased from her parents (a common arrangement), that Salisbury tied her to his horse "as the only practical way of leading her back to the paths of industry," and that her death was "so evidently the result of an accident that there was no arrest nor trial."[91] Van Deusen even explained the myth of the noose, saying that Salisbury might have worn a cord around his neck, as it was believed to prevent nosebleeds.[92]

Leaving aside for now that Claudius Van Deusen almost certainly never said that the girl was Hessian (as is suggested in Murray's letter), it is possible to discern in Murray's 1942 letter a local contest over the ghost in which the different assignments of race cleave to a large extent along local class lines, and indeed along family lines. On one side in Murray's letter is common knowledge—an anonymous, diffuse, popularly based authority—which holds that the ghost is that of a black slave, something that emphasizes a sense of injustice in the town's early history. That is, to say that the girl was a "Negro woman slave" is to make her more dramatically powerless, and to stress the abuse of power on the part of Salisbury specifically, and the slaveholding founding families by implication. On the other side of the contest in Murray's letter is a prominent, named descendant of the early families, who has attempted to counter what is perceived as an indictment of the old local elite by asserting that the girl in question was "German" or "poor white," and thus to a degree complicit in the system of servitude and social order.

The sense of the story as an item of local contest and the specific class- and family-based lines of division suggested in Murray's letter are corroborated in an account of the case by the county historian, Jesse Van Vechten Vedder, probably written close in time to Murray's. Vedder, whose maiden and married names also link her to the earliest settlers of Catskill, wrote on the story several times in the first half of the twentieth century.[93] Although in her 1922 book, *Historic Catskill,* Vedder half-indulged a storytelling impulse—giving what she says is the real story, but ending on more mythic notes—she was a good deal sterner in a later response to a newspaper article about the ghost.[94] Her letter demonstrates how, and with whom, the event and the stories about it still hit a nerve in Leeds. She writes:

> In your issue of Sunday Nov. 17th there is an interesting article[,] in substance probably taken from an old magazine of the 1860's which has attracted considerable attention and interest in this vicinity. At the request of citizens and descendants of the Salisbury family to whom it refers, I am sending a true version of the [erroneous] tale (the author of which doubtless was intent only on weaving an interesting story

from one [first] handed down through generations of super-stitious slaves).[95]

Where Murray's letter divides between common knowledge and Mr. Van Deusen, Vedder's letter effectively sharpens the divisions, placing on one side what she paints as the embattled Salisbury family and what she tellingly calls the "citizens" of the town, and on the other side "generations of superstitious slaves" (and, by implication, their descendants in the area) along with what she elsewhere calls "superstitious townfolks."[96] And to counter the accusations of common folk and slaves, Vedder's "true version," like Van Deusen's, operates from a sense of social order that is at once historically relativistic and conservative, laying blame for the tragedy not on a system of servitude that might be understood as unjust or undemocratic, but squarely on the girl who does not know her place: "In William's house was a bound girl, Anna Dorothea Schwartz [sic], who in spite of commands and warnings insisted upon visiting a family of more than doubtful reputation. In those days the master of a bound girl was held responsible for her good behavior. William had been sorely tried in this respect."[97] Vedder also enlists a variety of hard facts. "Indisputable court records" showed that the case never came to trial. And, to staunch the further flow of ghost stories, she says in conclusion that "Spook Rock disappeared when a state road was built," and "even the old gray mare is gone who occasionally [broke] from the pasture . . . sending the belated traveler scurrying back to town with wild tales."

Written from different perspectives, Murray's and Vedder's statements divide along very similar lines. What both accounts reveal is that the different types of ghost, the different assignments of identity, are intimately linked to underlying contests within the local populations over town history in terms of both content and mode. They are, in part, manifestations of a tug-of-war between official, documented, written history and the type of oral, popular tradition which William L. Stone stumbled across in the 1820s, and which was still hard at work in the accounts of the mid-twentieth century. It is a contest over *belonging,* in which each side asserts itself through claims of special historical knowledge, and situates itself with reference to a figure who is alternately painted as a social outcast who was tragically wronged by the local elite, and as a social misfit who brought about her own death by her failure to mind her place.

Of course, the two sides—one interested more in the figurative aspects of the case, the other interested more in the facts—are talking past each other. This, too, is evident in Vedder's account, and in what it, like Van Deusen's multiple efforts, fails to accomplish. Indeed, it is worth pausing further over Vedder's letter, as it represents a particularly crucial and paradoxical moment in the epic of Anna Dorothea Swarts's ghost story. If at some level the purpose of the ghost story was to draw attention to the incident and to the case, then Vedder's response, ironically, represents what might be seen as the apotheosis of the ghost; that is, Vedder, while trying to defend William Salisbury against indictments made by ghosts, is compelled to bring to light the original case, the actual bill of indictment, and, for the first time in generations, the dead girl's name. It is a strange moment: denying the ghost stories, Vedder seems to fulfill them; disparaging Anna Dorothea Swarts, she nonetheless resurrects her.

If the ghost stories emanated purely from what had been hidden and neglected, one might imagine for a moment that Vedder's rematerialization of the girl might mean the end of the ghost. Yet Vedder's attempt to contain the ghostly Anna Dorothea Swarts by calling up the historical one fails. First, there are simply not enough facts to fill the ghost-producing historical voids. Moreover, there is too large and varied a contingent of the public who prefer stories to fact. As Vedder's letter indicates, she, like Claudius Van Deusen, is fighting not one but several forces that, as we saw in William L. Stone's story, operate in an uneasy but productive collusion. Vedder guesses that the current article she is protesting is based on a "magazine article from the 1860's" (probably related to Harris's novel), which, in turn, she believes is based on stories told by local slaves. On one side are various "outsiders" who have seen in the local ghost various aesthetic and political potentials, and have drawn her accordingly. On the other are local vernacular and popular cultures in which the ghost also serves a number of purposes, from protesting class or racial disparities, to challenging the local elite, to perhaps simply enlivening the mundane local landscape and experience. Certainly, the local proliferation of the legend in the 1930s and 1940s may be related to the baneful effects of the Great Depression and World War II on the local economy, signaled by the closure of the Catskill Mountain House in 1942.[98]

The ghost is simultaneously too shifty and too well entrenched, too interesting and too useful. So, Claudius Van Deusen's assertions are undone: as Murray's letter indicates, not only has the idea that the girl was black (whether based in *The Sutherlands* or in the claims of slaves) survived in local culture, but somewhere along the short grapevine between Van Deusen and Ella Rush Murray someone has added yet another identity, claiming that the ghost was a Hessian, a move that allows this local tragedy, and thus the history of Leeds, to resonate with the most dramatic event to touch regional history, the Revolutionary War. Meanwhile, Vedder's account, which itself testifies to Van Deusen's failure to dispel the ghosts, is no more successful in staunching the perpetuation of stories, even though she has more facts to tell. She is mistaken in thinking that the ghost story is only about the original case. Her little dam of facts is easily breached or circumvented by the stories and desires of residents and visitors alike.

Most telling, in fact, among the materials to be found in the Jones Archives is a letter written in 1956 to Louis Jones (then director of the New York State Historical Association) by one of William Salisbury's descendants, who apparently was not one of the local descendants Vedder mentions in her account. This descendant *thanks* Jones—who had included a version of the Leeds ghost story in his recent children's book of Hudson Valley ghost tales—for "calling attention to my murderous ancestor! It has made my genealogical quest quite exciting."[99] Moreover, distressed at the neglected condition of William's house, called the "Ghost House" by the owner at the time (who had yet another version of the ghost story to tell), the letter writer wonders whether anything might be done: "As you pointed out, the N.Y. Thruway has an exit a mile to the east of Leeds and this may help revive this little village, including the haunted house." The note reads almost as a betrayal of Jesse Van Vechten Vedder's attempt to defend Salisbury against the allegations in the ghost stories. Even more, it underlines the problematic nature of ghostliness for Anna Dorothea Swarts; her potentially indicting ghost is once again co-opted—this time providing entertainment to one of Salisbury's descendants, who hoped to enlist her to revive the Salisbury properties, especially as the new highway connections promised to draw in a new generation of travelers.

And so, stories continued to be told in Leeds, and the ghost continued to change shades. In 1975 an article in the Catskill *Daily Mail* announcing the opening of an antiques store in William Salisbury's old house reported that it was "a young American Indian girl" who was indentured to William Salisbury, who was killed "in the vicinity of what is now the Thruway exit at Leeds," who "appears yearly at the anniversary of her death being dragged behind the riderless horse," and who, conveniently, "now haunts the manor house."[100] Thus it was that the antiques dealer was "offering '200 years of tradition' along with her fabrics, rugs, handmade ponchos and shawls." Anna Dorothea Swarts, dead two hundred years, was still serving in William Salisbury's house.

In many ways the ghost story of Leeds is unique, and is compelling for precisely that reason. Unlike, for instance, the nationally pervasive story of the ghostly hitchhiker, who exists both everywhere and nowhere, the ghost of Anna Dorothea Swarts belongs to Spooky Hollow and is about the village of Leeds in a way that is nontransferable.[101] The origins of the legends, the details of every version retain some link to the particular, peculiar case from the mid-eighteenth century; and the emergence and development of the ghost legend have to do with discrete local events, beliefs, people, and places. Each of the various renderings and debates about the ghost contains specific valences and meanings that resist generalization.

Yet the shifts and transformations in the story of Leeds are also broadly representative. Versions of this story coincide, either directly or tangentially, with ghost types prevalent throughout the Hudson Valley, while the variability of the ghost's identity exposes a more fundamental aspect of ghostliness, a relationship between vagueness and definition that allows us to fathom the social and political functions of hauntings. In essence, the shifting identification of Anna Dorothea Swarts's ghost points to a profound though not entirely antagonistic tension at the core of haunting, a dialectic between ghosts as impositions and as choices; as received, unbidden residues of the past and as adaptable, impressionable entities.

Recent scholars locate the psychosocial roots of hauntings in the Freudian concept of repression. Kathleen Brogan in her study of ghosts and ethnicity observes that "denied history reasserts itself, much like the return of the repressed."[102] The town of Leeds *is* haunted by the past; the ghost *is* in some way the reassertion of what was "ignored" in the case of William Salisbury and Anna Dorothea Swarts. Swarts's ghost signifies things hidden in a collective unconscious; she is the martyr and memory of a secret history, recalling, for instance, exploitative and violent systems of servitude that existed in the North, in New York, as well as elsewhere. She represents whole categories of people who have been tucked away from view—the sorts of people about whom Avery Gordon writes: "it is essential to imagine their life worlds because you have no other choice but to make things up."[103]

Certainly, this story is related to issues of gender. A female servant, completely subject to and overshadowed by her master, Anna Dorothea Swarts embodies in exaggerated form the problematic historical situation of women in general. From laws of coverture in the colonial period to the ideology of domesticity in the nineteenth century, gendered social structures have contributed to ghost stories, in part by making women vulnerable to exertions of masculine will, and thus to wrongs that could arouse haunting feelings of guilt or sympathy, particularly with the rise of a sentimental culture that at once lamented and idealized female suffering.[104] More basically, as they have been denied economic and political selfhood in life, women have been eclipsed historically, rendered obscure in ways that easily translate into ghostliness—hence the multitude of shady women roaming the roads, streams, and woods of Greene County and beyond.[105]

In Anna Dorothea Swarts's case, her haunting invisibility as a female is redoubled by her social status, her almost undoubted poverty; and thus the haunting of Leeds is founded in issues of class as well as gender. It is also—indeed, most obviously—connected to questions of race and ethnicity. With the possible exception of Stone's story, which assumes and exaggerates whiteness, the stories from Leeds are centrally concerned with assigning the ghost an ethnic identity. Even those that do not outwardly ascribe African, Native American, Scottish, or German ancestry usually make some qualifying reference: Van Deusen says "poor white"; Vedder renders the spelling of the girl's name ("Schwartz") to seem more German than Dutch.[106] On one level, this emphasis bespeaks an American privileging of race and ethnicity over social class. On another level, the necessity of an ethnic or racial description seems to reflect apprehensions of a more basic otherness that approximates, or can be understood as, race or ethnicity. Charles Skinner's phrase "a color of the supernatural" reads ghostliness itself as a racial designation.

Tied in her variations to social anxieties about underrepresented others lurking in regional as well as national history—women, the poor, Native Americans, slaves, immigrants—the ghostly servant girl's story more broadly relates to what might be called the problem of the past. The past is a foreign country, David Lowenthal asserts in the title of his book on memory.[107] In the case of the United States this is true both in the sense of a history inhabited by people largely from other places, and in the sense of the difference between pre- and post-Revolutionary affiliation. Notably, most versions of the Leeds ghost story in part attribute Salisbury's escape from execution to the discontinuity in government resulting from the American Revolution, which cemented in neglect and amnesia the injustice of the past. Locked in the history of "a foreign country," the case remains permanently unclosed, and the ghost unintegrated. Whereas Kathleen Brogan writes of a movement from possession to exorcism, or from bad to good haunting as ethnic writers are able to integrate their ancestry,[108] what makes the ghost of Leeds so difficult to exorcise, the reason why she continues to haunt in ethnic form, is her essential difference from the ghosts Brogan sees haunting recent ethnic literature: Anna Dorothea Swarts is not an ancestor. She is irretrievably other. Her ghost emanates from the lost history of a local tragedy, from the problematics of ethnic and racial diversity in the early settlement, and from the distance between the eighteenth and later centuries. Neither she nor the incidents surrounding her death can be entirely assimilated into the present landscape and culture. Thus the ascriptions of ethnicity, as well as blankness, and the inability of the ghosts to communicate fully—they howl, shriek, low, cry, moan, and laugh incomprehensibly—represent at the core of this haunting an inability to comprehend a history that seems alien, but refuses to go away. In part, then, the unresolved past haunts by virtue of its unresolvability, and the diversity of assignations represents attempts to estimate what has been lost or to give understandable form to what seems unexplainable or unassimilable.

But this is not all. First, the past is not entirely a foreign country, and ghosts haunt only insofar as they have not become entirely irrelevant. The main work of haunting is done by the living. As much as it may be haunted by the ghosts of the past, the town of Leeds is even more haunted by stories people tell. C. G. Hine, noting the number of variations of the story available in 1906, marked it as "showing how much can be made of little when the neighbors really take hold and help."[109] The phrasing is gruesomely appropriate. While the ghost of Anna Dorothea Swarts may represent a fearsome reassertion of things repressed or unresolved, she also embodies the exact opposite of agency: a servant, female, tied and drawn entirely against her will by a motive force that is not her own. While the various ascriptions of ethnicity to the ghost may encode apprehensions about the unknown past, they are also the colorings and interpretations of generations and individuals who have seen, in the vague, passive servant girl's ghost, an opportunity to draw her in the direction of their own desires.

The story of Anna Dorothea Swarts's ghost demonstrates how ghosts, who on one side may be undesirable or troubling eruptions of repressed history, also exist as a sort of "usable past" that may be cut and colored to suit a wide variety of frameworks and needs. The ghost waxes and wanes, evolves and multiplies with reference to discernible aesthetic trends and cultural models: folk culture, gothic and romantic literature, sentimentalism, a vogue for Indian ghosts, the heightened interest in folklore in the 1930s. And the variations of type are simultaneously motivated by political, social, or commercial demands, from the national to the personal. As a skeleton in a winding sheet, the ghost is turned into an inviting stereotype for nineteenth-century tourists looking for domestic romance. As a black slave, she can serve an antislavery agenda or be used to undermine local elite authority. Certainly, there is an ambivalence of fear and desire in hauntings: ghosts may represent those whose disappearance or death leave guilt or an appalling gap, or they may stand for ideal ancestors whose ghostly presence is enlisted to assert priority and ownership. Nonetheless, what the story of Leeds makes clear is that, as much as ghosts may be emanations of repressed pasts, they are also laden with present meaning. Anna Dorothea Swarts's ghost is itself haunted.

None of the stories of Leeds is pure fiction: each version is complex, double-sided. In her variations, the ghost is both vestige and novelty, positive and negative, powerful and powerless, a possessing force that descends upon the town and through history, and something passive that is possessed. It is in its double-sidedness, its ambivalence, its intertwining of imposition and interpretation, that the ghost really functions. What makes this haunting particularly effective is that, even though we can trace vectors of influence in the tale and detect where apparently deliberate switches in identification occur, it is impossible to distill out what is original or true and what are innovations (as in the case of Miriam Coles Harris's "Nattee"). What seem fictional liberties descend as the legendary inheritance of another generation. This confusion is what makes it so difficult to exorcise the ghost, especially as the mechanisms of decision and proliferation are most often hidden from view ("the tremulous tongue of superstition" and "common knowledge"). The double-sidedness of the servant girl's ghostliness—the combination of assertiveness and impressionability—makes the ghost simultaneously sticky and slippery. The ghost may not be provable, but, in the vagueness of history and the diffusion of storytelling, she is also not disprovable. The point is directly and arrogantly made by A. E. P. Searing, who wins the award for most implausible casting of the ghost, presenting her as Spanish and the lover of Captain Kidd, in *The Land of Rip Van Winkle* (1884). When her narrator is challenged about the accuracy of his story, he simply replies, "I have told my story . . . the burden of disproof lies with you."[110]

And there is no other place in our country where this poetry and romance are so strangely blended with the heroic of our history as along the banks of the Hudson. No other river where the waves of different civilizations have left so many *waifs* upon the banks.

—*Legends and Poetry of the Hudson*, 1868

LOCAL CHARACTERS

4

The late nineteenth and early twentieth centuries witnessed a second great awakening of hauntings in the Hudson Valley. A period of dramatic industrial development, urbanization, and immigration, these years were at the same time characterized by surging interest in "ancestors, memories, and legends" in American culture, as Michael Kammen writes in *Mystic Chords of Memory*.[1] The architectural historian Vincent Scully put it forcefully: "this was a self-conscious generation, tormented, as men of the mid-[nineteenth] century had seldom been, by a sense of history, of memory, and of cultural loss."[2] Marked by regionalism in literature, colonial revivalism in architecture, and the rise of historical and genealogical societies, including the American Historical Association and the Daughters of the American Revolution, this period also generated an unprecedented outpouring of written reminiscences, local histories, and collections of legends.

In the Hudson Valley, where a legendizing impetus had already been set in motion by the legacy of Washington Irving and by the region's central position as a tourist destination, this emergent fascination with the past had special resonance, yielding a bevy of works such as Henry D. B. Bailey's *Local Tales and Historical Sketches* (1874), A. E. P. Searing's *Land of Rip Van Winkle* (1884), Charles Pryer's *Reminiscences of an Old Westchester Homestead* (1897), Edgar Mayhew Bacon's *Chronicles of Tarrytown and Sleepy Hollow* (1897), and C. G. Hine's *West Bank of the Hudson River* (1906). Along with such printed works were thriving strains of oral folklore, whose traces can be found throughout local and state archives. Not surprisingly, this literature and lore is crowded with ghosts.

This chapter traces the hauntings that appear in Hudson Valley folklore and literature, beginning with the 1868 publication of *Legends and Poetry of the Hudson,* and encompassing late-nineteenth- and early-twentieth-century hauntings that resurface in folklore collections of the 1930s and 1940s. We start with a basic question: Who or what haunts the Hudson Valley in this period? Of course, this question immediately raises a series of problems and complications, not least because of the sheer number and variety of ghosts in the region. Attempts to categorize ghosts by type, location, and chronology are further compromised by their tendency toward indeterminacy, their susceptibility to changing identification, and their habits of recurring at different moments, or even in different places, to say nothing of the difficulties involved in establishing definitive moments of origin and currency. Moreover, the question of what haunts is not necessarily the same as the question of who haunts; the identities of ghosts may be determined by reaction to contemporary fears as much as they are related to historical questions. As haunting is the work of tellers as well as ghosts, to ask who haunts necessarily involves attention to the sometimes very different motivations and backgrounds of those who turn ghost stories loose in the landscape.

Nonetheless, patterns do emerge. Specifically, we can trace in the literature and lore of the late nineteenth and early twentieth centuries three predominant strains: "aboriginal" hauntings associated with Indian and Dutch presences, Revolutionary War hauntings, and industrial hauntings. These preoccupations are not entirely surprising; they derive from important aspects of regional history. Nor are the points of reference contained in these categories of haunting unique to the region or to the period in focus. Yet the predominance of these three types of haunting in the late nineteenth and early twentieth centuries, both in their typicality and in their variations, both in themselves and as they coexisted and contended with one another, serves to register the historical and social concerns of the region in this period, while also illuminating the functions of historical imagination more broadly.

Moving from ghosts of more ancient to more recent provenance, this chapter traces how hauntings operate at various distances from originating circumstances, suggesting an aesthetic transformation of ghosts over time from vehicles of protest or emblems of trauma to bulwarks of tradition. It also illustrates the work these hauntings performed in their social setting, a period of momentous demographic and physical changes. The various ghosts who roamed the Hudson Valley in this period, while related to particular pasts, and representing complex negotiations of those pasts, were configured and employed to fight contemporary battles over locality and regional character.

REGIONAL ABORIGINAL

Along with the local ghost stories and historical traditions he documents in his 1897 *Reminiscences of an Old Westchester Homestead,* Westchester native Charles Pryer describes a few of his own eerie encounters, among them an incident that occurred at his "Old Homestead" in New Rochelle some years earlier. After a stormy November night, one of Pryer's farmhands reports having seen "a light, which appeared to come from a lantern," moving along the property as if carried by a man inspecting the buildings and animals. Although Pryer admits to first thinking that it was "some person, probably of dark complexion," investigating his chickens with an eye to obtaining a cheap Thanksgiving dinner, his mind is turned to the possibility of a supernatural explanation when he hears that this mysterious light has appeared on other occasions, always during stormy weather. Thoroughly intrigued, when the next stormy night arrives, Pryer takes the opportunity to see what is haunting his land. After huddling in the rain for several hours, he and the farmhand are about to give up when in the orchard across the creek a flickering light does in fact appear. The two men wait breathlessly as a faint glow begins moving toward the very spot where they are standing. "What was our disappointment," Pryer recalls, to discover that the glow was only the pipe of a neighbor, very much alive, who was cutting across the fields on his way home.[3]

Yet, writing years later, Pryer is not entirely willing to give up the ghost. "Still," he contends, "as I look back on the affair from this far distant point of view, I am far from satisfied as to the cause of the light." Instead, he chooses to believe that "it may have been the return of some ancient Sachem, who came to visit his early hunting-ground; or again, one of the first Dutch settlers visiting the farmyard to see if the cattle and poultry had improved since he was a resident of this sphere."[4] Having moved between suspicion of dark-complexioned thieves and the prosaic reality of a familiar neighbor, Pryer's ultimate speculation regarding the "mysterious lantern" is both predictable and revealing. Local history and lore, as well as personal desire, lead him not only to believe that ghosts might very well wander this neighborhood, but also, more specifically and significantly, to expect that they might be the ghosts of either Indians or Dutch folk, or possibly both. A preoccupation with Indian and Dutch hauntings in the Hudson Valley of the late nineteenth and early twentieth centuries derived from an ambivalent, fragmentary sense of the region's prior inhabitants, and from a search for tradition and authority that arose as a reaction to the rapid development and population changes of the late nineteenth century.

"It requires no great effort of the fancy to picture the bark canoes of the aboriginals still plying upon the bosoms of the many romantic lakes," writes Philip H. Smith at the start of his 1887 book, *Legends of the Shawangunk:* "One would be pardoned for being deceived into the belief that the smoke from an embowered cottage arose from the embers of an Indian wigwam; and the traveler half expects to meet troops of goblin warriors . . . painted and equipped for battle, silently threading the forest over the Indian trails yet clearly traceable through the mountain fastness."[5] It took little imaginative effort to conjure up Indian spirits in the region because, although Native American tribes had disappeared as a real presence or force in Hudson Valley life by the second half of the nineteenth century, Indians came to occupy a preeminent place in Hudson Valley lore. One need only glance through the Hudson section of Charles Skinner's *Myths and Legends of Our Own Land* (1896) to see that Indians enjoyed a wide contemporary popularity here, as elsewhere; at least ten of the first twenty-one Hudson River tales involve Indians or Indian legends.[6]

Indians haunted the regional landscape in a variety of ways. First, the literature and folklore of the period incorporated a plethora of alleged Indian legends that attached spirits and supernatural creatures to landscape features throughout the region. The legends of "Ontiora" (the Catskill Mountains), which appeared, for instance, in *Legends and Poetry of the Hudson* (1868), in Skinner's *Myths and Legends of Our Own Land* (1896), and in Jesse Vedder's *Historic Catskill* (1922), told of spirits residing both in and on the mountains. According to the version that appeared in *Legends and Poetry of the Hudson,*

> They were called by the Indians, the Onti-o-ra's [*sic*], or Mountains of the sky, as they sometimes seem like clouds along the horizon. This range of mountains was supposed by the Indians to have been originally a monster who devoured all the children of the Red Men, and . . . the Great Spirit touched him when he was going down to the salt lake to bathe, and here he remains. . . . In these mountains, according to Indian belief, was kept the great treasury of storm and sunshine, presided over by an old squaw spirit who dwelt on the highest peak of the mountains.[7]

Other sites were haunted by association with a host of tragic "Indian legends" that seemed to grow in number during this period. While the author of the 1868 *Legends and Poetry of the Hudson* lamented that the region lacked any legends of lovers' leaps, it was a poor county that, by the early twentieth century, had not discovered within its boundaries some rock or cliff that was marked by an Indian tragedy.[8] Late-nineteenth- and early-twentieth-century stories told of leaping (or otherwise perishing) Indian maidens at Raven Rock in Tarrytown, at a cliff in Mahopac, at Spook Rock near Claverack, at Gypsy Rock in Hudson, at Mount Utsayantha in the Catskills, and at Kaaterskill Falls, where, A. E. P. Searing's narrator avers, "if you tune your thoughts aright, the silvery white garments seem to gleam through the waters of Kaaterskill, and the face will almost shape itself."[9]

In addition to haunting by legend, of course, the Indians haunted the region as ghosts. J. B. R. Ver Planck, for instance,

stream of water that plunged for the first time

d into
ing drops
he floating
came the
unlight on
the great
aughter to
saddened
vages went
way, not
reak their
he Catskill
d all the
hey never

THE MAID IN KAATERSKILL FALLS.

"The Maid in Kaaterskill Falls." From A. E. P.
Searing, *The Land of Rip Van Winkle: A Tour through
the Romantic Parts of the Catskills, Its Legends and
Traditions* (New York: G. P. Putnam's Sons,
Knickerbocker Press, 1884).

testified in court, in a 1913 railroad condemnation hearing, that the
ghost of "an Indian . . . caught stealing from the [Henry] Hudson
party" was supposed to "walk stealthily" about a field on the family
property in Fishkill; while C. G. Hine, Charles Skinner, and others
wrote of the ghost of Chief Croton and of "the walking sachems of

Teller's Point"—an outcropping of land in Croton where there was believed to be a Kitchawank burying ground.[10]

Although they are associated with particular places and figures, this proliferation of Indian hauntings is neither unique nor surprising. Indian ghosts have haunted the American imagination and landscape from at least as early as settlers landed at Plymouth, and they appear throughout the United States.[11] In part the rising popularity of Indian ghosts in the Hudson Valley in the late nineteenth century represented attempts to tap into, and in many cases capitalize on, a more widespread attraction to Indian hauntings. What makes the Indian hauntings of the Hudson Valley unique, what offsets and complements the impact of Indian ghosts, is the simultaneous presence of an alternate set of ghostly aboriginals. As the author of *Legends and Poetry of the Hudson* asserts, "Closely blended with these Indian traditions we have the early tales and legends of the first Dutch settlers along the rich valley of the Hudson."[12]

The Indian hauntings that proliferated in the late nineteenth and early twentieth centuries shared the field with hauntings of a Dutch character. Indeed, if just about half of Skinner's Hudson Valley tales in *Myths and Legends of Our Own Land* center on Indian characters and myths, an equal number feature Dutch-place legends and ghosts. The "Dutch" story of a white lady at Dobbs Ferry who absconded with a young Dutch bride and groom, and "Dutch" legends of the Storm Ship, of the devil at Spuyten Duyvil, of demons at the Duyvil's Danskammer reappeared time and time again in regional collections of the late nineteenth and early twentieth centuries.[13] Regardless of whether they were adapted from Irving or actually derived from Dutch folklore, these legends were stamped with Dutchness in guidebooks, collections, and local histories. Whereas Indian legend told of the old squaw on Ontiora who controlled the weather, Dutch legend told of the "Heer of Dunderberg Mountain," who, as Skinner tells it, "is a bulbous goblin clad in the dress worn by the Dutch colonists two centuries ago, and carrying a speaking-trumpet, through which he bawls his orders for the blowing of the winds and the touching off of lightnings. These orders are given in Low Dutch, and are put into execution by [imps], who troop into the air and tumble about in the mist, sometimes smiting the flag or topsails of a ship to ribbons."[14]

There were also, of course, Dutch ghosts, the most commonly invoked being the Dutch crew of the *Half Moon*, along with Henry Hudson himself, rendered into a Dutchman by the common spelling of his name—"Hendrick"—in regional stories.[15] And beyond invoking individual ghosts, writers of the period evince a more broadcast sense and expectation of a Dutch hauntedness. "Miss Rutherford," A. E. P. Searing's stand-in within the narrative of *The Land of Rip Van Winkle*, says of the town of Katsbaan: "Think of all the ghosts talking Dutch, as they must, of course, in this region."[16] Dutch manor houses—Van Cortlandt, Van Rensselaer, Ten Broeck, Van Wyck—were inevitably haunted, whether by family ghosts or others; and Dutch churches, farmhouses, and taverns throughout the region repeatedly appear as both the site and the *raison d'être* of stories. In Kingston, of all the "old stone houses [that offer] wonderful possibilities for a fruitful imagination" and that he suspects hold "a dozen or more good ghost stories," C. G. Hine is most drawn to the Old Dutch Church: "there is a mysterious something, as one stands below and gazes to the diamonded shingles and small windows, that gives the imagination play."[17]

Dutch settlement predated English takeover of the territory by only forty years, and descendants of the Dutch continued to inhabit the Hudson Valley region; some of New York's (and the country's) most prominent families were of Hudson Valley Dutch ancestry, and enclaves of Dutch speakers could be found into the twentieth century.[18] Both despite and because of these factors, Dutch folk even as they continued to dwell in the Hudson Valley were repeatedly pictured as ancient remnants in a way that aligned them with Indians. A process of figurative Dutch aboriginalization had been going on throughout the nineteenth century. For instance, in her 1843 *Letters from New-York*, Lydia Maria Child, who at another point speaks of Indians along the Hudson as "these ghosts of the Past," writes of Dutch-descended people in Tappan as "antediluvians," while also revealing a more widely held association of Dutchness with regional antiquity and ghostliness: "'An indefinable influence of the former inhabitants,' is indeed most visible; but then it needs no ghost to tell us that these inhabitants were thoroughly Dutch."[19] During the late nineteenth century, Dutchness took on even fuller qualities of antiquity, primacy, and authenticity. A reporter writing in Rockland County in 1877, for instance, acknowledged a debt to a local shopkeeper for sharing with him some of the "legendary lore of the Hudson . . . of original Dutch character."[20] And in the same way that writers invoked "Indian belief" to lend an air of authenticity to regional place legends, A. E. P. Searing proved that Overlook Mountain was the place haunted by Hudson's crew, by stating that it was there that "the early Dutch settlers believed that Hendrick Hudson kept vigil over his loved river."[21]

There were, of course, differences between Dutch and Indian hauntings. Different creatures haunted Dutch place legends than haunted those of the Indians. If Indian hauntings were associated mostly with natural features—rocks, trees, and simply ground which might contain Indian dead—it was often Dutch structures or their ruins that were haunted. While Dutch ghosts were often presented as comic, along the lines laid out by Irving, Indian ghosts tended to be either menacing or melancholy. These two groups, however, were clearly conjoined in late-nineteenth- and early-twentieth-century regional imagination—"closely blended," as the author of *Legends and Poetry of the Hudson* phrased it.

Indeed, the aboriginal pairing of the Dutch and the Indians was reflected not only in the implicitly parallel treatments of Dutch and Indian hauntings, but also in references and stories that explicitly intermingled Indian and Dutch elements. In *The Land of Rip Van Winkle,* Searing writes of a "marsh called by the Dutch, the Gröt Vly," which held "in its bottomless depths one of those Indian demons that the Dutch held in very respectful veneration."[22] Charles Skinner also cross-references Indian and Dutch legends and hauntings in a tale titled "The Catskill Gnomes":

> Behind the New Grand Hotel, in the Catskills, is an ampitheatre of mountain that is held to be the place of which the Mohicans spoke when they told of people there who worked in metals, and had bushy beards and eyes like pigs. . . . They brewed a liquor that had the effect of shortening the bodies and swelling the heads of all who drank it, and when Hudson and his crew visited the mountains, the pygmies held carouse in his honor and invited him to drink their liquor. The crew went away shrunken and distorted by the magic distillation.[23]

And the Indian who haunts the Ver Plancks' "Spook Field" is not just any Indian but, most dramatically, an Indian killed in 1609 by a crewman on the ship of "Hendrick Hudson."[24] It would be harder to find a ghost who better signified regional origins.

While Charles Pryer's speculations regarding the "mysterious lantern" suggest an interchangeability of Indian and Dutch ghosts, other tales of his explicitly place Indian and Dutch ghosts on the same ground. One of the most extended and interesting stories of Dutch-and-Indian haunting is recounted by Pryer under the title "A Bedford Courtship." It is unclear whether Pryer intended irony in this title—which ostensibly refers to a courting couple who are disrupted by the ghosts—as the story derives from a historical event which one nineteenth-century historian called "by far the most sanguinary [battle] ever fought on Westchester soil."[25] In the winter of 1644, during a period of hostilities between Indians and settlers of New Netherland, a force of men under orders from Governor Kieft

attacked a large encampment near what is now the village of Bedford, set fire to the huts, and killed anyone who tried to escape the
fires, thus wiping out virtually the entire camp—between 500 and
700 people. "The memory of the affair," writes Pryer, "was kept
fresh among the quiet people of the place by the reports of spirit
battles." In addition to "individual spooks" that were "to be seen
nearly every night that any one had the courage to walk past the fatal spot," among them "a headless sachem seated mournfully upon
a stump," Pryer writes that the ghastly battle scene replayed itself
twice a year: "the whole neighborhood would be illuminated by
what appeared to be the burning wigwams of the savages. Plainly by
the conflagration's light could [witnesses] see the Dutch burgo-
master-soldiers, holding aloft the bright yellow banner of 'My Lord
States-General,' and coolly relieving of his head every Indian that
issued from the flaming huts."[26]

Veering between gruesome violence and Irvingesque comedy
(one specter appears in "a pair of pantaloons that might have
graced the extremities of Tenbroeck, and had a nose that would
have done credit to any Beakman"), the tale nonetheless unites the
Dutch and Indians as inhabitants of an exclusive, original ghostly
sphere that periodically reoccupies the neighborhood as a sort of
semiannual pageant.[27] Pryer writes of the apparitions: "On each occasion the Indians went through the same performance of rushing
from their burning wigwams upon the Dutch and having their
heads cut off. How their heads were put on again for the next battle
is a complete mystery, but . . . enough for us to know there is one
patent out in the other world that has not *yet* descended to us."[28]
The phrasing is ingenious; borrowing the idea of patent from the
colonial system of land ownership, Pryer indicates that the Dutch
and Indian ghosts continued jointly to possess and occupy physical space by their haunting. The story's title, "A Bedford Courtship," is after all perversely fitting.

It becomes apparent that the tales of haunting that filled late-nineteenth- and early-twentieth-century regional lore reflected a sense of both Indian and Dutch aboriginality, and that these aboriginal hauntings held a preeminent place in the regional imagination. The question remains as to why this was the case. Looking closely, we discover that the implications of these aboriginal hauntings are multiple, complex, and often contradictory. At base, Dutch and Indian hauntings emerged from the prior inhabitancy and subsequent historical obscurity of both groups in the region. "Who were the people that lived here before our ancestors gained a home on the soil; and how did they live?" asks the author of *The History of Greene County* (1884), summarizing the problematic questions of Indian history in the area. "Indications of their existence are not wanting. We see them in the traces of their once frequented villages, their burial grounds, their stone arrow-points and instruments of various kinds, but in these there is little upon which to found a definite account of their history or themselves."[29]

In a way akin to but more apparent in the late nineteenth century than Indian sites and artifacts, Dutch houses and people existed as distinct yet perplexing evidence of earlier settlement in the region. Despite complaints of the lack of preservation that prefaced books like Helen Wilkinson Reynolds's *Dutch Houses in the Hudson Valley before 1776* (1929) and Rosalie Fellows Bailey's *Pre-Revolutionary Dutch Houses in Northern New Jersey and Southern New York* (1936), these works demonstrated that a number of colonial Dutch houses continued to stand well into the twentieth century. At the same time, Irving's assertion in "The Haunted House" of the general obscurity of New York's early colonial history continued to hold true. As a result of language barriers, of the fact that many Dutch colonial documents were housed in the Netherlands, of a lack of historical self-consciousness among Dutch colonists in the Hudson Valley (compared to that of Puritan New England),

and of post-Revolutionary immigration and history-obliterating "progress," Dutch colonial history *was* to a large degree a mystery to nineteenth-century inhabitants. According to historian Alice P. Kenney, as far as nineteenth-century historians were concerned, "the history of the province began in 1664 and it did not seem worthwhile to investigate the 'prehistoric' Dutch period in any detail."[30] And although enclaves of Dutch culture and language persisted through the nineteenth century, their difference from what had become mainstream culture, as well as a degree of clannishness and reticence within these communities, further contributed to an uncanny sensibility regarding them.[31]

The unclear, unexplained traces of both Indian and Dutch presences in the region lent themselves to ghostliness in a number of ways. At some level, aboriginal hauntings had to do with conquest and displacement, and with concomitant apprehensions of reprisal and return. Renée Bergland's comments on Indian ghosts are to the point here: "Europeans take possession of Native American lands, to be sure, but at the same time, Native Americans take supernatural possession of their dispossessors."[32] Hints of residual suspicion, guilt, and fear appear, for instance, in Charles Skinner's comments that the Indian ghosts of Teller's Point sallied forth nightly on "errands of protest," and in the projections of a Croton fisherman depicted in "The Crawbucky Tales" (1920): when he comes "to the open space where in old times the Indians used to camp," he begins to think, "Maybe they had a scalp dance, too, and other goings on. Perhaps they killed people there, too; there is no knowing."[33] The unsettling threat of aboriginal repossession through haunting is apparent as well in the fate of the young couple in Pryer's "A Bedford Courtship." Having unconsciously wandered onto the haunted ground and seated themselves "on the stump of a half-decayed oak, that must have been a flourishing tree in the time of the Indians," they find themselves confronted by "the form of a Savage, with head inverted, flying from a stalwart Dutchman." Although neither apparition "seemed to notice the couple intruding upon their premises" (note the plural possessive), the scene is enough to dispel the unwitting trespassers for good.[34]

Yet although Pryer offers the summation in "A Bedford Courtship" that "there is one patent out in the other world that has not *yet* descended to us," these possessions–the land and the hauntings–*had* descended to Pryer and others who were staking claims of sorts through their ghostly affiliations, or more accurately through their asserted inheritances of local traditions. The curses of vanishing aboriginals, Werner Sollors has argued, were akin to blessings, as both signified a line of succession.[35] As much as tales of aboriginal hauntings may have contained fearful potentials, they also conferred significant pleasures, consolations, and benefits to those who had the privilege of being haunted.

Clearly related to the contemporary surge of interest in folklore, tradition, history, and genealogy, the profusion of aboriginal Indian and Dutch hauntings in the Hudson Valley around the turn of the century was in part the product of efforts to attract tourists to the region. Here were *two* sets of aboriginals, one of which had the added attraction of being old-worldly at the same time.[36] Closer to home, though, this profusion also connected to a search for rootedness and legitimacy–for longevity and inclusion within the "patent"–which gained urgency in the context of the late nineteenth and early twentieth centuries. Aboriginal hauntings were activated by a sense of drastic changes in regional landscape and character, changes that included an ethnic aspect. The historian Arthur Abbott, who asserts in *The Hudson River Today and Yesterday* (1915) that "no page in the world's history is more interesting than the Dutch settlement along the Hudson River," and who imagines the Dutch spirit "brood[ing] over all like a spirit from out of the past," begins his book with this claim: "There has never been a time in the history of our nation when the story of its glorious past was so important as today. A large percentage of the millions of aliens flocking to our shores . . . know but little and consequently care less, of our institutions, their purpose and ideals."[37]

Gilded Age immigration and urban growth effected dramatic changes in the Hudson region, particularly in areas adjacent to New York City. In the 1870s and again in the 1890s, segments of lower Westchester were annexed by New York City. The remaining sections of the county were becoming less agricultural, while rapidly gaining population as a result of suburban development fostered by rail and trolley lines, and as a result of the arrival of immigrants, many of whom came to work in factories and on railroads and reservoir construction.[38] Between 1880 and 1900, immigrants made up 40 percent of Westchester's population.[39] Charles Pryer's writings are clearly informed by these social changes, which had noticeable impacts on his native town. During the years Pryer was collecting and writing, New York City had moved up to the doorstep of New Rochelle, two major rail lines had been joined in the town (which by 1901 had the highest assessed railroad valuation in the county), the population had nearly quadrupled since 1870, and among the new residents were a significant number of immigrants, as well as African Americans who had begun migrating to northern cities in large numbers in the 1880s.[40] All of these changes echo in Pryer's *Reminiscences*. A political conservative, he begins his book with a quote from Longfellow which refers to "the encroaching city" that might drive a man "an exile from the hearth of his ancestral homestead." He goes on to lament, "All things in this section have so changed, since those times so enjoyable to me," and describes the county as "now crowded and over-populated." He explicitly characterizes his efforts as deriving from a desire to go back to a time before the neighborhood "was spoiled by the locomotive, the summer cottage, and worse than all, the lands speculator." And, it is worth recalling, Pryer's first thought when he is told of the mysterious light, which he later imaginatively renders into the form of an ancient Indian or Dutchman, is that it was "some person, probably of dark complexion," looking to steal his poultry.[41]

Aboriginal hauntings emerged in the face of changes and perceived intrusions both as items of tradition to be defended and as claims of priority and legitimacy on the part of those haunted by aboriginal ghosts, those conversant with traditions of these hauntings. The author of *Legends and Poetry of the Hudson* (1868), for instance, writes in a language of inheritance and, to some extent, exclusivity. Referring to the "gabled-roofed" (read Dutch) houses, he writes, "We all have visited these old hearthstones; to some of us they are a part of our very childhood." The "strange stories and legends" collected in the book are from "our father's fire-sides."[42]

To a degree, the use of aboriginal ghosts to provide a sort of ancestral grounding paralleled broader genealogical and colonial revival movements of the late nineteenth and early twentieth centuries, which in the New York area led to the founding of the Holland Society of New York in 1886, a series of publications like Mrs. John Van Rensselaer's *The Goede Vrouw of Mana-ha-ta* (1898), and efforts to preserve Dutch properties.[43] In fact Dutch hauntings were occasionally employed in support of what might be called "Dutch pride." On Halloween in 1905, for instance, Albany sponsored a parade that included the "apparitions" of two hundred Dutch burghers from 1705. A verse storybook written on the occasion told how "Jan Van Schlichtenhorth" in 1705 made a brew that allowed the Dutch Albanians to sleep for two centuries so they could come back for the parade. Clearly drawing on "Rip Van Winkle," both the parade and the story emphasized Albany's particularly strong Dutch heritage; the burghers parade on horses for which their

> great-great-great-grandchildren pay,
> For our descendants still live here,
> To welcome us with hearty cheer.[44]

But one of the benefits of aboriginal haunting was that one did not need to be a lineal descendant to claim possession. Dutch genealogical and historical societies, in fact, more often sought to combat the relegation of Dutchness to a ghostliness that could also signify irrelevance. Such hauntings, it seems, tended more to be utilized in what Sollors, speaking of the reconfiguration of Indians as adopted ancestors in the nineteenth century, calls a "presumptuous reconstruction of American kinship."[45] Indeed, to anyone familiar with Westchester history, it is particularly striking that Charles Pryer evokes the spirit of an early Dutch settler on his New Rochelle homestead, since New Rochelle's major claim to regional distinctness is that it was settled by French Huguenots—something that Pryer, himself of French and English ancestry and a member of the Huguenot Society of New Rochelle, certainly knew.[46] In being haunted by Indians and aboriginalized Dutchmen, even non–Native American and non-Dutch Hudson Valley dwellers could align themselves through a sort of imaginative osmosis with an ideal regional ancestry, which conveyed a rootedness and legitimacy in a moment of social upheaval. In particular, the presence of the Dutch provided European Americans with a "white" aboriginal haunting that combined the ancestral with the uncanny, side-stepping on one side the implications of responsibility that might come with real ancestral hauntings, and on the other the racial distance and more violent implications contained in the ghosts of dispossessed Indians.

In being haunted by aboriginal ghosts, and in their possession of aboriginal traditions of haunting, Charles Pryer, A. E. P. Searing, and others sought to fill a contested territory with "natives" and to include themselves among the elect—to assert a kinship with the original inhabitants by legendary inheritance. Throughout his book, Pryer not only aligns himself with the old folk; he literally absorbs into his own *Reminiscences* a series of stories he has heard

from neighborhood ancients, including "Nicholas the Hunter"–
the putative source for "A Bedford Courtship" and the very stereotype of an old Dutchman. "The instant you look upon him," Pryer
writes, "you almost forget the days of the burgomasters are over."
The storytelling session begins as Nicholas "lights his long Dutch
pipe that seems coeval with the surroundings. And as the volumi-
nous clouds ascend they seem to shut out the world of to-day, and I
soon find myself transported back a century or more."[47] Pryer, it
seems, inhales the story along with the smoke, and the legends
and hauntings become his own. Although *Reminiscences of an Old
Westchester Homestead* purportedly incorporates tales from several
neighborhood storytellers, there is almost never any sense of a narrator separate from Pryer.

Thus not only does Pryer choose to haunt his old homestead
with original Indian and Dutch ghosts; he also conflates himself
with the old inhabitant, whose age and Dutchness he stresses, and
from whom he inherits legitimizing and grounding tales of haunting. Indeed, Pryer goes a step further. He may not be certain whose
ghost it is—Indian sachem or Dutch settler—that haunts his homestead, but he closes the book with the forecast: "I need not be curious much longer, for ere many snows shall fall, I, too, must join that
ghostly company."[48] He is, in other words, almost one of them.

Almost. There remains at some level in these hauntings both the
fact of and the potential for distance and displacement. Renée
Bergland speaks of "the ghosting of Indians"—the ways in which
Native Americans, even though they continued to exist, not only
provided a common source of ghost stories, but also were depicted
as ghostly in a way that supported contemporaneous policies of Indian removal.[49] Aboriginal hauntings have the capacity both to
ameliorate and to justify the disappearances they point to. The old
inhabitants, as ghosts, are still there, though not in any way that
truly challenges latter-day possessors; and their ghosts may be used

in ways that explain their disappearance or marginalization, allow-
ing inhabitants to inherit tradition—and also territory—without assuming blame.

What one finally notices in the tales of aboriginal haunting that
filled the Hudson Valley imagination in the late nineteenth and
early twentieth centuries is that they frequently involve acts of either self- or mutual destruction within the aboriginal sphere. In
one instance recounted in C. G. Hine's *West Bank of the Hudson
River* (1906), the Indians literally spook themselves out of the region. Describing a place outside New Paltz where "the last remnant
of the Indians" came to sell baskets, Hine writes: "finally one of
them was drowned in the Wallkill, and they came no more, claiming that the drowned man had 'spooked' them."[50] Other hauntings
implicate the Dutch in the disappearance of the Indians. Hints of
this appear, for instance, in the Fishkill-area story, mentioned earlier, of an Indian killed by one of Hudson's crew in 1609, and in a
story from Nyack of an Indian—the last of the Tappans—who returned to haunt the Dutch settlers who had forced him from his
ancestral home during the French and Indian War.[51]

The most striking exemplification of this tendency in regional
aboriginal hauntings to charge the Dutch in the disappearance of
Native Americans is Pryer's "A Bedford Courtship." The tale portrays what came to be seen as an appalling massacre of hundreds of
people, an incident that haunted local memory for generations.[52]
While Pryer, as we have seen, elsewhere works to attach himself to
the legitimacy of old Dutchness, his narrative in this case clearly
implicates the Dutch, and only the Dutch, as perpetrators of this
act. In describing the ghost battle that recurs in the neighborhood
twice a year, the narrative goes to great lengths to emphasize the
Dutchness of the attackers: Dutch banner, Dutch names, Dutch
stereotypes. Most interesting, though, is who is left out of Pryer's
ghost tale—Captain John Underhill, an Englishman, a "celebrated

Indian fighter from New England," and joint commander in the attack, in which both Dutch *and* English men participated.[53] In this regard, as well, it is worth noting that the town of Bedford, though within the originally Dutch borders, was first settled not by the Dutch but by Connecticut Yankees crossing over from Stamford.[54] By omitting Underhill and the English while spotlighting the Dutch elements, Pryer is able both to tap into regional tradition that relies on a foundation of Dutch and Indian ghosts and to lay blame for the disappearance of the Indians on the Dutch.

Thus even as the Dutch and Indians were invoked as quasi-ancestral, aboriginal spirits by those like Pryer who sought bulwarks against invading newcomers and those like Searing who sought to encourage tourist trade, Hudson Valley ghost tales like "A Bedford Courtship" also allowed local populations to inherit the benefits of possession while being exonerated from implications of dispossession. The aboriginals, according to the stories, had provided the basis for settlement by conveniently doing away with each other and themselves.

Revolutionary Travesties

"When Major André had been safely disposed of at Tappan," writes Edgar Mayhew Bacon, speaking of the British officer who had been hanged as a spy for his dealings with the American traitor Benedict Arnold, "that incident was thought to be concluded." The war was long over by the time Bacon published his *Chronicles of Tarrytown and Sleepy Hollow* in 1897; men had long ago looked to turn "from their swords to their plowshares," in Westchester as elsewhere. But then, Bacon reports, "before quiet had fairly settled upon the neutral territory"—the area of Westchester that had suffered between the British and American forces for almost the duration of the war—"it began to be whispered that a war reminiscence of an alarming character insisted upon recognition":

Down the post road, on still autumn nights, belated wayfarers sometimes heard the sounds of hoofs. A madly galloping horse seemed to approach, but no horse or horseman was visible to the keenest eyes. A few reported that they had seen a formless gray shadow whisk by in the neighborhood of the swamp that lay by the side of the highway, and others declared that the word "halt" had been pronounced in a soldierly tone just before the galloping ceased. All agreed that the hoofbeats stopped as though the rider had reined in suddenly, and that they were never heard further south than the immense old tulip tree, known as André's tree, that spread its gaunt, ghost-like arms in the moonlight.

"André's tree"—where André had been captured with the plans of West Point in his boot—no longer existed when Edgar Bacon was writing. It had been destroyed by lightning in 1801, allegedly on the day news of Benedict Arnold's death reached Tarrytown. And André's remains had been removed from Tappan, across the river, to be buried in Westminster Abbey in 1821. But if these facts suggested that André's alarming reminiscence should have long dissipated by the end of the nineteenth century, Bacon had other news. If this ghost was "more than usually unsubstantial," Bacon averred that he was also "pertinacious in his appearing, having been heard several times within the present decade, as the writer, among other witnesses, can testify."[55]

The Hudson Valley saw more than its share of the Revolutionary War. In addition to the battles that were fought here—at White Plains, at Stony Point, at the Highland forts—residents throughout the region, particularly those caught in the neutral ground, suffered daily insecurity, privation, and violence inflicted by both armies, by bandits known as Cowboys and Skinners, and by one another. These events left traces of themselves in Hudson Valley landscape and memory. And when, after a period of historical neglect in the late eighteenth and early nineteenth centuries, the combined forces of cultural nationalism, romanticism, and tourism resurrected Revolutionary landmarks and memories as items of intense interest, the Hudson Valley emerged as a major repository of Revolutionary recollection, as reflected in and fostered by the attention given in the earliest successes of American literature—Irving's *Sketch Book* and Cooper's *The Spy*—to the Revolution in this region.[56] Although the Civil War would supplant the Revolutionary War as the central event of local history in many other areas, the Revolution continued to hold a predominant position in Hudson Valley lore and memory into the twentieth century, fueled by centennial celebrations, increased tourism, and post–Civil War efforts to forge a cohesive national tradition. As Edgar Bacon's ghost story suggests, however, Revolutionary memory in the region in the late nineteenth and early twentieth centuries was multifaceted and conflicted, containing on one hand prolific evocations of patriotic spirits, and on the other haunting uncertainties that were amplified rather than diminished in the context of this period.

Nothing, wrote the author of *Legends and Poetry of the Hudson* (1868), in "the *poetry of this river*" could be "more interesting to the genius of our people" than the Revolutionary memories that dwelt there: "Here the great struggle for freedom has consecrated many a spot . . . the ruined ramparts they defended with their lives; redoubts and bastions, battered and broken: these are eloquent to every heart!"[57] With dramatic scenery and a stock of Revolutionary forts made all the more appealing by years of decay and neglect, the Hudson Highlands offered a good deal to the historical imagination, as guidebook writers and storytellers continually reminded. "No other area," asserted an 1884 article, "of equal extent on the continent is so replete with historic associations, or can so thrill the patriot's heart with tales of his country's struggle for freedom, as these hills."[58] Guidebook writer and poet Wallace Bruce also evoked a sense of patriotic memory embedded in the Highland landscapes. In "The Long Drama," a poem he read at the 1883 centennial of the disbanding of the Continental Army at Washington's Headquarters in Newburgh, he called for his auditors to pause a moment in the "proud and onward march" of American civilization, to envision in spectral "dress parade" those to whom the celebrants owed their liberty and prosperity:

> In silence now the tattered band—
>   Heroes in homespun worn and gray—
> Around the old Headquarters stand,
>   As in that dark, uncertain day.
>
> That low-roofed dwelling shelters still
>   The phantom tenants of the past;
> Each garret beam, each oaken sill,
>   Treasures and holds their memories fast.[59]

Amalgams of centennial-era sentiment and rising tourist desire for storied places, these images of a landscape immanent with patriotic spirits drew from a sort of historical imagination that was akin to hauntedness. But the "phantoms" conjured in these images seem deliberate and self-conscious. In the shadow of the airy patriotic images that populated the Highland fancies of Bruce and others, there was another type of Revolutionary memory at work in the region. This one spoke of presences that, though not entirely beyond manipulation, seemed to derive their existence less from poetic assertion and more from colloquial sources, presences that seemed to erupt unbidden into regional collective imagination. And if visions of the spirits of '76 registered no uncertainty about the War for Independence, no fear, guilt, or ambivalence, the *ghosts* of the war tell a somewhat different story.

The Revolutionary ghosts who inhabited local tales current in the late nineteenth and early twentieth centuries were rarely patriots.[60] Instead, they were the ghosts of foreign soldiers killed in battle: a Hessian soldier who haunted "Spook Field" in Fishkill; the Hessians who guarded "Bloody Pond" near Bear Mountain; a "body of phantom horsemen dressed in the uniforms of the British Regulars" that appeared in New Rochelle.[61] Along with these foreign soldiers were the ghosts of spies, Revolutionary War bandits, and others whose affiliations were difficult to determine. A spy hanged by order of General Putnam haunted Gallows Hill near Peekskill and, according to what C. G. Hine heard in 1905, scared into his grave the local farmer who had served as hangman.[62] An 1896 history of Yonkers reported that a headless Revolutionary War bandit, killed during a midnight raid on a tavern, threw "a veil of horror" over Valentine's Hill in Yonkers.[63] Pryer's *Reminiscences of an Old Westchester Homestead* contains numerous accounts of ambiguous Revolutionary apparitions. One tells of a "mysterious mass," once encountered by a local farmer, that "began to move slowly and silently across the road backward and forward, like a sentry on duty" at the crossroads of the Boston turnpike and the road to DeLancey's Neck. Pryer also offers three accounts of a ghost at the Skinner's Oak, a tree in Pelham Bridge on which wartime bandits called Skinners had been hanged. The ghost said to appear there was a figure of unclear allegiance: "a man, dressed in a dark suit, and a military coat with an overcape after the style of officers in the army toward the close of the last century." Hearing the tales, Pryer wonders, with a strange hint of pity, whether the ghost was "the spirit of one of the unfortunates who perished upon the oak."[64]

Then of course there was the insistent, quixotic ghost of the British major, John André, who had been hanged at Tappan as a spy for his dealings with Benedict Arnold, and who, according to Bacon's account in *Chronicles of Tarrytown and Sleepy Hollow* (1897), continued to haunt the place of his capture in Tarrytown. Even at the time of his execution, André had inspired an inordinate amount of sympathy, admiration, and regret among Americans; described time and again as "beautiful," "manly," and "noble," he continued to be a troublingly sympathetic figure in nineteenth-century American Revolutionary memory more broadly.[65]

Bacon's ghost story suggests that this fascination with André echoed with particular strength in the lower Hudson Valley at the turn of the century. Indeed, since Bacon himself was less favorably disposed toward André than most, his reference to the ghost's pertinacity, its continued appearance in the 1890s, points all the more strongly to a sense that André was nearly inescapable in contemporary regional historical imagination.[66] Historian William Abbatt's *Crisis of the Revolution* (1899) attests to the compelling hold André exerted over local, as well as national, memory of the Revolutionary War, as it recounts in minute detail the events of the last ten days of André's life, fetishistically retracing the routes and prolifically illustrating a host of sites and objects associated with André: the "André Window" and "André Table" at Treason House in West Haverstraw; the "André Well" in Mount Pleasant; the "André Brook" near the point of capture; the "André Step" in a Westchester farmhouse; and "André Hill," where he was finally executed. Of the last, Abbatt writes: "No spot in the county, indeed in the State, was better known or more accurately identified."[67] Even in the twentieth century, a number of the sites visited by André during those final days maintained reputations as haunted places.[68]

What do we make of these haunting alien or at best ambiguous characters in the Hudson Valley landscape of Revolutionary memory? And why did they appear as they did in the period from the centennial into the early twentieth century? These ghosts do not entirely overturn patriotic or nationalistic readings. While victors and heroes may come back as "spirits," it is the defeated who most often appear as ghosts, their very ghostliness attesting to the victory of their adversaries. Nonetheless, these hauntings do exist as questions, registering levels of uncertainty over both the experience and legacy of the Revolutionary War.

Embedded in the foundations of these ambivalent hauntings were recollections of the Revolution itself, a basic sense of horror and dismay over the actions and consequences of war. The ambiguities of these stories might suggest the distance of the war from contemporary memory, the inevitable distortions and uncertainties that arise over time, and perhaps the sense of fading connection that resonates even as early as Irving's "headless horseman." But to some extent, the abundance of ambivalent ghosts that haunted the lower Hudson into the twentieth century reflected the *closeness* of the war as well. According to federal census data, 20,000 Revolutionary War veterans were still living in 1840, and people alive during the Revolution could and did live into their eighties and nineties—into the latter half of the nineteenth century.[69] This means that people living and writing well into the twentieth century could and did hear reminiscences regarding local sites and events of the war from firsthand witnesses. William Abbatt, the Westchester historian writing about Major André in the late 1890s, could cite several firsthand sources, including John Romer, who was sixteen when André was brought temporarily to his family's house as a captive, and who lived to be ninety-one (until about 1855).[70]

Quite basically, something of the violence of the war, generally removed from airy patriotic centennial incantations, remained in regional and local memory, and viscerally haunted the imaginations of people living even into the twentieth century. This is evident in an account given by the noted outdoorsman William Thompson Howell of a hike he took in the Hudson Highlands in 1910 with a Peekskill man named Alzamore Clark. The two men had set out to explore the ruins of twin Revolutionary War forts—Montgomery and Clinton—that had been important during the war, and the site of a dramatic skirmish in 1777, but whose story, according to Howell, "has never been fully told; it is, indeed, not known even among historians."[71]

Clark, the great-grandson of a man who had fought at Fort

Montgomery, had heard tales from his grandfather and uncle and had "spent several summers at Fort Montgomery, one year living in a house . . . which stood within the very 'Bloody angle' where the British poured over the ramparts . . . and forced the greatly outnumbered Continentals over the bluff into the river." Where Howell saw only woods punctuated by a few piles of rubble, Clark mapped out something of the scene that came into his mind. "That," he said pointing at a small slough of water, "is itself a small 'Bloody Pond' for there it was that they threw such of the bodies of the dead American soldiers as were not burned after the battle, most of them having been burned." Clark had known a man, born in 1787, who claimed "that he himself had seen the remains of the bodies lying there"; the claim, if true, indicated that the remains had lain visible for years after the battle.[72] Clark himself had found "buttons and charred bones" that he believed were those of soldiers. Clark then pointed to a field nearby where the dead British soldiers were said to have been buried "in deep trenches": "Their bones have never been turned up by the plough, probably because they are too far down, but this British burial ground is well known as such throughout the region." These violent events not only left traces of themselves in the landscape; they also left deep impressions in local memory. "It is well known, of course," Clark tells Howell, "that the inhabitants of the . . . country shunned this spot for years after the battle, it being considered an uncanny locality." One hundred and thirty years after the fact, the site continued to affect Clark: "This is indeed an historic spot. I never come here but I feel like taking off my hat."[73]

Although Clark's ultimate reverence is compatible with patriotic memorialization, the sense of hauntedness he evokes is not without ambivalence. His statements reveal a deep trauma embedded in both the actual and the imagined landscape. Indeed, though surely he means the point literally here, his mention of unmarked graves, and especially of the British dead not yet turned up by the plow, is highly suggestive of the traumatic nature of the war in local memory, of things unintegrated into everyday functional life and consciousness, which thus continue to haunt memory and imagination. Michael Kammen writes of the plow as symbol of a return to peace and prosperity in post-Revolutionary iconography, reflecting both an actual return to peacetime pursuits and a symbolic turning from swords to plowshares.[74] A number of the Revolutionary War hauntings discussed here include reference to plows, but many of these also refer either to a failure to return to the plow or to sites untouched by the plow. Edgar Bacon's image of men turning "from their swords to their plowshares," for instance, is narratively interrupted by the ghost of André; and more than one visitor to André's gravesite in the early nineteenth century noted that the plow had spared the ground there.[75] The dead of both armies lay scattered throughout the region, in fields and ponds, in graves that were often unmarked.[76] These images of what the plow either declines or fails to reintegrate, of what remains hidden but suspected in the ground, resonate with fears over unmarked burial sites and unidentified bodies, and suggest psychological roots of hauntings by the Revolutionary dead.

Beyond basic recollection of the war's violence, the ghost stories of the late nineteenth and early twentieth centuries also point to a great degree of uncertainty lodged in the memory of the war regarding questions of territory, possession, and right, both legal and moral. In one instance, neighborhood men digging for treasure find themselves approached by "phantom horsemen dressed in the uniforms of the British Regulars"; the men run off, having "concluded that the spirit troop had a better right to the booty then they." A sense of the ambiguities of wartime justice and a fear of retribution are also suggested in stories of the Skinner's Oak, which, at least in Charles Pryer's retelling, reveal a moral confusion in the haunting of this spot: "The oak is still standing, and is a very large and vigorous tree, except that the arm extending over the road, and upon which the victims were hanged, is dead and now fast decomposing, and it has always been said that the limb was withered by the curse of the dead who there perished so ignominiously."[77]

These hauntings point to an enduring and problematic sense of the Revolution as a civil war rather than an international conflict, and it is not surprising that ghosts registering ambivalence might preoccupy Hudson Valley war reminiscence. Although estimates vary, and loyalties were often kept covert, New York and the Hudson Valley contained an extraordinarily high number of loyalists, including many of the region's landholding elite. At the war's end, large-scale confiscations of loyalist properties occurred in New York, and some loyalists found themselves permanently banned from returning to their former homes under the threat of death.[78] Between 20,000 and 35,000 loyalists left the New York region after the war.[79] Notably, the Haunted Brook written of by Pryer as having a powerful reputation for ghosts, and guarded by a mysterious sentry, is in the vicinity of property once belonging to the De Lanceys, a powerful New York Tory family that epitomized the problematic nature of guilt and loyalty in this war. On one hand, the De Lancey name was associated with the worst pro-British ravages of the lower Hudson countryside. Colonel James De Lancey, commander of the light horse brigade that notoriously pillaged and terrorized Westchester under the name of Cowboys, was the object of much hatred.[80] On the other hand, the plight of the De Lancey family also symbolized the acts of violence perpetrated by American forces against loyalists, and the legally tenuous confiscations of loyalist property. Patriots had burned one of the De Lancey houses to the ground, attacking three women staying there (among them James Fenimore Cooper's future mother-in-law). After the war, the family was exiled.[81]

The misnamed neutral ground embodied in microcosm the treacherous and internecine quality of the war. Beyond the devastation caused there by armies and bandits, Westchester residents of opposing loyalties, as one contemporary observer wrote, "have taken up arms, and become the most cruel and deadly foes."[82] More aptly called the "debatable land," it was a place where questions of loyalty and character constantly rattled.[83] And although André was British, not American, part of what was so haunting about André, it seems, was related to the shiftiness, the sense of travesty represented in that terrain. André–who even Washington said was "more unfortunate than criminal"[84]–was to no small extent a victim of the neutral ground, where allies and enemies were easily confused, and appearances were deceiving, where bandits became heroes, and "beautiful," "accomplished" young Englishmen were condemned as spies. Having already several times been lost, and having several times stopped at farmhouses to inquire as to the location of the American militia in the territory, André, himself out of uniform and carrying a false pass, was stopped at Tarrytown by three men whose character and allegiance would be the object of much subsequent debate.[85] Probably noticing that one of the men was wearing the uniform coat of pro-British German troops (he had recently escaped imprisonment under the British in New York City), André said to the men, "I hope you belong to our party."[86] When the men asked which party he meant, André indicated the British. It was a fatal misperception. When the men, having first asserted that they were British, then told him that they were in fact "Americans," André tried to recant. But the trio nonetheless searched him and, finding the papers hidden in his boots, discovered him to be "a spy." The details of André's ghostly appearance, as indicated in Edgar Bacon's 1897 account–the fact that the haunting leads up to and stops just at the moment of André's crucial mistake–suggest a sense that André's tragedy, his misfortune, was located in this moment of neutral-ground uncertainty.

The memories of violence and loss and the sense of uncertainty about the war and its legacy that were reflected in late-nineteenth and early-twentieth-century tales of ambiguous Revolutionary haunting were not new in the literature of the Hudson Valley. These shadows were, to some degree, present in the works of Irving and Cooper. Rip Van Winkle returns, having missed the Revolution, only to find that a contentious lot of Yankees have overrun his favorite tavern, and his friends have been killed in the war. Sleepy Hollow's war reminiscence takes the form of a headless Hessian who is at once an emblem of the violence that took place in the neighborhood and a representation of disintegrated historical understanding. And the shifting, problematic issues of loyalty and identity around which *The Spy* revolves are not entirely subdued by the fact that Cooper's peddler-spy, Harvey Birch, turns out to be in the American service.[87] Also, at some level, the ambiguities of Revolutionary hauntings in the late nineteenth and early twentieth centuries may simply reflect the imperfect apparatus of memory, especially secondhand memory, at an increasing temporal distance from the war.

Yet the insistence with which ghosts of the Revolution inhabited the literature and folklore of the region from the centennial through the turn of the century suggests that the concerns registered in Irving and Cooper did not diminish, but rather flourished, and took on added dimensions in the contexts of the period. Both an urgency to remember the Revolution—to affix national and local traditions of origins—and an ambivalence about the war's meanings and legacy were amplified by contemporary developments and events that had distinct regional as well as national resonances. One might see, for instance, in the memory and ghosts of the Revolution, reflections of the Civil War. The divisiveness of that more recent conflict served to sanctify the "old war," and a conciliatory nationalism certainly lent force to centennial memorializations. "Following the rancor of Reconstruction," writes Michael Kammen, "many Americans perceived the Revolution—or wanted to—as a . . . shared memory, a common core of national tradition that could banish the old bitterness."[88] At the same time, the

Civil War may have colored imaginative reconstructions of Revolutionary tales with more visceral and immediate images of battle and death, and also may have contributed to a continuing fascination with André and a resurrection of the memory of the loyalists, as it exposed the relativism of loyalty and rebellion. Notably, in his preface to the 1879 publication of the loyalist *History of New York during the Revolutionary War*–written in the 1780s but never before published–Edward Floyd De Lancey (note the name) writes: "The ideas of 'loyalty' and 'loyal men,' and 'rebellion' and 'rebels,' which have been current in the United States since the Revolutionary war, were rudely shocked, and quite changed, by the outbreak . . . of the late civil war at the South. Americans then learned . . . in a way never to be forgotten, that 'loyalty' was a virtue . . and that 'rebels' and 'rebellion' were to be put down at any cost."[89]

More immediately apparent in the turn-of-the-century Hudson Valley writings that focused on ambivalent Revolutionary memory and hauntings, though, were questions and concerns over urban growth and immigration that also animated aboriginal hauntings of the period. William Abbatt's pilgrimage along André's path, in *The Crisis of the Revolution*, for instance, is rife with a sense of impending change and loss. Abbatt considers as he moves from site to site how little seems to have changed: "I passed over almost every foot of the road [André] traversed, and realized that the landscape could not differ greatly from that which he saw." However, Abbatt has real reason to fear the loss of the sites of memory he surveys. Not only are places like Mabie's Tavern (André's last prison) falling to ruin, but the specter of the Croton reservoir system–expanding by thousands of acres in the 1890s to supply water to a rapidly growing New York City–is looming. Abbatt is keenly aware that a number of the houses along his path are on "reservoir land" and "must soon be removed or destroyed"; "by the time these lines reach the reader," he says, these houses "will probably be things of the past."[90]

Charles Pryer's interest in local Revolutionary lore was also apparently triggered by his acute perception of change in West-chester—in his case by a sense that an overflow of new populations into the region was rapidly destroying local ethnic and social character. As we have seen, Pryer clearly had the sense of a quickly passing order in Westchester. Writing of the "old Huguenot" from whom he had heard ghost stories of Skinner's Oak, Pryer says: "he was the scion of an old race and class, that I regret to say is fast passing from the face of the earth. Born when the Revolution was something more than the written story of the dead years in the minds of the people, he was full of the quaint old legends and traditions of that epoch . . . he was ardently attached to the old ways and old ideas; and as in these matters we were in perfect accord, many is the talk we have had together of the olden times."[91]

Pryer's statement reveals that Revolutionary remembrance, on the regional as well as the national level, could be activated in this period as part of a nativistic response to accelerated urban growth and immigration. And Pryer's comments point to underlying concerns with character and race that preoccupied the late nineteenth century. A connection between Revolutionary and racial heritage is evidenced also by Abbatt's dedication of his book "to the descendants of the men of 'Seventy-Six' as represented in our Patriotic-Heredity Societies." The irony, though, is that in this period of great social flux, the nativistic impulse that placed a premium on Revolutionary traditions often turned, in its focus on inimical and ambiguous ghosts, not to what had been achieved, but instead to what had been lost in the Revolution.

Carl Carmer writes in *The Hudson* (1939): "The exodus [of loyalists] from New York in the year 1783 was the removal of a considerable part of the Hudson River civilization."[92] The Revolution had severed the American connection to Britain and had opened a door to social change and upheaval locally and nationally. Ultimately, the regional preoccupation with André and the proliferation of hauntings that dwelt on a sense of travesty in the

Revolution were regionally focused manifestations of a larger contemporary, conservative reaction, which is strikingly apparent, for
instance, in the opening of historian Claude Halstead Van Tyne's
The Loyalists in the American Revolution (1902): "The formation of
the Tory or Loyalist party in the American Revolution; its persecu-
tion by the Whigs during a long and fratricidal war, and the banish-
ment or death of over one hundred thousand of these most conservative and respectable Americans is a tragedy but rarely paralleled
in the history of the world."[93] Although Charles Pryer points specifically to the "old Huguenot" as the repository of local Revolutionary memory, it was in part a wistful elitist regret and Anglophilia—activated by social and ethnic change—that animated the
ambivalent ghosts of the Revolution in the minds of conservative
men like Abbatt and Pryer.[94]

The heightened concern with character and race that both
aroused and qualified Revolutionary traditions in the late nineteenth and early twentieth centuries suggests why André's ghost in
particular lingered in the Revolutionary memory of the lower Hudson Valley. It was in part a sense of having amputated or sacrificed
Anglo-American character and civilization that haunted in André's
guise. This is suggested on the monument erected in 1879 on the
site of André's execution in Tappan through the combined efforts
of Arthur Penrhyn Stanley, dean of Westminster Abbey, and Cyrus
Field (the man responsible for laying the transatlantic cable), a
Tarrytown resident. It reads: "this stone was placed about the spot
where [André] lay, by a citizen of the United States against which
he fought, not to perpetuate the record of strife, but in token of
those better feelings which have since united two nations, one in
race, in language and in religion, in the hope that the friendly understanding will never be broken."[95]

Revolutionary tradition, which also contained egalitarian and
antitraditional resonances, mixed somewhat tenuously with the desire for racial rootedness and heritage that gained strength in the

late nineteenth century. Tales of Revolutionary hauntings, though, allowed room for the coexistence of nationalism and ambivalence. Overall, like aboriginal hauntings, the Revolutionary ghosts that proliferated in the Hudson Valley from the centennial into the early twentieth century contained multiple valences and motivations. On one level a register of the relative nearness of these events in public memory, the war haunted the generations once or twice removed from that direct memory. On one hand reflecting a troubled memory of the war, its means, and its consequences, the ghosts of Revolution also served to register later concerns over the legacies of the Revolution, and over perceived dissolution of national and regional character.

WORKING GHOSTS

Looking in one last time on Charles Pryer, we find him reading through old letters and papers he has found in a trunk at his old Westchester homestead. And he is transported: "As I turned the yellow, time-stained papers, I could almost see before me the stately dames and formal gallants of the colonial period. I seemed to breathe their air and be surrounded by their conditions; nor was there anything especially incongruous in my environment as I raised my eyes from the papers and looked about me. . . . I was still in the past." But then Pryer is unwillingly snapped back into the present by the "sound of a steam whistle," which forces him to realize "that the nineteenth, and not the eighteenth century, was dying."[96]

Pryer was far from the first to have his timeless reverie rudely interrupted by a passing locomotive. By the mid-nineteenth century, some of the best American authors had their pastoral visions dispelled by the thunder and blast of a train.[97] Nor is he the only late-nineteenth and early-twentieth-century Hudson Valley writer to depict the railroad as the antitype of the past, the destroyer of tradition and desirable hauntings. An inimical relationship between the railroad–together with the industrializing, modernizing forces it represented–and the haunting presence of the past echoes in other Hudson Valley scenes as well. After a day of wandering through sites "sacred to the Indian," the narrator of Searing's *Land of Rip Van Winkle* is similarly distraught at the arrival in Haines Corners of "the snorting little fiend of an engine" in "the stronghold of the great Manitou. What a desecrating thought!"[98] It was not just railroads that disturbed a haunting sense of the past. Tanneries, quarries, brickyards, and factories–intrusive and often earth-scarring activities, which also drew waves of immigrants into the region as workers–were castigated time and again for trampling history, despoiling scenery, and dispelling ghosts. C. G. Hine writes of the village of Catskill: "one by one, those buildings which linked the present-day village to the past have been demolished to make way for factory or brickyard, until to-day the place holds too little to attract the traveller."[99] All in all it seems that the industrial world and the haunted landscape should be mutually exclusive.

But to settle on this formula is to ignore the significant number of hauntings in which the industrial appears as instrumental or central; it is to overlook the fact that the presence and products of industrial society not only have been conducive to the proliferation of hauntings of various types, but have in many cases provided the locus and content of the hauntings themselves. The New York Central Railroad, for instance, appears in a surprising number of tales of haunting in the Hudson Valley, and in a wide variety of roles. In addition to serving as impetus to reactionary hauntings, as in the case of the Ver Plancks, who conjure a ghost on their property in response to their dispossession by the New York Central; and in addition to promoting the ghostly assets of the region in its own advertising to tourists, the railroad has itself been the site of ghostly activity.[100] One former railroad employee told a folklore collector in the mid-twentieth century that his wife had once been knocked down by an "angry spirit" along the tracks.[101] Another former worker told of the annual appearance on the tracks of a ghost train, carrying a skeleton orchestra and a coffin.[102] And beyond just serving as the site of ghostly activity, the railroad has also produced ghosts of its own, such as those of two men killed in 1912, who haunted the railroad yards just west of Albany; and that of another worker killed in 1913 who haunted a house in Rye.[103]

As this brief accounting of railroad hauntings begins to suggest, links between industrial development and regional hauntedness are not as counterintuitive as the comments of Hine, Searing, Pryer, and others might make them seem. These railroad hauntings are just one subset of a larger body of what might be called industrial hauntings—hauntings of industrial sites and hauntings by the ghosts of workers—that make up a significant portion of hauntings in the Hudson Valley in late-nineteenth- and early-twentieth-century literature and folklore.

One type of industrial hauntedness in the Hudson Valley drew from a base of culture and desire quite similar to that which populated the landscape with Revolutionary echoes and aboriginal ghosts. This variety of industrial hauntedness involved the transfiguration of abandoned industrial sites into scenes of melancholy and nostalgia. As with aboriginal and Revolutionary hauntings, the romanticizing of industrial remains in the late nineteenth and early twentieth centuries had some precedents in the early nineteenth century. Ironworks—the region's first type of heavy industry—began operating in the mid-to-late eighteenth century at various sites in the region. Intensive operations, they were also in many cases short-lived, with a number of furnaces having seen their last use before even the nineteenth century arrived.[104] With their slowly crumbling, Gothic-tower-like furnaces, in a period when some Hudson Valley residents were importing and even building ruins to fill a perceived gap in misty historical associations, abandoned ironworks were ripe even in the first half of the nineteenth century for romantic reinterpretation. For example, the ruins of the Augusta ironworks, just west of Tuxedo, which closed in 1813, provide a melancholy scene in *The Warwick Woodlands; or Things as They Were Twenty Years Ago* (1850), by the sportsman-writer "Frank Forester": "The roof-trees broken, the doors and shutters either torn from their hinges, or flapping wildly to and fro; the mill wheels cumbering the stream with masses of decaying timber, and the whole presenting a most desolate and mournful aspect."[105] A similar depiction of the Augusta ruins prefaced an 1848 novel by E. Oakes Smith titled *The Salamander,* a mystical "history" set in a Rockland County ironworks and involving lost angels, fire demons, and a greedy German-born ironmaster.[106]

The early iron industry continued to be represented within the landscape of industrial hauntedness that developed in the latter half of the century.[107] And as the general rise of Hudson Valley industry through the nineteenth century inevitably produced further instances of industrial failure—adding to the landscape not only decaying furnaces but also dilapidated factories, abandoned quarries, and overgrown railroad tracks—romantic reconstructions of this failure occurred with increasing frequency, and sometimes with startling rapidity.[108] Just a few months after a strike shut down work at a Westchester marble quarry, the author of an 1872 article in the Yonkers *Statesman* wrote: "A stranger visiting the marble quarries . . . must be struck with the deathlike silence which now prevails, where a few short months since, the hillsides and rocks teemed . . . with busy life. But the merry music of mallet and chisel is hushed . . . and the whole scene is a forcible reminder of 'The Deserted Village.'"[109] This writer was not the only one in the region to reconfigure industrial abandonment in terms of Oliver Goldsmith's proto-romantic poem on pastoral loss.[110] In 1884 A. E. P. Searing similarly described an abandoned tannery in the Catskills as "a veritable 'Deserted Village.'"[111]

These instances suggest how, in an age hungry for romantic tradition, the industrial presence was drawn into a landscape of nostalgia similar to that inhabited by more antique ghosts. A broadcast, versatile sense of melancholy akin to hauntedness was applied to industrial residues in a way that, for the most part, had little to do with industry itself. Although the article in the *Statesman* evinced a desire for work to resume at the deserted quarries, this type of industrial hauntedness generally necessitated, and to a degree celebrated, the end of industrial activity and the partial reversion of industrial sites to nature. The tanneries whose remnants Searing turns into items of nostalgia were the scourge of Catskill tourists. Only when they had been abandoned could they be drawn into nineteenth-century mythic geography. The factory ruins, not the factories, are what C. G. Hine, in *The New York and Albany Post Road* (1905), explicitly says "lend an added charm" to Wappinger Falls.[112] Like ghosts of Indians, Dutch folk, and Revolutionary enemies, these ghosts of industry enter the landscape of haunted imagination only insofar as they are no longer viable presences or threats.

But there is another facet to what I am calling industrial hauntings, one that involves both the haunting of functional industrial sites and hauntings by industrial workers. Almost entirely absent from the written sources examined thus far, these hauntings thrive in local folklore available from the early decades of the twentieth century. This is not to say that working ghosts were absent from the nineteenth century; these hauntings hold affinities, for instance, with ghost stories involving slaves and servants, such as the case from Leeds discussed earlier. Yet worker ghosts seem to surface with increased frequency in the early twentieth century, probably both because the number of industrial sites and workers had reached a critical mass by that time, and because the capture of local oral folklore that included this type of haunting occurred primarily in the 1930s and 1940s.

Industry haunts Hudson Valley folklore of the early twentieth century in a number of ways. There are industrial-site hauntings that have little to do with the work done at those sites, but instead reflect a general sense of these places as uncanny locations in the landscape, as places of danger.[113] More interesting and important are the hauntings by ghosts of workers whose deaths resulted from industrial activities. In addition to the ghostly railroad workers noted earlier—two killed in the yards at Colonie, another from Rye—another railroad worker, killed while building the railroad in Dutchess County, haunted a farm in Boston Corners.[114] A man named John McGowan killed in a landslide at a Haverstraw brickworks returned as a ghost, along with his horse and cart; a Haverstraw woman "heard him say 'giddap' to his horse as though he was there in the road."[115] Another fatal landslide, at a Glasco brickworks, also led to tales of haunting by two dead workers.[116] And more than one account in the Jones Folklore Archives tells of the ghosts of workers killed during the building of the Mid-Hudson Bridge at Poughkeepsie in the 1920s. According to one version, the night watchman hears the cries of the three men from the top of the caisson that had given way, killing them; another account claims they return looking "very much alive and are wearing their work clothes."[117]

One senses immediately a difference between these industrial hauntings and those of the "deserted village" strain. These are not the images of picturesque industrial decline. These hauntings operate with reference to tragic incidents within an ongoing, more or less contemporary industrial order. These are working ghosts. And the content, background, and tone of the accounts that reveal their presence imply that they are also working-class hauntings, with origins and currency in the working populations of the region.

Pause to consider the people telling these tales. The story of the Glasco brickworkers was told by a Mrs. Francello, while the account of the two men killed in the Colonie railroad yard was given by a man named DeTommasi. The section of Rye where the ghostly railroad worker returns is called Dublin. The New York Central

Railroad worker who spoke of an "angry spirit" along the tracks was an African-American man born in Virginia. Although one version of the story of ghostly Mid-Hudson Bridge workers was told by an old Dutch woman, she had heard it from workmen, gathered "from all over the country," who were staying in her boardinghouse during the construction.[118] As Warren Sherwood, an amateur folklore collector and writer from Ulster County, explained in another account of the Mid-Hudson Bridge ghosts, the bridge construction workers "lived in little shacks near the place of construction and here swapped tales and superstitions."[119] What begins to become clear in this survey of those who told stories about ghostly workmen, and what makes the set particularly significant, is that almost all these stories of industrial hauntings arose and circulated in communities and subcultures of migrant and immigrant populations whose presence in the region was concomitant with industrial development.

This said, it is not easy to determine or categorize the political and social implications that filter through these often short references to worker ghosts. Seeming to represent the presence of what has been termed "preindustrial" cultural mindsets operating within the modern industrial sphere, they reveal communities of workers negotiating their position in a modern system by way of beliefs and stories in a manner that seems at once potentially conservative and potentially radical.[120]

At some level we expect these hauntings to contain working-class accusation and protest against the industrial order that produced these tragedies. We expect worker ghosts to behave like the ghosts of dispossessed Indians among Native Americans, and the ghosts of slaves among slaves and their descendants. And these expectations are answered, at least in some instances. Suggestions that hauntings served as a way of registering protest against negligent employers and bad conditions run through references to the ghosts of industrial tragedies. Sometimes the hints are very slight.

When Margaret May of Haverstraw speaks of John McGowan who was killed in a brickyard landslide, she says, "He came back because it wasn't time for him to go yet," implying that his death was unnatural and wrong; and the common belief that McGowan returns from the dead "as a very fine man," rather than as a workman, might suggest a sort of poetic justice in haunting, a reversal of fortunes.[121]

A more substantial sense of accusation, and of the deployment of working-class hauntings as a protest statement, surfaces in Elvira Francello's account of the haunting at the Glasco brickyard:

About 15 y[ea]rs ago there was a very serious accident at the brickyard in Glasco. A huge clay bank slid down the valley, killing two of the workers. This was before the use of steam shovels. The workers were buried alive. Their bodies were not unearthed until about 1 year later. The owners finally purchased steam shovels and one night this workman went to work on the steam shovel and he tried to light his kerosene lantern. He made three or four attempts and each time it went out. There was no wind that night and he believed it to be the ghosts of the 2 men. He refused to work there at night. Many of the people in the town believed this to be true.[122]

Francello's account suggests protest on several layers. First, although she speaks of the worker's death as an accident, and implies that this brickyard was not unusual in not having steam shovels, her subsequent statements evince a perception of callous disregard on the part of the employers, both in a lack of effort to retrieve the bodies of the dead workers who were gruesomely "buried alive" and in an implied delay in the purchase of steam shovels—"the owners *finally* purchased steam shovels" she says—which would, presumably, prevent similar accidents from befalling excavating workers. That the activity of the alleged ghosts centers on the steam shovel further suggests resentment and vengefulness in this regard.

What is also worth noticing in this account is how this haunting takes a wider place in the community in a way that suggests participation by the local workers in this postmortem protest against conditions. The steam-shovel operator begins a tale of haunting based on awfully slight evidence: he cannot light his lantern. Yet, rather than reject the operator's interpretation of this minor incident, the people of the town accept and perpetuate the story. "Many of the people," Francello concludes, "believed this to be true." That these tales of industrial ghosts seem to rest on sometimes slim origins only heightens their social significance as items of community response and comment, their dispersal registering a series of individual and group decisions about what matters.[123]

It also might be remarked that the steam-shovel driver uses his asserted belief in the haunting to insist on not working nights. Whether or not this represents a deliberate use of "superstition" toward the surreptitious achievement of material ends (akin to Uncle Julius's use of "conjure" tales in the stories of Charles Chesnutt) is unclear in this instance, although other contemporary examples from the region imply that recourse to ghost stories was taken as a way of asserting control over work.[124] A woman from Cohoes, for example, told this story, which apparently explained why some workers at her father's brickyard missed work on Monday mornings:

One time about fifty years ago [about 1890] my father went south to get some Negroes to work in the brickyard in Crescent. Every Saturday night they would go to Troy to have a good time and they would stay overnight. If they didn't get home by Sunday afternoon they wouldn't go home because they wouldn't pass the Wide Waters after dark. A man had drowned there and they said that every night after dark you could hear him calling for help.[125]

Even if we assume that all tales of ghost workers contain an implicit protest, simply in the memorialization of these events among communities, these stories still seem a far cry from a radical indictment of industrial capitalism. Whatever protests might be registered in these hauntings seem to rest mainly at the level of specific abuses; at most they serve as shadowy parallels to calls for eight-hour days and work-site safety. Indeed, it might be argued that these tales of haunting operated as a sort of mourning mechanism that defused or mitigated a more potent sense of outrage, and thus more active class consciousness or protest. These ghosts do not seem to question larger industrial development, nor are they in any way environmentally concerned. In fact these hauntings strangely support the industrial presence in the region, as they serve to incorporate the industrial landscape into a mythic sense of place. A perhaps unanticipated alliance between ghost stories and industrial development is suggested especially in the case of the Mid-Hudson Bridge, as told by Warren Sherwood: "The bridge workers had a sort of superstition about having a man killed on the job. They would be jittery and nervous until the first death. . . . This old superstition came from Roman times when pagan gods were worshipped. A victim had to be sacrificed to the god of the bridge before the construction could get under way."[126] Whether or not the historical data are accurate, what is significant in this account is that the workers not only possess a ready-made way to mythologize the death of fellow workers; they also *expect* that someone will be killed during the construction. It is necessary to the building of the bridge. Construction and ghosts thus go hand in hand.

Yet if these stories seem to resist radical political interpretations, there is nonetheless something radical in all this. The working ghosts who haunted the region's railroads and brickyards were simultaneously accepting and assertive. In the haunting of the Mid-Hudson Bridge—a story that seems to have achieved a significant currency in the area—a population not yet rooted in the region can be seen projecting itself onto the industrialized landscape. The workers haunt the bridge they built; they maintain possession of the product of their labor by haunting it with tales of ghosts—and, notably, ghosts in workmen's clothing. At base, the stories of ghostly workers that accumulated in the early to mid-twentieth century allowed industrial tragedies to take on mythic qualities, attached mythic meanings to the industrial landscape, and, most significantly, worked toward inscribing working-class immigrant and migrant cultures, presences, and experiences onto a landscape that others would rather have filled with more "native" hauntings. These tales of ghostly workers redrew the map of the haunted Hudson Valley to allow the new populations that accompanied regional industrial development to locate and affix their own stories in place and history.

The three strains of hauntedness traced in this chapter—"aboriginal" Dutch and Indian hauntings, Revolutionary War hauntings, and industrial hauntings—occupied overlapping territories of time, space, and imagination in the period from the last decades of the nineteenth century to the first decades of the twentieth. The question remains whether there was any common ground among these varieties of hauntings that not only contained contradictions and varieties of intent within themselves, but that from one to the next represented divergent and conflicting visions regarding local, regional, and even national character.

Clearly, there were affinities between the Revolutionary War and aboriginal hauntings, which, for all the uncertainties of history and legacy they registered, were equally invoked as touchstones of origins, nativity, and authority in a period of rapid change. A sense of conjuncture between the Revolutionary and the aboriginal is evident, for instance, in the assertion of the author of *Legends and Poetry of the Hudson* that it was entirely "fitting" that the graves of the

Revolutionary dead "should be scattered, as we find them, among the mounds of a strange people who once possessed these broad hunting grounds," or in Charles Skinner's claim that the ghost of Chief Croton appeared to urge one of the Van Cortlandts to join the Continental Army.[127]

These two sets of "original" hauntings clearly operated at some distance from the industrial hauntings that came from and populated the landscape with precisely the elements that those who invoked the former hauntings usually wished to escape or obscure. But to stop there is not to tell the whole story. There were connections and similarities here as well. Most basically, all these ghosts served needs arising out of specific contemporary circumstances; they were all "working ghosts," recruited to serve in battles over place and belonging that were waged in the tumultuous decades around the turn of the century.

Industrial sites and immigrant workers were not entirely resistant to the process of ghostly transfiguration that made regional icons of headless Hessians, walking sachems, and Dutch sailors. In a culture hungry for antiquity and tradition, obsolescence might make attractive ghosts even out of factories, tanneries, and railroad workers. Indeed, although the stories of working ghosts we have seen here point to events from the late nineteenth century to the 1920s, and seem to have been current during that period, it is important to note that these tales, as they are available today, were collected mainly in the 1930s and 1940s. While industrial activity did not completely disappear from the Hudson Valley in the twentieth century, a number of regional industries had been in decline from at least the turn of the century, and many were dealt a fatal blow by the Depression. In this context, workmen, too, were becoming items of romantic memory. A broadcast industrial nostalgia, incorporating both abandoned industrial sites and vanished working populations, is evident in a chapter of Carl Carmer's *The Hudson* (1939) titled "Ghost Towns and Ghost Trades." Along with images obviously within the romantic ruin tradition—defunct brickyards described as "picturesque weathered ruins . . . their chimneys standing lonely beside tumbled, weed-grown walls and staring empty windows"—Carmer includes wistful, past-tense depictions of "roistering" immigrant workmen. "A few of the old-timers are back in the ghost-town, Rosendale," he writes of a town once known for its cement works, but "there is no roaring of bully-boys as there was in the wild Irish days."[128] When told in the context of the 1930s and 1940s, tales of worker ghosts and tales of industrial ruins were both, to some extent, elegiac.

Still, worker ghosts never quite crossed over from local, primarily oral folklore to become staples of regional imagination. While Revolutionary and aboriginal hauntings were still prominent in regional stories into the late twentieth century, the hauntings by worker ghosts—at least those described here—have all but dissipated.[129] This is another product and sign of what we have seen here—that ghosts themselves are functions of the clienteles they haunt, dependent on those who use them. As turn-of-the-century industry disappeared, as extant immigrant populations assimilated and reinforcements were blocked by anti-immigrant legislation of the 1920s, the primary purposes and bases of these ghosts vanished. Compounding this marginalization, worker ghosts, because of the ethnic makeup and the limited political cogency of the populations from which they emerged, also lacked attributes that would allow them to signify regional origins. Ironically, the ghosts with the most power in the material world tended to be those furthest removed from the present, ghosts whose promise of roots held wide appeal for a restless population.

Why, this new world is not so bad. I am left in possession of the field.

—A Dutch sailor's ghost, in Maxwell Anderson,
High Tor, 1937

5

POSSESSING HIGH
TOR MOUNTAIN

*I*t is getting dark on High Tor mountain when Biggs and Skimmerhorn, representatives of a traprock quarrying company, come searching for Van Van Dorn, the mountain's irascible and fiercely independent owner. The men have come to try to force Van Dorn to sell his mountain. But the shadows are creeping up around them on the rocky crag, and the unscrupulous pair begins to think that there may be something moving there in the dark. "You think High Tor's just so much raw material," Van Dorn says to them knowingly, "but you're wrong. A lot of stubborn men have died up here and some of them don't sleep well. They come back and push things round these dark nights."[1]

In this play, *High Tor,* by Maxwell Anderson, which appeared on Broadway in 1937, ghosts do in fact materialize on the mountain–the ghosts of Dutch sailors, part of Henry Hudson's fleet, stranded and presumed killed by Indians in 1609–and they do indeed "push things round." They trap Biggs and Skimmerhorn in the scoop of a steam shovel. They get into a gunfight with a trio of dimwitted bank robbers. They drink and carouse and roll bowling balls at the mountain's airplane beacon. One of them–the ghost of the captain's wife–even has a brief romantic interlude with Van Dorn. And then, after being on the mountain for over three hundred years, they disappear into the sunrise on a ghost ship that finally comes for them. Such goings-on led critics to hail Anderson's play as "the first distinguished fantasy by an American in many years."[2] But *High Tor* was more than just a fantasy. Behind the play was an actual mountain "whose features, inhabitants, and traditions," wrote Anderson's biographer, were "inextricably bound up with that amazing work."[3] And the ghosts of the play pushed things around there, too, in a fight to save the mountain from real destruction.

Ghosts have consequences. They can scare off intruders (as in the case of Ichabod Crane). They can reveal or defend treasures (as in the case of the spirit troop that scares off money diggers in Charles Pryer's *Reminiscences*).[4] They can cause buildings or lands to be left uninhabited.[5] After all, a haunting is by definition an intervention, an occupation, a claim of priority and possession–if shadowy then all the more difficult to refute. Tales of haunting are riddled with references to property and rights. And there are examples of ghosts crossing over into the real world to take on physical (and fiscal) dimensions. In 1991, for instance, the New York State

Supreme Court ruled a Nyack house legally haunted, ordering a re-
fund for the buyer on the basis of its impaired value, and further-
more finding that because the seller had deliberately fostered the
belief that her house was "possessed" she had not, strictly speaking, delivered the premises "vacant" as stipulated in the contract.[6]
While this example is admittedly exceptional, it nonetheless relates
to much broader ways in which ghosts have made their presences
felt in the region's landscape and economy—most noticeably in its
tourist economy. In the twentieth century hauntedness has intersected with conservation and historic preservation efforts, which,
as they seek to reclaim and remove sites from the processes of development, have put ghosts to tangible social use. The story of
High Tor, in its relationship to the mid-twentieth-century mu-
seumization of the lower Hudson Valley, provides a unique opportunity to investigate how hauntedness links into a complex politics
of possession whose stakes involve control over place and property,
both replicating real-life power structures and complicating social
and cultural dichotomies.

THE MOUNTAIN AND MAXWELL ANDERSON

The story begins one spring afternoon in 1936 when playwright
Maxwell Anderson set out to climb to the top of High Tor. Anderson could see the mountain from his home of fourteen years, four
miles away on South Mountain Road in the still mostly rural New
City.[7] Thirty miles north of New York City, on the west shore of
the Hudson, and adjacent to the river's widest point, High Tor was
the northernmost point of the Palisades, and the boundary between the towns of Haverstraw and Clarkstown. High Tor's less-
than-mountainous 832 feet were made sublime by their steep ascent
from the Hudson River and the town of Haverstraw below. It was
the highest point in the view from South Mountain Road. This,
along with its distinctive shape, made it a favorite landmark among
Anderson's neighbors—something of a colony of artists, writers,

"Haverstraw, or Warren Landing." From Jacques G. Milbert, *Itinéraire pittoresque du fleuve Hudson* (Paris, 1828–1829). Courtesy of the Milstein Division of United States History, Local History and Genealogy, The New York Public Library, Astor, Lenox and Tilden Foundations.

and theater people. The mountain often appeared in their paintings and poems.[8]

That day when he climbed to the top of High Tor, Maxwell Anderson could see the wide expanse of the river below. He could see Connecticut in the east and the Ramapo Mountains in the west. To the north he could pick out Dunderberg and Bear Mountain, the southern gate of the Hudson Highlands. From parts of the mountain he might even have caught a glimpse of the growing number of tall buildings on Manhattan island. Anderson could see the hand of civilization here, too, in this stretch of the river valley spread out below: in the towns—Haverstraw, Stony Point, Croton, Ossining, Tarrytown—and in the railroad tracks that ran along both shores of the river. Just below, he would have been able to make out where the tracks came out of the West Shore Railroad tunnel, and he could see remnants of the brickworks that had once lined Haverstraw's shore.

Breathtaking as the view from High Tor could be, there were things in it that were unsettling to Max Anderson. When he had first come to New City, in the days before the George Washington Bridge had been built, his house had been without electricity, the road had been unpaved, and he preferred it that way. Indeed, when Rockland Power and Light had tried to run a high power line across his property, he had gone out at night to pull up the surveying stakes every time it had tried to place them; eventually the company had to put the line elsewhere.[9] But the modern world was inexorably encroaching, and portents of a new order were all around him. There was already an automobile factory across the river at Kingsland Point in North Tarrytown, and down at the foot of the mountain on which he stood stretched the paved surface of Route 9W, which, now along with the bridge, smoothed the way for automobile tourists and commuters to come pouring out from the city.[10]

Most immediately disturbing to Anderson was the view to the south where Middle Mountain stood. Behind a placid east face, the mountain was being chewed away, to be made into pavement for roads like 9W. "The great gouges in the mountain were an ugly sight and a real eye-opener," Anderson's son later recalled. "It was a real crisis around here at the time."[11] Anderson knew that the same thing was happening at other mountains along the Hudson, and he

could not help but fear for this mountain of rock that seemed so solid beneath his feet.[12] The New York Trap Rock Company had been trying to buy High Tor, and the only thing stopping it was the stubbornness of its current owner, Elmer Van Orden. The land on the mountain had been in Van Orden possession since before the Revolutionary War, and Elmer, a farmer and hunter, then well into his seventies, still lived alone on the mountain in a one-and-a-half-story farmhouse, the last habitation before the summit.[13] Van Orden was "pretty churlish" toward trespassers, as actor Burgess Meredith observed when he went up to do publicity shots for *High Tor*.[14] Yet there were other presences here that might be even more

Quarrying at Mt. Taurus (1938). Photograph by Hudson River Conservation
Society. Courtesy of the Franklin Delano Roosevelt Library,
Hyde Park, New York.

unsettling to the encroaching quarrying company. If on paper
High Tor was the property of Elmer Van Orden, Van Orden was
not the only one who possessed it.

So much history had passed on and around High Tor mountain. It was on High Tor, according to legend, that the local Lenape
tribespeople first spied a ship full of Dutchmen coming up the
river in 1609.[15] At its feet the Dutch, slowed at first by "Indian
raids," came to settle along the river's shore, joined over the seventeenth and eighteenth centuries by German, Huguenot, and possibly Danish and Flemish settlers, as well as an increasing number of
migrants from New England.[16] During the American Revolution,

signal fires had burned on the mountaintop to warn of the approach of British ships; and it was in the mountain's shadow that British major John André came ashore for his infamous and fateful meeting with Benedict Arnold.[17] High Tor stood through the rise of industries—ice works at Rockland Lake, textile factories in Garnerville and along the Minisceongo Creek, and brickworks, which dominated Haverstraw's economy in the nineteenth century. These industries had drawn new groups of people into the area and had also left marks on the mountain as the industrial appetite for wood denuded its slopes.[18] The mountain remained after most of these industries fell to ruin in the early twentieth century.

There were visible traces of this history in Anderson's view from High Tor—the "dead lagoons" of the abandoned brickyards; the graveyard, Mount Repose, on the mountain's northern side; the remnants of Dutch Town; and the sign marking the spot where André came ashore.[19] There were also less tangible emanations from the past lurking in the neighborhood. Perhaps it was the way the mountain brooded over Haverstraw, or the eerie emptiness of the mountain next to the bustle of the town below. Over the centuries, High Tor had been inscribed with legends and stories; it was a kind of storehouse of the supernatural, a place where the strange and ghostly were to be expected. Native American legend supposedly held that High Tor had been present at the creation of the world; it was the place where Manitou imprisoned evil spirits, who later escaped to roam the terrain when an ancient lake broke through the mountain to form the river.[20] Another legend said that one of the magi had come to High Tor and erected a stone altar for the purpose of converting the Indians. When a war party tried to rush up the mountain, the river broke through, swallowing up the warriors in a torrent of water.[21] Another legend, related to a group of German ironworkers who came to High Tor in 1740, told of a giant salamander who brought chaos to the mining colony when the ironmaster refused to let the forge fires be extinguished after seven years, as was the old-country custom.[22] That the mountain was still perceived as haunted into the twentieth century was attested by Daniel DeNoyelles, a local historian whose family had owned one of the main brickmaking operations of Haverstraw, who remembered rumors from his boyhood "about ghostly lights twinkling over the mountainous cliffs so we children often gazed at the darkened peak at bedtime."[23] Even Elmer Van Orden said there were ghosts sharing his craggy peak, and the ghost of his long-dead fiancée reportedly haunted the vicinity.[24]

Of course, it wasn't just High Tor that was haunted. Ghosts might have been found just about anywhere Maxwell Anderson might have rested his eyes that day. The Dutch, long out of power, were believed still to sail in ghostly vessels on the river below. In the dark of night one might hear the oars of Rambout Van Dam, an unfortunate Dutchman condemned eternally to row there for breaking the Sabbath centuries before. Or one might see the dramatic silent "storm ship."[25] A haunted house stood on Treason Hill, two miles north, while night travelers on Storm King Highway reported seeing the ghost of "Mad" Anthony Wayne, hero of the battle of Stony Point, riding by.[26] Up north on Dunderberg lived imps responsible for the storms that battered boats on the river below. To the south were stories of a mysterious lone Indian on Hook Mountain, and another in a place called Spook Hollow in Nyack.[27] Across the river, in Ossining, shad fishermen told stories of ghosts who protected buried treasure, while in Tarrytown there once rode on horseback a Hessian who had lost his head. (According to some he still rode there, although he was confused since the moving of his favorite bridge.)[28]

How many of these legends Anderson knew is hard to determine. Some said that he had heard stories from Van Orden.[29] He was almost definitely told of the "Guardian of Hook Mountain."[30] Nonetheless it is clear that Anderson saw spirits as he stood on the mountain that day. According to a 1937 *New York Times* article, Anderson said that he thought of "'the evanescence of civilizations,' for he was reminded of the Dutch fleet which had sailed up the river and of the Indians who had once dwelt on the mountain. By association the legend of Rip Van Winkle came to mind."[31]

Maxwell Anderson thought of theater as having a function in society, that "above and beyond entertainment" theater was supposed to "point out and celebrate whatever is good and worth saving in our confused and often desperate generations."[32] As he stood on the top of High Tor that spring day, he felt all around him the presence of history and myth, but he also saw that the present threatened to obliterate this heritage. "An echo and an image," the ghost of the captain's wife would say in the play Anderson began formulating that day, "one by one forgotten, fading out like an old writing, undecipherable, we lose our hold and go . . . could it be true?"[33] Anderson felt there was something at stake here, and when he descended the mountain that day he had an idea. A few days later he went to the small cabin on his property in which he did his writing, and worked to fill in the fading lines. Then, beginning on January 7, 1937, for 171 performances, on a stage set with a rock, a steam shovel, and the light of an airplane beacon, Maxwell Anderson's *High Tor* came to life on the stage of the Martin Beck Theatre.[34]

One hundred and seventy-one times the curtain opened on an old Indian, the last of his tribe, hearing the voices of his ancestors buried on High Tor, calling him to join them. One hundred and seventy-one times, Van Van Dorn, a doubly Dutch ditto of his ancestors, a twenty-four-year-old version of Elmer Van Orden, rejected the offer of Biggs and Skimmerhorn, representing the New York Trap Rock Company, which was trying to pirate this mountain from him. One hundred and seventy-one times, Biggs and Skimmerhorn found themselves stuck on the mountain by a rock slide that knocked out the easy trail. And one hundred and seventy-one times, at the end of the first scene, as the lights dimmed, and thunder came up sounding like rumbling bowling bowls, Maxwell Anderson's ghosts of High Tor materialized on this Broadway stage—six sailors, the captain, and the captain's wife, the crew of a ship lost in 1609, part of Henry Hudson's fleet.[35]

The ghosts claim possession of High Tor as "the earliest inhabitants, not counting Indians and Patagonians," and like Van Dorn and his real-life counterpart, Van Orden, they are pretty churlish about intrusions, especially the encroachments of the modern age. Although they are "wraithlike, half-effaced," they are not entirely without power. As the ghost captain says: "The life we keep is motionless as the center of a storm, yet while we can we keep it; while we can snuff out to darkness their bright sweeping [beacon] light, melt down the harness of the slow machines that hew the mountain from us. When it goes we shall go too. They leave us this place, High Tor, and we shall have no other." It is hinted that the ghosts caused the death of the steam-shovel operator a week earlier.[36] This night on the mountain they continue to foil the trespassers' best-laid plans. They trick the traprock men into their steam shovel and hoist them up. They scare the bank robbers off without their loot. "A poor Dutch wraith's more man than the thickest of you!" one of them calls after the retreating men.[37] These are, it seems, no lightweight specters.

As the play progresses, though, the ghosts begin to lose hold and fade; and as dawn approaches, the fate of the mountain becomes more and more insecure. This is also true of the Indian and Van, who seem like ghosts even in life. Van says late in the play:

God knows they haven't left me much. . . . Look, where the new road winds along the ledge. Look at the jagged cut the quarries make down to the south. . . . The West Shore tunnel belches its train above the dead lagoons that line the brickyards. Their damned shovel hangs across my line, ready to gouge the peak we're standing on. Maybe I'm a ghost myself trying to hold back an age with my hands; maybe we're all the same, these ghosts of Dutchmen and one poor superannuated Indian and one last hunter, clinging to his land because he's always had it.[38]

When morning arrives, the crew see their ship coming down the river; they vanish into the dawn, and at the end of the play Van agrees to sell, in part because the ghosts that gave the mountain meaning are gone, leaving it "barren," but also on the unexpected advice of the dying Indian, who, it seems, has seen ghosts come and go before. Citing an old sachem who also once lived on the mountain, he tells Van:

Our god is now the setting sun, and we must follow it. For other races out of the east will live here in their time, one following another. Each will build its cities . . . but none will live forever. . . . Let them come in despoiling [for] these will not endure. . . . I heard the wise [sachem] looking down when the railroad cut was fresh and the bleeding earth offended us. There is nothing made, he said, and will be nothing made by these new men . . . that will not make good ruins.[39]

The Indian's speech reassuringly predicts other ghosts to come. But there is something final in this moment. Without the mountain there is no longer a place for Van, for the Indian, for the ghosts who link this place to the past; and in the end, without the ghosts, the mountain is just rock to be made into roads.

In part, *High Tor* and the story behind its creation compel attention here simply because they so clearly reflect recurring trends and issues of Hudson Valley hauntings. The play points broadly to the region's history of unrest. (Indeed, the crew's ship in the play is called the *Onrust*—a word akin to "unrest," actually the name of the first ship built in New Netherland.)[40] And Anderson's description of the ghosts emphasizes the connection between historical erasure and ghostliness; the play is full of references to the ghosts as faded print or suggestive outlines whose meanings are becoming increasingly elusive over time.[41] The bowling Dutch sailor ghosts, and the fact that Anderson's reverie on the mountain inevitably arrives at "Rip Van Winkle" (without conscious reference to Washington Irving), emphasize the pervasiveness of Irving's influence. The play clearly echoes the regional predilection for Indian and Dutch hauntings, the association of both with antiquity and roots, and the sense of their self-removal from the territory, while the dying Indian's speech also suggests the possibility of industrial hauntings to come.[42] In all these ways, *High Tor* is a microcosm of major themes of Hudson Valley haunting. But what makes *High Tor* most interesting is the way that the haunting it portrayed onstage gained realization offstage.

The real story of High Tor turned out very differently from the ending of the play. Most people who went to see *High Tor* had probably never heard of the mountain before. By the time they left the theater, though, they had heard plenty—enough to make them want to save this mountain. Maxwell Anderson made them feel that this endangered mountain was a special, near-sacred place. Those who had not seen the play might nonetheless read about the mountain in the string of articles on High Tor that appeared in New York City newspapers in its wake—something that both reflected an interest in the behind-the-scenes issues of the story and generated further awareness.[43] Two years after the play appeared on Broadway, Elmer Van Orden was being celebrated in the *New York Times* as "The Savior of High Tor" for his refusal to sell. Five hundred guests, including the casts of *High Tor* and *Knickerbocker Holiday* (Anderson's current show with Kurt Weill), attended a party for him, and Van Orden was regaled with scenes from both shows and with pageants performed by local schoolchildren.[44] When Van Orden died in 1942 at age seventy-nine, and the western slope of High Tor was thrown open to the market, the Hudson River Conservation Society and the Rockland County Conservation Association turned their attention to the case, forming a Committee to Save High Tor, with Maxwell Anderson as chairman.[45] In a letter to Archer Huntington (son of Collis P. H. Huntington of the New York Central Railroad), who owned an estate at the base of High Tor, Anderson wrote: "High Tor is on the market. . . . It could be a state park—or the quarry could buy it. Probably it's no use trying to hold back the march of industrial machinery, but if you want to give a chunk of that sum I think I could raise the rest."[46]

The campaign to save High Tor included a variety of means to draw attention and funds to the mountain. Committee members put together an exhibition about the Tor, as well as a children's Christmas book. They sounded the alarm in articles written for local and New York City papers.[47] They circulated letters like the one written by the president of the Rockland County Conservation Association: "High Tor, one of Rockland County's most beautiful and historic spots, is for sale. This, as you know, is the Hudson crag that has inspired poets, playwrights and artists over the years. It is the highest eminence in the Hudson highlands and one of the richest in cultural and historical associations. If it is left to commercial exploitation, our children may know it as simply another great, raw gash along the Hudson's shores."[48]

And donations came. Donations came from Rockland County residents and from onetime residents. Funds came from young men and women in the armed forces "to make sure the Tor is still there when I get home," as one wrote.[49] Money came in from "concerned citizens from New York to Albany" and from "garden clubs, historical societies and many other organizations on both sides of the Hudson," recalled committee member Isabelle Savell.[50] Donations were mailed in from the West Coast and from Newfoundland, showing just how much "a mountain [may] matter . . . even to a transient visitor," explained one of Anderson's neighbors in a 1943 article.[51] In the end the campaign raised $12,000 to purchase High

Tor and the mineral rights, and in 1943, 492 acres on the mountain were donated to the Palisades Interstate Park Commission in perpetuity.

"There were important historical and geological reasons for all this fervor over High Tor," noted Savell. "But it is as a symbol, and a mystical one, at that, that High Tor holds the loyalties and concern of the countryside."[52] It is clear that the sense of mythic significance evoked by Anderson's play was of utmost importance in the campaign. As the chairman of the Hudson River Society claimed in a 1952 article, "many contributions to the cause had been directly inspired by this work."[53] Anderson's influence also echoes in subsequent accounts of the mountain: a 1980 article in the *Poughkeepsie Journal*, for instance, states that "High Tor . . . is where Rip Van Winkle slept. It is the haunt of the crew of Henrik Hudson's voyage up the river"; and a piece written in 1992 by a Haverstraw resident mentions "the lost crew from one of Henry Hudson's ships, who climbed up High Tor to keep a lookout for the fleet that never came," and portrays "the ghost of an old tribesman . . . praying to his ancestral spirits buried beneath the mountain."[54]

THE POLITICS OF POSSESSION: RESTORATIONS

When in *High Tor* Skimmerhorn Sr. asks Van what it is that he wants, Van cries out: "I want to have it back the way it was before you came here."[55] Despite the dispersal of the ghosts of the past at the end, the play was a call for restoration—both in the sense of returning property to rightful owners, and in the sense of a physical reversion of the site to a corresponding condition. The very success of the play in this respect demands investigation. Why, in the contexts of the Great Depression and World War II, would people not just in Rockland County but around the world care about preserving a haunted mountain, and care enough to send money? As one of the few vocal objectors to the campaign to save High Tor argued, "We are forced in these times to pay high taxes; we are asked to buy war bonds; we are asked to contribute to the U.S.O., to help relieve the French, the Greeks, the Russians, and the Chinese. . . . It seems to me that the Hudson River Conservation Society and the Rockland County Conservation Association might well bend their efforts in these times to more sensible problems."[56]

Certainly, the response *High Tor* engendered had to do with a sense of heightened endangerment from the quarrying industry, the most obviously destructive of the industrial activities that took place in the region, and one that had therefore become the most conservation-provocative bogey in the early twentieth century.[57] Yet scenic or historical value had not prevented quarrying at other mountains along the river. If the outcome of this case seems inevitable, if it seems natural that such storied places should warrant physical preservation, this sensibility is in large part one that developed in the period in which *High Tor* appeared on stage. At the turn of the century, Tarrytown historian Edgar Mayhew Bacon had lamented that his town was not foresighted enough even to preserve the "Katrina Van Tassel" house, knocking it down to build a new high school on the property; at that time, not even Irving's stamp guaranteed preservation.[58]

All tales of haunting assert claims. *High Tor* was able to make its claims tangible because it struck into a new cult of folklore in the 1930s and 1940s and intersected with conservation and preservation movements that were then enjoying unprecedented support from both private and governmental sources. Anderson's epiphany on the mountain, the play that this epiphany produced, and the conservation efforts the play inspired were linked to a broader contemporary cultural and political matrix. Empowering Anderson's ghosts was a yearning for rootedness and meaningful heritage that grew from the traumas of the Depression and that continued to flourish in the heightened nationalism of World War II. As one critic later wrote of this period, "attempt[s] to come to terms with the problems of the present prompted, at the same time, a remarkable effort to take possession of the American past—the hidden, unofficial past, the past that lay buried in the folklore and folk art and local legend."[59]

These impulses drove a whole series of efforts to capture regional and local identity, including such Work Projects Administration undertakings as the Historical Records Survey and the folklore collections and guidebooks produced by the Federal Writers Project. The 1930s and 1940s yielded a battery of regional collections and studies, from Zora Neale Hurston's *Mules and Men* (1935) to Benjamin A. Botkin's *Treasury of New England Folklore* (1947). In addition, Depression-era desires for senses of place and heritage propelled new support for conservation and historic-preservation movements, which had begun gathering steam in the age of Theodore Roosevelt but had since fallen into a lull. The new surge of conservation and preservation sentiment in the 1930s and 1940s was reflected not only in the rise of private societies and activities, but also in an extraordinary degree of government support under New Deal programs and legislation, including the Civilian Conservation Corps, the 1935 Historical Sites Act, and a reorganization of the National Parks Service that quadrupled the number of historical areas administered by that agency. Overall, the period 1932–1945, Michael Kammen writes, represented "a dramatic breakthrough in the government's sense of responsibility for America's historic and physical inheritance."[60]

As in the case of the romantic cultural nationalism of the previous century—and in large part because of it—these impulses found the Hudson Valley congenial ground. Indeed, Anderson's play operated between two nodal points: a New York City theater culture that in the 1930s nurtured an ideal of social commitment, and a local history and folklore movement centered in Albany, where in 1934 the New York State College became one of the first in the country to offer courses in American folklore, and where in the 1940s Louis Jones was amassing what would become his New York folklore archives.[61] *High Tor* resonated with a regional folklore renaissance that yielded studies like E. E. Gardner's *Folklore of the Schoharie Hills* (1937) and Harold W. Thompson's *Body, Boots and Britches: Folktales, Ballads, and Speech from Country New York* (1939), as well as such popular works as Paul Wilstach's *Hudson River Landings* (1933), Carl Carmer's *The Hudson* (1939), and Croswell Bowen's *Great River of the Mountains: The Hudson* (1941), all of which in some way catered to the renewed appetite for supernatural lore and ghost stories.[62]

The conservation and preservation sentiments that were gaining ground nationally also found new strength in the Hudson Valley in the 1930s and 1940s.[63] Indeed, some of the country's most vital supporters of conservation and restoration—Franklin D. Roosevelt and John D. Rockefeller Jr.—were Hudson Valley natives and dwellers who supported projects in the region.[64] Rockefeller's acquisitions of Hudson Valley sites in this period laid the basis for Sleepy Hollow Restorations (now Historic Hudson Valley), a set of historic site and house museums stretching up the east side of the river.[65] Adding to noteworthy advances from earlier periods (the first state-sponsored historic landmark in the country had opened in Newburgh in 1850, and the Palisades Interstate Park Commission had been created in 1900), regional support for conservation and preservation swelled in the 1930s.[66] Notably, the Rockland County Conservation Association and the Hudson River Conservation Society, both of which were involved in the case of High Tor, had been founded in 1930 and 1936 respectively.[67] By the end of the decade, a formidable network of preservation-supportive individuals and agencies had come into place in the Hudson Valley.[68]

Maxwell Anderson was no New Dealer. (*High Tor,* in fact, takes a swing at a prominent member of Roosevelt's cabinet.)[69] Nor was he a folklorist or historian. Yet he was clearly in tune with larger sentiments and movements, cutting across party lines in the Depression years, that placed new value on salvaging connections to American heritage, history, and myth, and that held as particularly precious a sense of regional roots and origins. Claiming historical and mythical, as well as scenic, significance for High Tor, Anderson both intuitively and deliberately turned to the Indians and Dutch ghosts that were the region's most prized (and also most easily recognizable) spirits of place—ghosts whose perceived aboriginality corresponded closely with a desire to preserve a more primordial landscape. *High Tor* staged a haunting that appealed to the idea of roots at a time when cultural propensities, political power, and governmental and institutional supports were in place to *realize* that haunting in the landscape, to physically preserve or restore the region's historical and legendary inheritances. It was a climate in which ghosts, with their suggestive, elusive, undisprovable claims, gained substantial power from real-world defenders. The success of the campaign, and the fact that support came from around the globe, reveal the degree to which Anderson's ghosts hit their marks.

THE POLITICS OF POSSESSION: REMOVALS

If Maxwell Anderson had lived to stand on High Tor thirty years later, say in 1967, he would have seen many things. He would have seen that they were still making cars at North Tarrytown, and still digging away at Middle Mountain. He would have seen even more tall buildings on Manhattan, and the Thruway bridge that now spanned the Tappan Zee. He would have seen where the Bowline Power Plant was soon to be built near the old brickyard lagoons, and where the Indian Point nuclear plant was already operating just a few miles upriver. He might have been aware of a controversy over Consolidated Edison's plan to gouge out Storm King Mountain to make a pumped-storage hydroelectric plant.[70] Suburban development in Rockland County was proceeding at a roaring pace, and the pollution of the river was becoming an item of increasing concern. Yet there would also have been other things in that view. Along the west bank of the river, from High Tor south to the George Washington Bridge, was a string of state parks (High Tor, Rockland Lake, Hook Mountain, Nyack Beach, Blauvelt, Tallman Mountain) administered by the Palisades Interstate Park Commission. A few miles to the north was Stony Point, now a state historical site acquired by the park commission in 1946; and just beyond that, the commission was solidifying its possession of Bear Mountain and Harriman State Parks—more than 50,000 acres, stretching southwest from the river to the New Jersey border.[71] In fact, over a quarter of Rockland County was now parkland. Across the river, too, probably not discernible but there nonetheless, were Sunnyside, Philipsburg Manor, and Van Cortlandt Manor—the sites restored and maintained by Sleepy Hollow Restorations—as well as Lyndhurst, the Gothic-revival mansion of Jay Gould, now a national historic landmark. The state legislature had just created a Hudson River Valley Commission charged with preserving the riverfront landscape; the federal government had just passed the National Historic Preservation Act.[72]

What happened at High Tor in the 1930s and 1940s was part of a larger trend in the Hudson Valley in the twentieth century—one in which portions of the landscape were increasingly set aside as part of a preservation and restoration agenda that promised emotional and imaginative access to the past via physical sites. As the Hudson River Valley Commission asserted in 1969, history "is found not only in aging manuscript or upon the printed page. The landmarks of the Valley are an even stronger link with the past. The values of our forebears can be sensed in well preserved historic sites, in aging elm-lined streets, even in the decaying ruins of abandoned factories and farms."[73] Along with specific stories of ghosts, this broader idea of haunting as the desirable recolonization of the present by the past was invoked to support the transformation of much of the lower Hudson Valley into what one historian has called "part of our culture's great preserved landscapes of nostalgia."[74]

These realizations of hauntings—the actual work done by haunting in the material world—constitute a politics of possession. And the accomplishments of the conservation and preservation movements in the region—the removal of scenic and historic sites from the path of destruction or destructive exploitation—have by and large been objects of praise. As the museum director of Bear Mountain State Park told a reporter in 1993, "The park took land that had been shot out, burned out, dug out, and trapped out . . . and the animals came back. We have a treasure here. We have a wilderness in the middle of development."[75] Yet there is another aspect of the politics of possession that must also be considered. Lodged within this culture of restorations is a profound political problem linked to recurrent questions of right and possession, questions of control over definitions of place and historical worth that consequently influence decisions regarding territory. The popularly sanctioned, publicly supported hauntings represented by the case of High Tor, even as they promised to preserve regional character and history from the encroachments of the modern age, were themselves construed as intrusions and impositions that displaced actual people and overran local history, culture, and property in the name of a mythic regionalism.

Look again at High Tor. The widespread support for saving that parcel of riverfront from quarrying obscures, but does not entirely subdue, a social, political, and cultural cleavage in the concept of place that translates into real differences over land usage and control. Perhaps the strongest articulation of this divide appears in a letter to the editor of the Rockland County *Journal-News* in December 1942, at the height of the Committee to Save High Tor's rallying activities. Headlined "Why Fuss about High Tor?" the letter raises an issue of imposition on interrelated levels:

In the first place, High Tor has no particular historical significance and seems to depend for its position in the lime-
light almost entirely on the recent play of the same name, a
painting of it, and some poetry about it. Search of the local
histories fails to give it more than passing mention. . . . [Also]
the avowed purpose of the movement is to make the property
a part of the Park system, and thereby a permanent loss to any
private interests and to the county for tax purposes. Those of
us who pay taxes and who like to reside in the county watch
with some gloom the continued encroachments of a park
whose avowed purpose is to own al[l] the riverfront from
Newburgh to the Palisades and as far west as the Ramapos.

Floyd D. Frost, Tompkins Cove[76]

Although Frost is wrong in his suggestion that High Tor is without
historical or mythic significance, he does have a point as he suggests
that the haunting of the mountain by Maxwell Anderson represents not a triumph of local memory, but an application of popular regional ghostlore. (There is no evidence that High Tor had
any lore of Dutch sailor ghosts before 1937.) Moreover, this transplanted haunting (itself based on a fiction) directly corresponds to
a territorial imposition in the service of a broader, cosmopolitan
culture and desire. The pliable, irrefutable claims of ghosts have
been employed in what Frost points out is an extraction of property from local control, a colonization that alienates possession
(and tax revenues) from local jurisdiction. Frost's points gain support, ironically, in the response he received from the president
of the Rockland County Conservation Association, who in part
bases High Tor's historic significance on the fact that many contributions came "from unknown people in faraway places," and who
further states that the association only wishes to "insure [the land's]
proper development in a residential countryside."[77] Floyd Frost
may seem like a crank, and his objections regarding tax revenues

petty and shortsighted. Yet his letter exposes a more thoroughgoing pattern in which new colonizations, justified by a romanticized view of history, nature, and folk, override local views and wills.[78]

The deeper conflicts become more apparent when we start tugging at the loose ends of the story of High Tor. Consider the differences between the two primary characters in the story, Maxwell Anderson and Elmer Van Orden, both of whom make claims on the mountain, yet with different perspectives on it, literal and otherwise, which are easily obscured by their shared desire to keep the mountain whole, and by the fact that both saw the mountain as haunted. Van Orden was about as "local" as one could be in this part of the world. This property had been in his family since before the Revolution, and he lived his entire life on the mountain. Anderson, born in Pennsylvania, a graduate of the University of North Dakota and then Stanford University, came to High Tor with a continent full of experiences, as well as a cultural background in which, his son wrote, were interwoven "the words, the music and the images from the Greeks to Greenwich Village."[79] A year before his death, Anderson wrote that before he had finished eighth grade he had "discovered and read most of the well-known novelists, Dickens, Stevenson, Scott, Dumas, Cooper, and a vast sampling of others," to which he added in high school the poets, "first Keats, then Shelley and Shakespeare . . . and then all the major names from Tennyson, Browning and Swinburne on into the past."[80]

In the play, Van describes the ghosts as "a kind of memory of things you read in books, things you thought you'd forgotten."[81] Anderson may have felt what Kent Ryden describes as "a world of local experience which glimmers and resonates elusively in our sympathetic minds."[82] He may have heard local stories, and have felt something meaningful, yet mysterious, in the historical fragments that were laid out around him. And his play does include references to local circumstances and lore. But the things we are told he thought about on the mountain—Indians, the Dutch, the legend of Rip Van Winkle—and the ghosts he presents in *High Tor* are general, regional, and literary rather than specific, local, and personal, as, for instance, the ghost of Van Orden's fiancée might have been. Although he was interested in a very particular parcel of land, Anderson was unconcerned with specificity or accuracy in terms of locating stories. The Guardian of Hook Mountain becomes the Indian of High Tor. Most glaring, of course, is the migration of Dutch sailors downriver from the Catskills, where Washington Irving set them in "Rip Van Winkle."[83] Anderson to a large degree conflates region with locality here, or rather he makes use of the transient, undisprovable aspects of haunting to link this mountain to the region's most evocative myths. Anderson's musings on the mountain and his play participate in a type of cultural shorthand, the result of more than a century of legendizing and literary production of haunted images in the Hudson Valley, through which Anderson could efficiently communicate significance to a far-flung audience versed in American literature and popular culture.[84]

The differences in cultural background and social attachments between Anderson and Van Orden correlate to a subtle but important difference in the view of place and landscape values. Anderson, his son tells us, "developed a very deep affection for South Mountain Road and Rockland County as it was" when he first moved there in the 1920s, considering it primitive, preferring it in Thoreauvian style.[85] Anderson's biographer depicts Elmer Van Orden similarly as "a foresighted conservationist."[86] Yet the distinct difference between the two men begins to emerge from a statement made by Van Orden in 1937. "Time was," Van Orden said sadly, according to a New York *Sun* article, "when all that country was real farm land, with cows in the meadows and fertile fields as far as [the] eye could reach. Now the city folks have moved in and I'm one of the few farmers left in those parts."[87] The working countryside that Van Orden evokes is not the same as the primitivist "wilderness" that Anderson and other urban exiles envision, the recreational and residential countryside–the one that is set in place by making the land a state park. And Van Orden's reference to the "city folks" suggests that, while Maxwell Anderson and the South Mountain Road contingent, as well as those "unknown people in faraway places," believe that they are preserving and protecting local character, the local character senses impending displacement at the hands of people who think of themselves as beneficently restoring an original landscape, haunted by aboriginal ghosts. Van Orden sees himself in opposition to and in territorial contention with the city people, and he sees that he and his type are losing ground.[88] If Maxwell Anderson developed some awareness of local folklore and a real attachment to the local landscape, he was at the same time tied into the wide world represented by the growing number of skyscrapers thirty miles downriver. In fact Anderson was part of the avant-garde of a new era of tourists and suburbanites. In the end, the ghosts of Van Orden's High Tor are overrun, and little exists to reveal how Van Orden actually conceived of the mountain or thought about place. He becomes subsumed into the more public narrative of which Maxwell Anderson is representative and conservator.

In the 1910s the hiker William Thompson Howell, photographing the mountain people of the Highlands, wrote: "They are genuine, and mark a type which will largely have gone out with their generation. The coming of the State Parks means the passing of the old ways."[89] A triumph of conservation, the case of High Tor is at the same time linked to a broader marginalization of the local, as the valley of romantic myth was increasingly incorporated into suburbs, parks, and museums in the twentieth century. Some of this marginalization occurred at the level of rhetoric. As Jane S. Becker argues in *Selling Tradition,* the casting of people as "folk," even as it seems to place value on them as the source of tradition, also tends to mute their contemporary social and political voice by suggesting that "their significance lies in the past rather than the present."[90] And indeed, regional treatments of Hudson Valley "folk" in the 1930s and 1940s often relegated them to a level of quaintness and antiquity in ways that both augmented their local colorfulness and justified their marginalization, similar to the nineteenth-century "ghosting" of Indians and the Dutch. Anderson himself does this in *High Tor* as when he has Van say, "Maybe I'm a ghost myself trying to hold back an age."[91] Several of the articles that appeared at the time similarly equate Van Orden with the ghosts of *High Tor*. In the 1937 *New York Times* article "Mounting High Tor," Van Orden is said to have "appeared" and "startled" Burgess Meredith. Another article in the New York *Sun* depicts Van Orden as a sort of museum piece, quoting him in dialect and describing him as "out of Franz Hals."[92] These descriptions echo in more sweeping midcentury treatments of Hudson Valley folk. Here, for instance, is Croswell Bowen, writing within five years of Anderson: "Strange people live high among these mountains that line the river . . . people with mixed strains of blood in their veins, and in their minds beliefs in supernatural things. Civilization seems to have passed them by."[93] A somewhat similar alienation of local sensibilities can be detected in attempts by some of the region's historic house museums, many of which had local reputations for being haunted, to exorcise ghost stories once the sites became "museumized"—something that reflects a distancing of these houses from the living neighborhood.[94]

Such rhetorical dismissals and folkloric eviscerations attended (and obscured) more substantial removals being effected by the increasing presence of suburbs and parks in the valley. High Tor, largely uninhabited, and not of much practical use (other than for quarrying), was a site at which conservation required no real displacement of people. But there are other instances in which the Palisades Interstate Park Commission effectively evicted people from their homes. At the beginning of the twentieth century, hundreds of people lived in towns, settled before the Revolutionary War, that now lie in the Bear Mountain and Harriman State Parks; by the mid-1960s the park system had moved them all out, leveled the towns, and in some cases flooded them to make lakes.[95] In the years after the last of the residents left these towns, references to the destruction and alienation that accompanied the parks' creation began to emerge. Perhaps not surprisingly, where ideas of haunting helped create the park system, it is in images of ghostliness that these latter-day remembrances are couched. "Today, Doodletown is a ghost town," says a 1989 article on one of the towns, whose streets were "once trodden by the British and Colonial armies during the Revolutionary War."[96] "Here and there a stairway climbs to nowhere, and the stones of heaved foundations lie scattered and sinking," says a 1993 article: "The voices of the children seem to echo still from the meadow where Sandyfield school used to stand." The director of the park's museum more directly asserts: "There are ghosts in the old towns in the park."[97]

These hauntings in part represent the surfacing of protest on the part of the "natives," who "still refer to the old villages as 'up home.'" According to park historian Andrew Smith (whose family lived for generations in one of the towns destroyed by the park), "Former residents yearn for the past."[98] The last of the displaced families in nearby towns lament the loss of place, the desecration of family cemeteries still within park confines: "There's a lot of history there," says one former resident; "I'd like to see it respected and preserved."[99] These latter-day hauntings leave us finally at the crux of a dilemma—a choice between variants of hauntedness, both of which seem to hold a valid claim to the territory. This dilemma is perhaps best articulated by Jack Focht, the park's museum director. Focht, as we saw earlier, praises the park for restoring the natural environment ("We have a treasure here. We have a wilderness in the midst of development"); but there is an uneasy subtext that emerges as he continues: "we have to acknowledge the people who sacrificed to allow us this. They left homes they had known for generations, and they left behind a trail of tears."[100] The allusion to Native American removals is not entirely uncalled for (and not only because some of the area's "mountain people" have Native American ancestry). The coming of the parks, the proliferation of historic preservations—such acts of restoration have also been acts of dispossession, similar to other displacements resulting from battles of interpretation that were also battles over territory. Yet the irony is that, as with the appeals to Indian ghosts, the sympathetic references to the park's ghost towns that appeared in the late 1980s and early 1990s echo an underlying protest that has little power to effect any real restitution, both because the last of the "natives" are vanishing, and because the park resurrects their history and memory as its own. At the time these articles appeared, Focht and Smith were in the process of collecting for the museum the stories and memories of the "park's people," a tellingly inappropriate designation whose lack of alternatives reveals how completely the former inhabitants have been left bereft of history and place.[101] Public sympathy for these ghosts, as with the ghosts of Indians, Dutchmen, and loyalists, has expanded only as real contention diminishes. Displacements yield hauntings, the embrace of hauntings evidences the larger powerlessness of the displaced, and the susceptibility of their ghosts to reinterpretation and cooptation.

The story of High Tor is not a grand one—a play about Dutch ghosts that combined melodrama and farce, a peak along the Hudson that could be bought for all of $12,000. It is, though, a small story that suggests powerful interactions of culture, social life, politics, and economics and raises large questions—about who and what define "place," and about how decisions regarding territory and historical worth are to be made in a region that has been the object of so many competing claims and desires over time. Embodying a politics of possession set within a particular context—the rise of official support for hauntings, via conservation and preservation, in the twentieth century—the story of High Tor also raises in high relief complications that have reverberated throughout this study, and shows how varied and contending recourses to hauntedness are linked to perennial questions regarding control over memory and territory.

Most basically, the story of High Tor demonstrates that hauntedness affects the real world, that memory, narratives, and historical imagination have social, political, and physical implications. In particular, it highlights the enduring consequences and blessings evolving from the romanticization of the Hudson Valley, set in motion in the early nineteenth century. Beyond the more obvious cause-and-effect elements, however, the haunting of High Tor also forces us to confront a complex regional cultural and social politics—a contest that is not necessarily one of tradition against development, but rather one in which ghosts may contend with other ghosts. The case of High Tor suggests a sociocultural divide in the region that breaks down to some extent along lines of class, as the preservation agenda here has been championed and financed by Morgans, Rockefellers, and Roosevelts, along with a cultural elite represented by artists and authors to whom a sense of local history and character appealed, but who were often unconcerned with (and sometimes appalled by) the lives and desires of their less cosmopolitan neighbors. To some extent, as well, class lines intersect with a divide between insiders and outsiders, or perhaps older residents versus newer residents and visitors. Something of this dynamic echoes in the 1996 debates over changing the name of North Tarrytown to the more mythically resonant Sleepy Hollow. The measure (which ultimately passed) was supported by newly arrived, generally well-to-do suburbanites, who, according to the *New York Times,* felt that the village should seek "a new identity—or more precisely, return to an old one—by reaching back into history and legend." The measure, however, was strongly opposed by the town's older working-class community, who felt that the name change ignored its history in the town, which had been a blue-collar neighborhood focused around the General Motors factory for a hundred years. As the *New York Times* summarized: "The campaign has stirred passions to a high pitch in a village . . . already uneasy about the fault lines between the half-million-dollar homes on its leafy margins and a large working class core, between old-timers and arrivistes, and among whites and Latinos. The controversy has also raised wider questions about what it means to live in a particular place."[102]

Yet, while we can begin to label contending parties, what the cases of High Tor and Sleepy Hollow finally demonstrate is that there is no easy dichotomy between good/conservationist/local and bad/exploiter/outsider, and that the region's hauntedness is not singular but multifarious and ambivalent in type and purpose. "Invocations of the past (as tradition)," writes Michael Kammen, "may occur as a means of resisting change *or* of achieving innovations."[103] Ghosts may be pitted against machines, the past employed against development, but in many cases, the contest is one between different versions of memory and myth which vie over the same place, each with a compelling claim, and each supporting a different view of who or what belongs there. What the case of High Tor reveals—indeed what all of the stories in this book reveal—is not only that hauntings are intimately tied to the social life of the region, but that they uniquely mirror the complexities and ambivalences within that life. There are layers of hauntedness: regional and local, common and epic, old and new, sanctioned and dismissed, literary, popular, and folkloric—a sense of hauntedness that is like the "memory of things . . . read in books," and one that arises from the accumulation of lived experience and history in a place. These different types of hauntedness—while they may at times overlap and indeed influence each other—are often irreconcilably opposed, corresponding to differing ideas of place, different cultural and social backgrounds and values. The dilemma raised by High Tor, and by the haunting of the region more broadly, is the enduring dilemma of judging whose place this is, whose ghosts should haunt, after repeated mythification and restless change have thrown history into shadow.

There was a lot of history in the area, he supposed, George Washington and Benedict Arnold and all of that, but history didn't do mu[ch] for him. Fact is, he'd never even read the insc[rip]tion on the thing.

Never even read it . . . it was nothing to hir[m.] Something along the side of the road, that's a[ll.] Slow Down, Bad Curve, oak tree, billboard, h[is-] torical marker, driveway. Even now he would[n't] have given it a second glance if it weren't for [the] shadow that suddenly shot across the road in front of him.

–T. Coraghessan Boyle, *World's End* (1987)

HAUNTINGS WITHOUT END

Walter Van Brunt was riding his motorcycle home through Peterskill-on-Hudson in the predawn hours after his twenty-second birthday in 1968. And he was feeling a bit unsettled. A self-avowed existentialist, Walter had never known or cared much about history, and surely he no longer believed in the stories his grandparents had told him as a child: bits of Indian and Dutch lore, stories about the Imp of Dunderberg Mountain across the river, about the wailing woman who appeared during snowstorms along a nearby ridge, about the headless Hessian down in Sleepy Hollow. Yet since the previous morning, Walter had been suffering an "attack of history," in which ghosts both ancient and recent, legendary and familial, were indiscriminately intruding into a world that had before seemed to him without meaning or connection to any relevant past. During the day, his dead mother and grandparents had appeared to him, as had the Dunderberg Imp, dressed in his traditional pantaloons and sugarloaf cap. That night he had seen the Imp again—recognizable, though now dressed in contemporary work clothes—along with the apparition of his long-absent father, who, Walter would later discover, was not even dead. Walter hoped the attack was over as he sped along the familiar roads. But as he rounded a curve, he saw something, a moving shadow, dart across his path—a fateful shadow that caused Walter to crash into a state historical marker on the side of the road in a "collision with history" that cost him his right foot.[1]

So opens T. Coraghessan Boyle's 1987 novel, *World's End*, a "historical fugue" centering on a plot of land in "Peterskill" (Boyle's native Peekskill).[2] Alternating between the seventeenth and the twentieth centuries, the novel traces the complicated and troubled history of three sets of people whose lives have been intertwined since the beginnings of Dutch colonial settlement: the Kitchawank Indians, who are betrayed out of their ancestral lands; the Van Warts, who gain manorial title to much of upper Westchester; and the Van Brunts, whose founding ancestor first set foot on the cursed ground as Van Wart's tenant. Although much has changed in the town over the centuries, and waves of other settlers have since arrived—a family of Yankees named Crane, nineteenth-century Italian immigrants, Jewish communists living in "Kitchawank Colony"—remnants of the old families continue to dwell around the fateful spot: Jeremy Mohonk, "the last of the Kitchawanks," who tries to reclaim his ancestral territory; Depeyster Van Wart, the twelfth heir, living in a manor house that has always belonged to his family; and, of course, Walter, the last of the Peterskill Van Brunts.

What is it that haunts Peterskill? The place seems to have been cursed from even before the Van Warts and Jan Pieterse (after whom the town is named) swindled the Kitchawanks. An inscrutable, devouring spirit seems to afflict generations of settlers there; and a dwarf called "Piet," the underlying, noxious spirit of "Pieterskill," the Dunderberg Imp made flesh, appears time and again to instigate trouble for the Van Brunts.[3] Yet the novel's hauntings also stem from generations of interracial, interclass, and interfamily conflicts at this site, from the original dispossession of the Kitchawanks, to the violent, anticommunist "Peterskill riot" of 1949, in which Walter's "patriot" father betrayed his friends and family.[4]

Despite Boyle's copyright-page disclaimer that the book "bears small relation to actual places and events, and none whatever to people living or dead"—that it is "pure fiction"—the book is a canny (and sometimes campy) compendium of regional history and lore. Boyle draws on Irving (the Heer of the Dunderberg, the white woman of Tarrytown, a man with "a head like a pumpkin," the Yankee Cranes, the Dutch Van Brunts); on Native American, Dutch, and African-American lore; on Revolutionary legends; on the peculiar manorial history of the region; and on later regional history.[5] This is not, however, a stale rehash of old material. Boyle dispels the quaint atmosphere around Irving's legacy and rejects any sense of history and lore as comfortably segregated into a distant past. *World's End* is Irving refiltered through Faulkner. Like the insidious pollution of the river that runs through the novel, the accumulated residues of the past have contemporary, palpable, and far from benign effects. Walter may be "unconscious of the impact of history and the myths that shaped him." The ghosts may deliver cryptic messages and speak in inscrutable tones (Walter hears the ghost of his grandmother like a static-plagued long-distance connection).

And it is never made clear where the origins of these hauntings lie (the book suggests, in varying parts, individual psychosis, "genetic memory," history, the subconscious influence of legends, and perhaps simply supernatural forces). Yet, impenetrable as these ghosts and the past they represent are, they, like the Dutch wraiths in *High Tor*, are potentially damaging forces. Boyle drives this point home viscerally by having Walter lose his foot (an event that echoes his seventeenth-century ancestor's loss of a foot to a snapping turtle, the Kitchawanks' totemic symbol, hiding at the bottom of a murky pond).[6] Walter tries to unravel the mystery which has thrust itself upon him: "the accident, the marker, the ghosts . . . were pieces of a puzzle." Even when Walter eventually learns the significance to his family history of the events on the fateful sign, the knowledge seems utterly irrelevant to him, yet it dooms him still. The shadows that promise revelation close up "like a fist."[7]

Boyle's back-and-forth chronological strategy in part promises a deconstruction of myth and legend; in some cases it exposes how historical events become twisted and fuzzy in folklore and ghost stories.[8] And the apparitions in the book draw us, like Walter, to look for deeper meanings and for explanations—to try to solve them. Yet the book refuses to answer all its questions, or to deny or explain all the hauntings it raises, and instead becomes more about how unresolved, unresolvable pasts—how tangles of heredity, history, and myth—continue to affect the present in ways that seem at once potent and indeterminate: ghostly, in other words.

World's End reconfirms much of what I have argued about the haunting of the Hudson Valley. It suggests a legacy of haunting based in a series of contentions over territory and culture—a legacy that continues to reflect on an original sin of colonial dispossession but that gains material and emphasis from whole series of subsequent events. It echoes the enduring problems of rights and possession. The question "Who gives you the right?" is posed more than once to a settler on the unlucky ground, without satisfactory response.[9] The book highlights how the accumulation of changes and the passage of time create a situation fertile for haunting, in which history becomes "murky," even though it leaves suggestive traces in the present. Informed by historical possibilities, the hauntings in the novel really arise from the book's engagement with what Boyle has called "the problem of pastlessness" (or, as he implies in the novel, a lack of historical footing).[10] *World's End* further spotlights how a myriad of literary and folkloric traditions of haunting have struck roots in the region's social and historical cracks, making hauntedness a cultural force to be reckoned with here. In particular, it reveals the degree to which Irving's stories continue to resonate in regional image and culture. The book reflects, once again, the degree to which the Dutch and Indian pasts continue to feature in the region's "unique heritage," while also raising ghosts left by more recent "waves of civilization." And, of course, the novel is—like this study—driven by the idea that the apparently immaterial is far from inconsequential.

World's End also makes a fitting endpoint for our discussion because it reveals how the haunting of the Hudson Valley continues to evolve. Boyle's reconjuring of the region's old ghosts, and his addition of new ones, suggest how hauntings are tied to past issues, yet descend to the present as both problems and opportunities. And while the novel seems at one level Boyle's attempt to come to grips with the restless history and mythic inheritances of his native region, it also reflects how the region's hauntedness opens itself to creative reconfiguration. Very much aware of the potential for reinvention that his own "very uncertain" past, and that of his region, allow him, Boyle is not simply replaying old ghost tales;[11] he is using hauntedness to current purposes, employing the region's ghosts to explore the impacts of ethnicity, heredity, and history—an inquiry that links *World's End* to prevailing concerns in contemporary American literature and scholarship.[12]

The end of *World's End* hints at a resolution, or at least an end to its particular apparitions. Having committed a vicious act of betrayal akin to those committed by his father and earlier ancestors, Walter Van Brunt dies without children, while Depeyster Van Wart, whose wife has just given birth, willfully overlooks the fact that this long-wished-for heir, to whom he will leave his property, is in fact the progeny of Jeremy Mohonk (and thus represents an Indian repossession of that much-disputed acreage).[13] Despite this fictional restitution, the sum product of *World's End* is to suggest a place irrevocably littered by its accumulated pasts, which leave multiple traces in the form of place-names, ownerships, historical markers, museums, pollution, genes, legends, and ghosts. *World's End* ultimately suggests an endlessly haunted world. And even as the book focuses on this one spot of land, with its peculiar set of historical contingencies and storied inheritances, its implications range out over the rest of the continent, where conflicts and displacements have multiplied.[14] "The book," Boyle writes, "is never closed."[15]

How can we know or adjudicate whose place this is? How can we resolve the past, especially when that past is obscured by a tangle of myths and contending claims, apparently lost in the shadows of change and neglect, trampled under the feet of restless populations? These are vexing questions, becoming more unanswerable over time. And so, the Hudson Valley—like the United States more broadly—continues to be multifariously, ambivalently haunted, as the issues and dilemmas that have troubled it historically continue to linger while new conflicts and hauntings continually emerge. Ghosts congregate here not in spite of the social and historical discontinuities; they congregate here because this is a complex, contentious place, and because they themselves are shifty creatures, drawn to uncertainty and capable of reflecting back to a diverse, restless society the spectrum of its desires and anxieties. I began this book with a question: Why is the Hudson Valley haunted? Perhaps a better question after all is: How on earth could it not be?

CCHS Columbia County Historical Society, Kinderhook, New York
GCHS Greene County Historical Society, Coxsackie, New York
JFA Louis C. Jones Folklore Archives, Supernatural–Ghosts Files, New York State Historical Association Library, Cooperstown, New York
PCHS Putnam County Historical Society, Cold Spring, New York
HSRC Historical Society of Rockland County, New City, New York
WCHS Westchester County Historical Society, Elmsford, New York

Introduction

1. Yi Fu Tuan, *Landscapes of Fear* (Minneapolis: University of Minnesota Press, 1979), p. 127.

2. Washington Irving, *The Sketch Book of Geoffrey Crayon, Gent.* (1819–1820), ed. Haskell Springer (Boston: Twayne, 1978), p. 273, referring specifically to Sleepy Hollow; Henry James, *The American Scene,* in *Collected Travel Writings: Great Britain and America,* ed. Richard Howard (New York: Library of America, 1993), p. 483; Maud Wilder Goodwin, *Dutch and English on the Hudson: A Chronicle of Colonial New York* (New Haven: Yale University Press, 1919), p. 120; Ellen Guiley, *Atlas of the Mysterious in North America* (New York: Facts on File, 1995), p. 114.

3. Charles Pryer, *Reminiscences of an Old Westchester Homestead* (New York: G. P. Putnam's Sons, Knickerbocker Press, 1897), p. 20.

4. Among works on memory and place that provide contexts for this study are Michael Kammen's exhaustive *Mystic Chords of Memory: The Transformation of Tradition in American Culture* (New York: Alfred A. Knopf, 1991); Lewis Perry's *Boats against the Current: Revolution and Modernity, 1820–1860* (New York: Oxford University Press, 1993), which focuses on the problematic nature of tradition and memory in an antebellum cul-

ture of revolution and novelty; Jill Lepore's *The Name of War: King Philip's War and the Origins of American Identity* (New York: Vintage, 1998), which investigates the link between victory and the shaping of memory; Kent C. Ryden's *Mapping the Invisible Landscape: Folklore, Writing, and the Sense of Place* (Iowa City: University of Iowa Press, 1993); David Thelen and Roy Rosenzwieg's *The Presence of the Past: Popular Uses of History in American Life* (New York: Columbia University Press, 1998); Alfred F. Young's *The Shoemaker and the Tea Party: Memory and the American Revolution* (Boston: Beacon Press, 1999); Henry Glassie's *Passing the Time in Ballymenone: Culture and History of an Ulster Community* (Philadelphia: University of Pennsylvania Press, 1982); and Pierre Nora's *Realms of Memory: Rethinking the French Past,* 3 vols., ed. Lawrence D. Kritzman, trans. Arthur Goldhammer (New York: Columbia University Press, 1996–1998).

5. Avery Gordon, *Ghostly Matters: Haunting and the Sociological Imagination* (Minneapolis: University of Minnesota Press, 1997), p. 8.

6. Kathleen Brogan, *Cultural Haunting: Ghosts and Ethnicity in Recent American Literature* (Charlottesville: University Press of Virginia, 1998), pp. 4–5. Bergland similarly writes: "Ghosts may have become subjective experiences, but they have not stopped being historical or political"; Renée L. Bergland, *The National Uncanny: Indian Ghosts and American Subjects* (Hanover, N.H.: Dartmouth College, University Press of New England, 2000), p. 8.

7. Gordon, *Ghostly Matters,* p. 23.

8. Bergland moves toward a more localized investigation of the uses of haunting in her conclusion, where she briefly explores how Indian spirits in Stephen King's *Pet Sematary* operate with regard to a late-twentieth-century land dispute in Maine; *The National Uncanny,* pp. 164–167.

9. The following chapters focus mainly on the counties of Westchester, Putnam, Dutchess, Columbia, and Rensselaer on the east bank, and Rockland, Orange, Ulster, Greene, and Albany on the west bank.

10. These works include the anonymous *Legends and Poetry of the Hudson* (New York: P. S. Wynkoop and Sons, 1868); Charles M. Skinner's *Myths and Legends of Our Own Land* (Philadelphia: J. B. Lippincott, 1896); Charles Pryer's *Reminiscences of an Old Westchester Homestead* (New York: G. P. Putnam's Sons, Knickerbocker Press, 1897); Edgar Mayhew Bacon's *Chronicles of Tarrytown and Sleepy Hollow* (New York: G. P. Putnam's Sons, Knickerbocker Press, 1897); C. G. Hine's travel narratives *The New York and Albany Post Road* (New York: privately published, 1905) and *The West*

Bank of the Hudson River: Albany to Tappan (1906; reprint, Astoria, N.Y.: J. C. and A. L. Fawcett, n.d.); A. E. P. Searing's 1884 collection *The Land of Rip Van Winkle* (New York: G. P. Putnam's Sons, Knickerbocker Press) and her 1926 memoir *When Granny Was a Little Girl* (Garden City, N.Y.: Doubleday, Page); Wallace Bruce's guidebooks from the 1870s to the 1900s; Paul Wilstach's *Hudson River Landings* (Indianapolis: Bobbs-Merrill, 1933); and Carl Carmer's *The Hudson* (New York: Rinehart, 1939).

11. O'Brien writes: "In the Hudson a neat categorization between residents and visitors ('insiders and outsiders') is difficult; the line is blurred between those who live in the valley and those whose views and opinions actually bear weight in terms of land-use decisions. It has in fact been this way historically. . . . It might thus be argued that the only real 'outsiders' were perhaps, and only perhaps, the European visitors"; Raymond J. O'Brien, *American Sublime: Landscape and Scenery in the Lower Hudson Valley* (New York: Columbia University Press, 1981), p. 15.

12. Alan Taylor, *William Cooper's Town: Power and Persuasion on the Frontier of the Early American Republic* (New York: Vintage, 1995), p. 8. Taylor uses the expression to describe a tendency in community studies.

13. O'Brien, *American Sublime*, p. 277.

1. "How Comes the Hudson to this Unique Heritage?"

Epigraph: Washington Irving, unfinished article, quoted in Pierre M. Irving, *Life and Letters of Washington Irving*, rev. ed., vol. 1 (New York: G. P. Putnam and Sons, 1869), p. 19. The passage refers to Irving's first journey up the Hudson in 1800.

1. C. G. Hine, *The West Bank of the Hudson River: Albany to Tappan* (1906; reprint, Astoria, N.Y.: J. C. and A. L. Fawcett, n.d.), p. 70. Biographical information comes from Henry Charlton Beck's introduction to the reprint of Hine's 1908 book *The Old Mine Road* (reprint, New Brunswick, N.J.: Rutgers University Press, 1963). Hine (1859–1931) published about a dozen books, several of which document walking trips in the Hudson Valley. He was the editor of the *Insurance Monitor*.

2. Paul Wilstach, *Hudson River Landings* (Indianapolis: Bobbs-Merrill, 1933), p. 26; Maud Wilder Goodwin, *Dutch and English on the Hudson: A Chronicle of Colonial New York* (New Haven: Yale University Press, 1919), quoted in Wilstach, pp. 26–27.

3. Frank H. Pierson, "The Crawbucky Tales," unpaginated manuscript,

1920, WCHS. The manuscript contains five tales collected from Croton-area fishermen. Some authorial interposition by Pierson is evident.

4. Yi Fu Tuan, *Landscapes of Fear* (Minneapolis: University of Minnesota Press, 1979), p. 6.

5. For samples see Roland Van Zandt, ed., *Chronicles of the Hudson: Three Centuries of Travelers' Accounts* (New Brunswick, N.J.: Rutgers University Press, 1971).

6. Robert Boyle writes that "much of the wonder . . . about the Hudson is caused by its diversity . . . and the main key to its character is the extraordinary variety to be found both in it and along its shores"; Robert H. Boyle, *The Hudson River: A Natural and Unnatural History* (New York: W. W. Norton, 1969), pp. 15–16. Paul Wilstach writes: "The diversity of its water stretches, its tumbling banks sweeping up to miniature mountains, the changing lights of sunshine and cloud-shadow, the inexplicable variety of color in calm or storm, on field or forest or peak, all . . . convey the diversions of pleasure or awe with undeviating, inescapable directness"; Wilstach, *Hudson River Landings*, pp. 15–16.

7. Wilstach, *Hudson River Landings*, p. 158. For patterns of development and reversion, see Raymond J. O'Brien, *American Sublime: Landscape and Scenery of the Lower Hudson Valley* (New York: Columbia University Press, 1981).

8. Tuan, *Landscapes of Fear*, p. 7.

9. Ibid.; John R. Stilgoe, *Common Landscape of America, 1585 to 1845* (New Haven: Yale University Press, 1982), p. 7. For the seminal discussion of the aesthetics of mountains, see Marjorie Hope Nicolson, *Mountain Gloom and Mountain Glory: The Development of an Aesthetics of the Infinite* (Ithaca, N.Y.: Cornell University Press, 1959). For an extended discussion of forests in Western culture, see Robert Pogue Harrison, *Forests: The Shadow of Civilization* (Chicago: University of Chicago Press, 1992).

10. Stilgoe, *Common Landscape*, pp. 7–8; Venetia Newall, "West Indian Ghosts," in *The Folklore of Ghosts*, ed. W. M. S. Russell and Hilda R. Ellis Davidson (Cambridge: D. S. Brewer for the Folklore Society, 1981), p. 74. For the anthropomorphic potential of trees, see also Douglas Davies, "The Evocative Symbolism of Trees," in *The Iconography of Landscape*, ed. Denis Cosgrove and Stephen Daniels (Cambridge: Cambridge University Press, 1988).

11. Stilgoe, *Common Landscape*, p. 11.

12. O'Brien, *American Sublime*, p. 106.

13. See, for instance, Wilstach, *Hudson River Landings:* "the brooding serried jagged agglomeration known as the Catskill Mountains" (p. 270). This language continues to infuse descriptions of the riverside mountains. Raymond O'Brien, for example, writes of the "brooding highland formations" in *American Sublime* (p. 60).

14. Edgar Mayhew Bacon, *Chronicles of Tarrytown and Sleepy Hollow* (New York: G. P. Putnam's Sons, Knickerbocker Press, 1897), p. 103; Charles Elmer Allison, *The History of Yonkers* (1896; reprint, Harrison, N.Y.: Harbor Hill, 1984), p. 109.

15. Jesse Van Vechten Vedder, *Historic Catskill* (1922; reprint, Astoria, N.Y.: J. C. and A. L. Fawcett, Inc., n.d.), p. 98.

16. Harold W. Thompson, *Body, Boots and Britches: Folktales, Ballads, and Speech from Country New York* (New York: Dover, 1939), p. 109.

17. Augusta Knapp Osborne, "The Green Fly Monster," *New York Folklore Quarterly* 11 (autumn 1955): 214-215. For other supernatural stories of swamps, see JFA, entry 61.54, about the "vly" in Glenford; and entry 142.8, about "Dark Hollow" in Wittenberg, Ulster County.

18. Wilfred B. Talman, "Names on Our Land: The Jersey Devil," *Rockland Independent,* May 4, 1967, Folklore file, New City Library, Rockland Room, New City, N.Y.

19. According to John Bierhorst in *Mythology of the Lenape: Guide and Texts* (Tucson: University of Arizona Press, 1995), Lenape (Delaware) myth contained unpredictable creatures called the Thunders (p. 11). Following Washington Irving, thunderstorms have been attributed to the ghosts of Dutch sailors bowling in the Catskills and elsewhere, and to the "Heer" of Dunderberg mountain, who is said to brew up storms when not paid the proper respects by passing ships.

20. In describing his first trip up the Hudson, Irving writes: "of all the scenery of the Hudson, the Kaatskill Mountains had the most witching effect on my boyish imagination. . . . As we slowly floated along, I lay on the deck and watched them through a long summer's day, undergoing a thousand mutations under the magical effects of atmosphere; sometimes seeming to approach, at other times to recede; now almost melting into hazy distance"; quoted in P. Irving, *Life and Letters,* 1: 19. Irving's "Rip Van Winkle" begins similarly. See also Wilstach, *Hudson River Landings,* pp. 15-16.

21. Henry James, *The American Scene,* in *Collected Travel Writings: Great Britain and America,* ed. Richard Howard (New York: Library of America,

1993), p. 479. In *History of the Valley of the Hudson, River of Destiny, 1609–1930,* 5 vols. (Chicago: S. J. Clarke, 1931), Nelson Greene writes: "On a still summer night, when the mists are forming over the broad waters of the [Tappan] Zee, one can almost see the Indians' canoes plying the surface or the Phantom Ship slipping along silently through the gathering gloom" (1: 43).

22. Irving, quoted in P. Irving, *Life and Letters,* 1: 19; Elisabeth L. Dugger, "Hiking the Hudson Highlands," *Hudson Valley,* March 1979, p. 32. In *When Granny Was a Little Girl* (Garden City, N.Y.: Doubleday, Page, 1926), A. E. P. Searing recalls the response of a river fisherman when she as a child expressed a desire to spend a night on a boat in the river: "There's strange noises out on this here river nights . . . hoot owls, loons, an' things that come cryin'" (pp. 254–255).

23. Tales of supernatural encounters in a "Spook Vly" in Ulster County and in Dutchess County's Green Fly Swamp, for instance, suggest that the creature in question might have been a bear; see JFA, entry 142.8; and Osborne, "The Green Fly Monster." Of early-twentieth-century sightings in Spring Valley of the "Jersey Devil"–described by witnesses as resembling a flying serpent–a local historian hints that it may have been a large crane; Talman, "Names on Our Land."

24. Pierson, "The Crawbucky Tales."

25. According to Van Zandt, "Although Plymouth, New Amsterdam, and Jamestown were all founded within a few years of each other with approximately the same number of people, Massachusetts had 16,000 by 1643, Virginia had 15,000 by 1649, but as late as 1653 New Netherland still had only 2,000 inhabitants. In 1664 when England acquired New Netherland by force of arms, Virginia had 40,000, New England had 50,000, and the conquered Dutch province had about 10,000. By 1698, Virginia and Massachusetts each had 58 to 60,000, whereas New York still languished with less than 20,000"; *Chronicles of the Hudson,* p. 3. On Dutch culture and language in the Hudson Valley, see Alice P. Kenney, *Stubborn for Liberty: The Dutch in New York* (Syracuse: Syracuse University Press, 1975); and Van Cleaf Bachman, Alice P. Kenney, and Lawrence G. Van Loon, "'Het Poelmeisie': An Introduction to the Hudson Valley Dutch Dialect," *New York History* 61 (April 1980): 161–185, which reports that Dutch was still spoken in enclaves of the valley into the twentieth century.

26. Goodwin, *Dutch and English on the Hudson,* p. 121.

27. For a detailed discussion of Native American tribes in the region,

see E. M. Ruttenber, *History of the Indian Tribes of Hudson's River* (Albany: J. Munsell, 1872). According to Patricia Edwards Clyne in *Hudson Valley Tales and Trails* (Woodstock, N.Y.: Overlook Press, 1990), Native American settlement in the region can be traced back at least nine thousand years, and from 1500 to 1700 the Native population in the region was composed of four major groups: "west of the Hudson, the Delawares (also called the Lenni-Lenape or Munsee) extended north to the land of the Mohawks, while east of the Hudson the Wappingers occupied the region roughly from Manhattan island into Dutchess, and north of them were the Mohicans (also spelled Mahicans or Mohegans)" (pp. 28–30). In *The Hudson River*, Boyle cites estimates that that in 1600 there were about 3,000 Mahicans, 4,750 Wappingers, including those in Connecticut, and 8,000 Delawares (p. 42).

28. For a detailed history of relations between colonists and Native Americans in the region, see Ruttenber, *Indian Tribes of Hudson's River*, pp. 99–157.

29. For New York–New England border disputes, see Dixon Ryan Fox, *Yankees and Yorkers* (New York: New York University Press, 1940). According to Fox, "between New England and New York the 'warfare,' with pen and sword, lasted actively from the sixteen twenties to seventeen ninety, the counterclaims were not entirely subdued until the eighteen seventies, and . . . the Supreme Court of the United States was pronouncing on the issues as late as 1932" (p. ix).

30. See David Steven Cohen, "How Dutch Were the Dutch of New Netherland?" *New York History* 62 (January 1981): 49–60. The first record of African slaves in the region appears in 1626. The African slave population in New York was 2,170 in 1698, and 21,329 in 1790; Edgar J. McManus, *A History of Negro Slavery in New York* (Syracuse: Syracuse University Press, 1966), pp. 4, 197, 200. According to historian Oliver A. Rink, New Netherland was "the most culturally heterogeneous European colony in North American"; Rink, "The People of New Netherland: Notes on Non-English Immigration to New York in the Seventeenth Century," *New York History* 62 (January 1981): 34.

31. Colonial observers noted the particular animosities between the Dutch and the English. For instance, the Swedish botanist Peter Kalm, visiting in 1749–1750, wrote: "The hatred which the English bear against the people of Albany is very great, but that of the Albanians against the English is carried to a ten times higher degree. . . . They are so to speak perme-

ated with hatred toward the English"; quoted in David M. Ellis, "Yankee-Dutch Confrontation in the Albany Area," *New England Quarterly* 45 (June 1972): 264. For scholarly accounts emphasizing the discord of colonial New York, see especially Patricia Bonomi, *A Factious People: Politics and Society in Colonial New York* (New York: Columbia University Press, 1971).

32. Bonomi, *A Factious People*, p. 15.

33. Douglas Greenberg, *Crime and Law Enforcement in the Colony of New York, 1691–1776* (Ithaca, N.Y.: Cornell University Press, 1974), p. 135. Greenberg argues that the high crime rate in New York as compared to New England reflects the fact that "neither New York City nor the rural counties were composed of 'consensual communities' where aggressiveness was limited by social structure" (pp. 55–56).

34. "Statistically," writes Roland Van Zandt, "the State of New York had borne a disproportionate share of the burdens and suffering of the war. Though it ranked only seventh in population, one-third of the total battles and engagements of the Revolution (an estimated 92 out of 308) had been fought on or near the banks of the Hudson"; *Chronicles of the Hudson*, p. 39. See Chapter 4 for a discussion of the Revolutionary War in regional memory.

35. Fox, *Yankees and Yorkers*, p. 197.

36. O'Brien, *American Sublime*, p. 131.

37. For details of railroad development, see Greene, *History of the Valley of the Hudson*, 2: 691–700. At one time there were six railroad lines running through Westchester (Laura L. Vookles, "Westchester: County of Railroads," in *Next Stop Westchester!: People and the Railroad* [Yonkers, N.Y.: Hudson Valley Museum of Westchester, 1996], p. 11). Putnam County had at least four railroads running through it by the end of the nineteenth century ("Chronology of Putnam County," compiled by the Putnam County Historical Society Workshop, 1957, PCHS). Rockland County was crossed by five railroads (O'Brien, *American Sublime*, p. 195). There were railroads running through the Catskills by the 1880s (see Roland Van Zandt, *The Catskill Mountain House* [New Brunswick, N.J.: Rutgers University Press, 1966], pp. 225–241). Albany, meanwhile, was a major railroad hub.

38. For discussions of social and economic changes in the region in the nineteenth century, see Thomas S. Wermuth, *Rip Van Winkle's Neighbors: The Transformation of Rural Society in the Hudson River Valley, 1720–1850* (Albany: State University of New York Press, 2001); Martin Bruegel, "The

Rise of a Market Society in the Rural Hudson Valley, 1780–1860" (Ph.D. diss., Cornell University, 1994).

39. The *Guidebook of the Hudson River with Notes of Interest to the Summer Tourist* (Albany, 1889) notes "extensive brickyards" as well as factories and ironworks. The author of the 1884 *History of Rockland County* writes of the "thousand wheels of extractive factories" along the Minisceongo creek (quoted in O'Brien, *American Sublime,* p. 234). Between 1860 and 1880 the number of manufacturing establishments more than doubled in Albany; Brian Greenberg, *Worker and Community: Response to Industrialization in a Nineteenth-Century American City, Albany, New York, 1850–1884* (Albany: State University of New York Press, 1985), p. 17. For a broad discussion of industrial developments in the lower Hudson Valley, see O'Brien, *American Sublime.* For individual industries, see James M. Ransom, *Vanishing Ironworks of the Ramapos* (New Brunswick, N.J.: Rutgers University Press, 1966); Daniel DeNoyelles, *Within These Gates* (Thiells, N.Y.: privately published, 1982), on the Haverstraw brickyards; and Lucius F. Ellsworth, *Craft to National Industry in the Nineteenth Century: A Case Study of the Transformation of the New York State Tanning Industry* (New York: Arno, 1975). County and town histories also offer accounts of local industrial development.

40. Ellis, "Yankee-Dutch Confrontation," p. 269. Ellis writes that this "Irish invasion . . . reached a floodtide in the 1840s and 1850s," accounting for 40 percent of Albany's population by the Civil War (p. 269). According to federal census data from 1880, every county along the river had a sizable Irish immigrant population, as well as immigrants from England, Scotland, Wales, Germany, France, and Scandinavian countries.

41. Vookles, "Westchester," pp. 18, 13 (caption).

42. For a discussion of American tourism in the nineteenth century, see John F. Sears, *Sacred Places: American Tourist Attractions in the Nineteenth Century* (New York: Oxford University Press, 1989). Regarding the Hudson Valley, see also Van Zandt, *The Catskill Mountain House;* and Kenneth Myers, *The Catskills: Painters, Writers, and Tourists in the Mountains, 1820–1895* (Yonkers, N.Y.: Hudson River Museum of Westchester; Hanover, N.H.: University Press of New England, 1988).

43. Van Zandt, *The Catskill Mountain House,* p. 223.

44. These included the Croton reservoir system, begun in 1842, and enlarged several times thereafter; and the Ashokan Reservoir in the Catskills, built between 1906 and 1915. For histories of the reservoirs and aqueducts,

see Frederick Shonnard and W. W. Spooner, *The History of Westchester County* (1900; reprint, Harrison, N.Y.: Harbor Hill, 1974), pp. 610–614; Mary Josephine D'Alvia, *The History of the New Croton Dam* (N.p.: privately published, 1976); and Alf Evers, *The Catskills: From Wilderness to Woodstock* (Garden City, N.Y.: Doubleday, 1972), pp. 590–597.

45. In Haverstraw, for instance, there were thirty-eight brickworks operating at the turn of the century; by 1942 there were none; see DeNoyelles, *Within These Gates*. Similarly, Putnam County had experienced an industrial boom between the Civil War and the 1880s, but then from 1891 to 1938 the historical record marks closing after closing; "Chronology of Putnam County," PCHS.

46. O'Brien, *American Sublime*, p. 25. The 1920s and 1930s saw the inception or completion of the Palisades Parkway, the Storm King Highway, the George Washington Bridge, the Bear Mountain Bridge, the Mid-Hudson Bridge, and the Rip Van Winkle Bridge. Another wave of highway and bridge building in the post–World War II period added the New York State Thruway and Tappan Zee Bridge.

47. For one instance, see documents and letters regarding the building of interstate highway 684 in Westchester in the 1960s, at the Westchester County Archives and Record Center, Elmsford, N.Y.

48. See, for instance, the foreword to Beatrice Hasbrouck Wadlin, *Times and Tales of Town of Lloyd* (Highland, N.Y.: privately published, 1974): "At the point in time when this book is going to print, the Township of Lloyd is in a dilemma about . . . the proposed atomic energy plant which might locate in the north end of the town." Between health and environmental concerns, and the need for new energy sources and the promise of a significant reduction in local taxes, the foreword states, "Personal feelings are running high on both sides." Such battles are not limited to the local level. In the foreword to Frances F. Dunwell's *The Hudson River Highlands* (New York: Columbia University Press, 1991), Robert F. Kennedy Jr. writes: "Since the early 1960s an uncompromising collection of environmental associations . . . have fought to maintain the river's biological and aesthetic integrity. . . . During the past decade and a half, Hudson River environmentalists have succeeded in stopping the construction of two major Hudson River highways, two nuclear power plants, and the proposed pumped storage facility on Storm King Mountain" (pp. ix–x).

49. *Legends and Poetry of the Hudson* (New York: P. S. Wynkoop and Sons, 1868), p. 22.

50. James Fenimore Cooper, *The Deerslayer, or, The First War-Path* (1841), ed. James Franklin Beard et al. (Albany: State University of New York Press, 1987), p. 15.

51. Renée Bergland, *The National Uncanny: Indian Ghosts and American Subjects* (Hanover, N.H.: Dartmouth College, University Press of New England, 2000), p. 11.

52. In sorting out how the Danskammer (the "Devil's Dance-chamber"), a site along the river near Newburgh, came to be so named, various sources suggest that the Dutch here observed Indians engaged in religious ceremonies, and thought them either to be demons or to be worshiping the devil; see Dirck St. Remy, *Stories of the Hudson*, 3d ed. (New York: G. P. Putnam and Sons, 1871), p. 46; Ruttenber, *Indian Tribes of Hudson's River*, p. 28; and Wilstach, *Hudson River Landings*, p. 258. It was not only the Dutch who read Native Americans as uncanny. In the 1840s Lydia Maria Child, visiting the Hudson Valley, wrote of Native Americans she met there as "ghosts of the Past"; L. Maria Child, *Letters from New-York* (New York: Charles S. Francis; Boston: John Munroe, 1843), p. 18. There are several twentieth-century accounts of indecision as to whether a figure is a living Native American person or a ghost. See, for instance, E. E. Gardner, *Folklore of the Schoharie Hills* (Ann Arbor: University of Michigan Press, 1937), p. 87. Renée Bergland explores depictions of Native Americans as ghostly in *The National Uncanny*. Chapter 4 further examines Indian and Dutch associations with regional ghostliness.

53. H. A. Von Behr, *Ghosts in Residence* (Utica: North Country Books, 1986), p. vii.

54. "The Spook Hole, or Haunted Cave, Clinton Point-(Barnegat)-On-The-Hudson," *Poughkeepsie Telegraph*, September 24, 1870, p. 1. Alternate explanations presented in this article also point to a suspicion of strange others: one story has to do with the pirate Captain Kidd; another says that the cave was the hiding place of a "negro murderer."

55. JFA, entry 32.30.

56. Tuan, *Landscapes of Fear*, p. 127. See Lewis Perry, *Boats against the Current: Revolution and Modernity, 1820–1860* (New York: Oxford University Press, 1993), for a discussion of the contending pulls of memory and "anti-history" in the antebellum period.

57. Introduction to Henry D. B. Bailey, *Local Tales and Historical Sketches* (Fishkill Landing, N.Y.: John W. Spaight, Fishkill Standard Office, 1874), p. 9.

58. Henry Brace, "Old Catskill," in *The History of Greene County* (New York: J. B. Beers, 1884), p. 86.

59. Hine, *The Old Mine Road*, p. 148.

60. Bergland, *The National Uncanny*, p. 5. Similarly, the editors of *Ghosts: Deconstruction, Psychoanalysis, History* write that ghosts and literature share "simulacral qualities; like writing, ghosts are associated with a certain secondariness or belatedness"; Peter Buse and Andrew Stott, eds., *Ghosts: Deconstruction, Psychoanalysis, History* (Hampshire: MacMillan; New York: St. Martin's, 1999), p. 8.

61. Avery F. Gordon, *Ghostly Matters: Haunting and the Sociological Imagination* (Minneapolis: University of Minnesota Press, 1997), p. 200.

62. JFA, entry 32.89.

63. Bacon, *Chronicles of Tarrytown and Sleepy Hollow*, p. 103.

64. Charles Pryer, *Reminiscences of an Old Westchester Homestead* (New York: G. P. Putnam's Sons, Knickerbocker Press, 1897), pp. 21–22.

65. Charles Wilde, "Ghost Legends of the Hudson Valley" (Master's thesis, New York State College for Teachers, 1937), p. 12; JFA, entries 32.26, 32.82, 32.48, and 53. See Louis C. Jones, "The Ghosts of New York: An Analytical Study," *Journal of American Folklore* 57 (October–December 1944): 237–254, for a discussion of trends in the ghostlore collected by his students in New York State.

66. A number of women in white, or sometimes in black or gray, appear throughout the region. Some of these will be discussed in Chapter 3. Other examples appear near the gatehouse at Lindenwald, in Kinderhook; at Forbes Manor, near Albany; in a graveyard in Dover Plains; at a mansion in Dobbs Ferry; and along Call Hollow Road in Rockland County (Wilde, "Ghost Legends of the Hudson Valley," pp. 24–25 and 10; JFA, entry 19; *Legends and Poetry of the Hudson*, p. 57; Andrew Smith, "Forgotten and Overlooked History of the Hudson Valley and Highlands" [Master's thesis, Columbia Pacific University, n.d.]). In addition to Irving's headless horseman (discussed in Chapter 2), there are tales of a headless man who rides on passing wagons, a headless woman who rummages in cellars, and "the Headless Parson," in Columbia County; and a white thing, headless, floating in the air" near an Albany church (Mayme O. Thompson, "Witchcraft! Halloween Ghosts Roam Year-Round over Taghkanic Hillsides," *Chatham Courier*, October 30, 1969, p. B1; W. V. Miller, "Folklore Tales of Columbia County: What Mission Sent the Headless Parson Coursing across a Moonlit Sky?" *Chatham Courier*, March 20, 1958, Folk-

lore file, CCHS; Wilde, "Ghost Legends of the Hudson Valley," p. 14). The Jones collection contains references to a "headless Negro riding on a white horse" in Albany County, a procession of silent headless men in Rensselaer County, headless horsemen in Pine Plains, a headless man driving a wagon led by headless horses in Crescent, and a ghost from Ulster County whose head is replaced at times by a "ball of fire" and at other times by a "white floaty mass" (JFA, entries 143, 14, 146, 175.19, and 147.3). More headless ghosts appear in Yonkers, Kinderhook, Yorktown, Warwick, and Hurley (Allison, *History of Yonkers*, p. 109; "Yankee Visits Sleepy Hollow," *Yankee*, July 1953, p. 34; JFA, entries 147.2 and 61.51; Hine, *West Bank of the Hudson*, pp. 105–106).

67. According to Louis Jones, only 10 percent of the ghost stories in his collection contain speaking ghosts, "while every third ghost makes one of a wide variety of noises. European stories tend to contain the element of discourse more frequently than American stories"; "The Ghosts of New York," p. 250.

68. Washington Irving, *The Sketch Book of Geoffrey Crayon, Gent.* (1819–1820), ed. Haskell Springer (Boston: Twayne, 1978), p. 34. Any number of examples of ghostly silence or incomprehensibility might be cited here. A ghost in Coxsackie would not respond to questions in either English or Dutch, and vanished when the disconcerted questioner threw a rock to try to provoke a response (JFA, entry 32). A Dutchess County man came to believe that his hay barn was haunted because he "heard noises and people talkin'." He found that "I could never understand what they said. The words weren't clear enough" (JFA, entry 32.66). At a mansion in Livingston, witnesses heard "all the sounds of guests for a gay evening . . . save those of human voices"; Eileen Thomas, "Tales of Old Columbia," October 25, 1946, Folklore file, CCHS.

69. A man from Berne, New York, encountered a spook in the woods there that he "feared to describe" (JFA, entry 32.16). A man from Pine Plains, who one night followed the local headless horseman to the cemetery, became "completely unnerved and [would] shake violently" whenever he tried to tell what he had seen there (JFA, entry 146). Ice-cutters who told of a Columbia County "Woman in Black" recalled feeling as if she had "cast a spell over them. Not a word was spoken"; "Folk Lore of Columbia County: Who Was the Woman in Black on a Lonely Poolesburg Road?" *Chatham Courier*, 1954, Folklore file, CCHS.

70. Washington Irving, "The Storm-Ship," in *Bracebridge Hall; or, The*

Humourists (1822), ed. Herbert F. Smith (Boston: Twayne, 1977), p. 283; Charles M. Skinner, *Myths and Legends of Our Own Land*, vol. 1 (Philadelphia: J. B. Lippincott, 1896), p. 50.

71. Pryer, *Reminiscences of an Old Westchester Homestead*, p. 25.

72. JFA, entry 32.65.

73. *The New Shorter Oxford English Dictionary* (1993 ed.) offers as definitions of *waif:* "a homeless and helpless person, *esp.* a neglected or abandoned child," and "a thing carried or driven by the wind; a puff of smoke, a streak of cloud."

74. Skinner, *Myths and Legends of Our Own Land*, p. 57. Skinner and others also attribute the wandering habits of regional ghosts to the wealth of "lost" graves, a mark of historical neglectfulness and abandonment. See Skinner's story about Thomas Paine, whose remains were moved from their original burial place and whose ghost thus hovers "between the two burial-places, or flitting back and forth . . . lamenting the forgetfulness of men"; ibid. pp. 103–104.

75. According to Louis Jones in "The Ghosts of New York," bridges are as likely as cemeteries to be considered haunted (p. 248). Haunted bridges appear in Kinderhook, Wittenberg, Rosendale, Glenford, Centerville, and Kerhonkson (JFA, entries 78b, 170, 32.43, 61.54, 32.60; Hine, *The Old Mine Road*, p. 67). Two haunted taverns appear in Ghent, and others are found in Germantown, Fishkill, and Albany. See "Gone with the Wind: The Mystery of Mammy Doodle's Wayside Inn Deepens," *Chatham Courier,* December 13, 1946; "The Old Gray Ghost of Ghent," *Knickerbocker News Union-Star,* July 24, 1972; W. V. Miller, "Folklore of Columbia County," *Chatham Courier,* March 13, 1958, Folklore file, CCHS; Bailey, *Local Tales and Historical Sketches,* p. 119; and JFA, entry 32.34. On ghostly fiddlers haunting bridges in Dutchess County, see "Fiddling Ghosts at Frosts Mills," *Poughkeepsie Daily Eagle,* September 10, 1908, p. 8; JFA, entries 142.4 and 97.91. Ghosts of gypsies are reported in the towns of Highland and Clarksville (JFA, entries 86 and 32.71).Of ghostly hitchhikers, Louis Jones recorded more than seventy-five occurrences in the region; Alex Silberman, "A Handful of Hauntings," *Hudson Valley,* October 1996, p. 36.

76. William Leete Stone includes a tale titled "The Murdered Tinman" in his *Tales and Sketches, Such as They Are* (New York: Harper and Brothers, 1834). In the story, which takes place in Ulster County, a local resident reports seeing the apparition of a peddler, which leads the community to be-

lieve that the peddler was murdered by the new tavernkeeper. The apprehensions in the story derive in large part from cultural misunderstanding: the Dutch locals do not understand that a Yankee peddler is subject to wandering. (They also distrust the new Yankee tavern owner.)

77. Bailey, *Local Tales and Historical Sketches,* pp. 121–122. In Bailey's story the ghost of the tavern owner figures more prominently than that of the peddler. However, other versions of this story focus on the peddler's ghost—including a version in the *New-York Tribune* of May 18, 1902, and one given by a local man to a Poughkeepsie newspaper (Helen Myers, "Countian Recalls Tales of Restless Ghosts That Haunted Famous East Fishkill Tavern," *Poughkeepsie Sunday New Yorker,* July 11, 1954, p. C1).

78. Bailey, *Local Tales and Historical Sketches,* pp. 123, 8.

79. JFA, entry 61.54. Similar accounts of peddler-related hauntings occur in Crescent, Warwick, Hyde Park, and Ballston, and at "Packpeddler's Hill" in Columbia County (JFA, entries 50, 61.53, 127.5, and 127.21; Thompson, "Witchcraft!"). See Hine, *West Bank of the Hudson,* p. 10, for an analogous story from Coeymans, in Greene County, centering on mysterious strangers, an unidentified skeleton, and the subsequent proliferation of ghost stories.

80. Jones, "The Ghosts of New York," p. 242.

81. For a discussion of peddlers as historical agents of change, see David Jaffee, "Peddlers of Progress and the Transformation of the Rural North, 1760–1860," *Journal of American History* 78 (September 1991): 511–535. Regional sources suggest how transient figures aroused anxiety and fear. One story tells of gypsies kidnapping children (JFA, entry 32.71), while a woman in Putnam County, who lived along the Albany Post Road, told C. G. Hine that in the period after the Civil War she spent a considerable part of her day feeding tramps who came to the door: "she, being afraid of them, never refused" (C. G. Hine, *The New York and Albany Post Road* [New York: privately published, 1905], p. 45). E. B. Hornby similarly recalls, in *Under Old Rooftrees* (Jersey City, N.J.: privately published, 1908): "Ere the county poorhouse was built, Warwick township literally swarmed with what is now called the 'tramp.'" (p. 181).

82. According to *The New Shorter Oxford English Dictionary* (1993 ed.), the Wandering Jew is "in medieval legend, a man who insulted Jesus on the day of the Crucifixion and was condemned eternally to roam the world until the Day of Judgement."

83. Stephen King, *'Salem's Lot* (1975), quoted in Manuel Aguirre, *The Closed Space: Horror Literature and Western Symbolism* (Manchester: Manchester University Press, 1990), p. 187.

84. Hine, *West Bank of the Hudson*, p. 135.

85. In addition to Irving and Maud Wilder Goodwin, numerous writers and historians point to the Dutch as the source of regional hauntings. An 1876 travel narrative, for instance, flatly asserts: "The old Dutch colonists were very much given to ghostly fears" (Daniel Wise, *Summer Days on the Hudson: The Story of a Pleasure Tour from Sandy Hook to the Saranac Lakes* [New York: Nelson and Phillips, 1876], p. 24). Maud Wilder Goodwin, while highlighting the Dutch, also names "the *wilden*" (i.e., Native Americans) and African slaves as co-conspirators in generating the region's supernatural sensibilities (Goodwin, *Dutch and English on the Hudson*, p. 120). For other attributions to African slaves, see Hine, *West Bank of the Hudson*, p. 70; and Wilfred Blanch Talman, *How Things Began in Rockland County and Places Nearby* (New City, N.Y.: Historical Society of Rockland County, 1977), p. 276. For a discussion of the treatment of folk sources in Irving, Cooper, and James Kirke Paulding, see Donald A. Ringe, *American Gothic: Imagination and Reason in Nineteenth-Century Fiction* (Lexington: University of Kentucky Press, 1982).

86. See, for instance, W. V. Miller, "Ghostly Teutonic Phantoms Haunt Old Burial Grounds," *Chatham Courier*, February 20, 1958, Folklore file, CCHS. A Rockland historian argues that it was not to the "matter-of-fact" Dutch that the region owed its peculiar heritage, but to "the sprightlier Frenchmen among them—perhaps a little to the later Scots, maybe some to the Danes, Swedes, and Germans of later days"; Talman, *How Things Began in Rockland*, p. 272.

87. See chapter 2 for Irving's depiction of the New Englander Ichabod Crane. Regarding later immigrants, Charles Pryer, for instance, describes an Irish gardener in Westchester as "a very good specimen of an Irish servant of the olden times . . . a firm believer in ghosts" (*Reminiscences of an Old Westchester Homestead*, p. 28), while a student folklore collector remarked about a ghost story told her by children in Rensselaer, that "these children were Polish, and probably drawing on their imagination" (JFA, entry 32.55).

88. Motif indexes compiled in the mid-twentieth century—including Stith Thompson's massive *Motif Index of Folk-Literature*, rev. ed. (Bloomington: Indiana University Press, 1966; CD-ROM, InteLex Corp.,

1993); and Ernest Baughman's *Type and Motif Index of the Folktales of England and North America,* Indiana University Folklore Series, no. 2 (The Hague: Mouton, 1966)—suggest origins and analogues for types appearing in regional ghostlore.

89. Talman, *How Things Began in Rockland,* p. 272. For Lenape myths and beliefs, see Herbert C. Kraft, *The Lenape: Archeology, History, and Ethnography* (Newark: New Jersey Historical Society, 1986); and John Bierhorst, *Mythology of the Lenape: Guide and Texts* (Tucson: University of Arizona Press, 1995). Bierhorst includes accounts from Swedish and Dutch colonial commentators from as early as 1650, as well as late-twentieth-century accounts given by Lenape people living in Oklahoma, where many of them eventually settled. For related Mohawk and other Iroquois beliefs, see Daniel K. Richter, *The Ordeal of the Longhouse: The Peoples of the Iroquois League in the Era of European Colonization* (Chapel Hill: University of North Carolina Press, 1992); and Anthony F. C. Wallace, *The Death and Rebirth of the Seneca* (New York: Alfred A. Knopf, 1970).

90. See, for instance, JFA, entry 175.18, in which a man of Native American ancestry recounts following the tracks of a mysterious animal, which lead into the woods but then disappear.

91. A Catskills-area man, born in 1909, for instance, recalled hearing "stories of ghosts and other weird happenings" from a Native American woman in his youth; quoted in Janis Benincasa, "Ghosts in the Catskills?" *Catskill Weekender,* July 26, 1986, GCHS. For parallel lore, see "The Spring Monster at East Jewett," in Doris West Brooks, *Short Stories and Tall Tales of the Catskills* (N.p.: privately published, 1983), in which the author's grandmother recalls sightings of a "horrid little animal" with fangs and horns. The monster turns out to be a snake swallowing a frog, but the sighting becomes local legend and is associated with a series of "strange and awful" events. The motif resonates with a "horned serpent, or great horned snake" which Bierhorst identifies as "one of the most consistently menacing supernaturals in Lenape lore" (*Mythology of the Lenape,* p. 11). Notably, an enclave of people of mixed Native American, Dutch, and African American ancestry live in the vicinity Brooks writes of, and Brooks has also produced a book of the lore of this group, *The Old Eagle-Nester: The Lost Legends of the Catskills* (Hensonville, N.Y.: Black Dome Press, 1992).

92. The story of a woman who falls from the sky and who lands on the back of a turtle, which ultimately becomes the foundation of the ground, appears throughout Lenape and Iroquois belief. In some versions, she is

noted as the creator of the heavenly bodies. See, for instance, Bierhorst, *Mythology of the Lenape*, p. 38, abstract no. 45; and Richter, *The Ordeal of the Longhouse*, p. 10. In "The Catskill Mountains," Irving says that he heard the story of the weather-making woman from an "Indian trader" during his first journey up the Hudson, along with "many stories, also, about mischievous spirits who infested the mountains in the shape of animals"; in *The Home Book of the Picturesque* (New York: G. P. Putnam, 1852), pp. 73–74. Alf Evers speculates that the "Indian trader" may have been Irving's brother William, who was involved in trade with Native Americans in upstate New York; *The Catskills*, p. 322.

93. A. E. P. Searing, *The Land of Rip Van Winkle: A Tour through the Romantic Parts of the Catskills, Its Legends and Traditions* (New York: G. P. Putnam's Sons, Knickerbocker Press, 1884), p. 113. According to Searing, this water demon had a particular interest in young women. The tale coincides with Lenape stories of a water monster that, according to Bierhorst, "displays an unwholesome interest in sex"; *Mythology of the Lenape*, p. 11.

94. See Eric Lott, *Love and Theft: Blackface Minstrelsy and the American Working Class* (New York: Oxford University Press, 1995), pp. 6–7.

95. Elizabeth Paling Funk, "Washington Irving and His Dutch-American Heritage" (Ph.D. diss., Fordham University, 1986). To show that Irving utilized Dutch-based folklore in his writing, Funk delineates aspects of folklore in the Netherlands, describing Dutch demons and spirits and suggesting a lore of little people, resembling figures in Hudson Valley lore, who dwell near hills. She also points to the presence in Dutch lore of riding ghosts, of headless ghosts, and of white women—all types that appear in the Hudson Valley as well. In addition, Funk notes that place-names denoting demonic influence, akin to "Spuyten Duyvil" and "Hellgate" in New York, are numerous in the Netherlands (p. 201).

96. Bachman, Kenney, and Van Loon, "'Het Poelmeisie,'" p. 181. In the introduction to this tale, Kenney writes that the woman who told the story asserted that she could tell it only in "Low Dutch"—the Dutch dialect spoken in the Hudson Valley—because the story did not have the same effect in English, something that further suggests a distinctly Dutch strain of storytelling at work. Kenney argues that the existence of a larger body of regional Dutch ghost stories has remained largely hidden, in part because of a reticence on the part of Low Dutch speakers to expose themselves to further stereotyping (p. 165).

97. There are Spook Rocks in Rockland, Westchester, Columbia, and Greene Counties; Spook or Spooky Hollows in Rockland, Putnam, Greene, Ulster, and Rensselaer; and two different Spook Fields, along with a Spook Hole, in Dutchess.

98. Hornby, *Under Old Rooftrees*, p. 88.

99. Interviewed by one of Louis Jones's folklore students, a Kinderhook man told a story about the ghost of Martin Van Buren's cook, "Aunt Sarah," which he had heard from his family's "old colored servants" (JFA, entry 87). Another of Jones's students wrote that stories of ghosts at Van Buren's mansion, Lindenwald, circulated among local farmers and black servants (JFA, entry 109); and another folklorist in the 1930s heard stories regarding the mansion's gatehouse from an African-American man who lived there (Wilde, "Ghost Legends of the Hudson Valley," pp. 24-25).

100. Jones, "The Ghosts of New York," p. 249. The Jones Folklore Archives are composed primarily of materials collected in the 1940s by students in Jones's folklore classes at what was then New York State College for Teachers at Albany. Jones finds that 96 of the 460 items collected between 1940 and 1944 were of European origin and setting, including examples from Italy, Ireland, Poland, Sweden, Great Britain, Finland, Russia, Germany, and Armenia.

101. Jones had his students submit "informant sheets" giving the background of people from whom folklore was collected. A sampling of those from whom ghostlore in the Hudson Valley was collected includes "a German girl whose family has kept contact with their relatives in Germany"; a woman "born in Sweden in 1887 [who] came to the U.S. at 15"; a twenty-two-year-old woman from Georgia, of German and English ancestry, who reported that "she got her ghosts from the negroes and from some unknown man down the street"; a man of Dutch descent whose family had lived for generations in Greene County; a French and Dutch Ulster County woman, who lived "among very superstitious people"; a seventeen-year-old Italian boy from Westchester; a sixty-year-old Irish man living outside Albany; an Ulster County man of Native American, Scottish, and Irish ancestry, born in the "Pang Yang" religious community; an African-American barber in Poughkeepsie; and a twenty-eight-year-old Polish woman who taught grade school in Columbia County. Speaking of growing up in Westchester, one of the collectors wrote of the "mixture of chil-

dren there, Irish, Greek, German, American, Italian, and Jewish [who] taught and learned rimes [*sic*] from each other" (JFA, informant sheets). Overall, Louis Jones asserts, the 460 items of ghostlore collected by his students from 1940 to 1944 came "from every social stratum, from nearly every racial and religious group in the state" ("The Ghosts of New York," p. 237).

102. JFA, entries 32.55, 32.83, and 97.96.

103. Searing, *When Granny Was a Little Girl*, p. 255.

104. JFA, entry 81.

105. JFA, entry 32.89.

106. One woman cited in the Jones Folklore Archives, for instance, recalled that "her father used to tell her many German ghost stories, but unfortunately she can't remember them. She tried to tell me a very interesting one about a blue light burning in a field, and money being found . . . but she was unable to remember the details"; JFA, entry 25.

107. "Mrs. Pierre (Catherine Beck) Van Cortlandt's written account of the Van Cortlandt Ghost, and Miss Van Wyck's experience with it," typescript, dated 1945, Westchester County, N.Y.–Folklore vertical file, WCHS. The date of Mrs. Van Cortlandt's original is not given. However, 1848 was the year the "rappings" that gave impetus to the spiritualist movement occurred at the Fox house in western New York; see Werner Sollors, "Dr. Benjamin Franklin's Celestial Telegraph, or Indian Blessings to Gaslit American Drawing Rooms," *American Quarterly* 35 (Winter 1983): 466.

108. For a history of spiritualist and parapsychological movements in the United States, see R. Laurence Moore, *In Search of White Crows: Spiritualism, Parapsychology, and American Culture* (New York: Oxford University Press, 1977).

109. For an overview of romanticism in Europe, see Lilian R. Furst, *Romanticism*, 2d ed. (London: Methuen, 1976).

110. Ringe, *American Gothic*, p. 10. Ringe writes that gothic titles began appearing in American book catalogues for the first time around 1793 and "increased year by year until at the end of the century they represented a substantial part of the offerings" (p. 14). Translations of the Grimms' *Märchen* and other German romantic works were published in the United States in the 1820s (p. 67). See also Sister Mary Mauritia Redden, *The Gothic Fiction in the American Magazines, 1765–1800* (Washington, D.C.: Catholic University of America Press, 1939).

111. For "imaginative furniture," see Daniel Hoffman, *Form and Fable in*

American Fiction (New York: Oxford University Press, 1965), p. 32. For discussions of the surge of interest in tradition and history in nineteenth-century American culture, see David D. Hall, "Reassessing the Local History of New England, Part One: The Rise and Fall of a Great Tradition," in *New England: A Bibliography of Its History*, ed. Roger Parks (Hanover, N.H.: University Press of New England, 1989), pp. xix–xxxi; Lawrence Buell, *New England Literary Culture from Revolution through Renaissance* (Cambridge: Cambridge University Press, 1986); Michael Kammen, *Mystic Chords of Memory: The Transformation of Tradition in American Culture* (New York: Alfred A. Knopf, 1991), part 1; and Perry, *Boats against the Current.*

112. Hall, "Reassessing Local History," p. xxvi.

113. Among the most prominent of these complaints is that found in Hawthorne's preface to *The Marble Faun* (1860): "No author, without a trial, can conceive of the difficulty of writing a Romance about a country were there is no shadow, no antiquity, no mystery, no picturesque and gloomy wrong, nor anything but common-place prosperity, in broad and simple daylight, as is happily the case with my dear native land"; Nathaniel Hawthorne, *Novels*, ed. Millicent Bell (New York: Library of America, 1983), p. 854. Ringe points out, however, that all the prominent authors from Charles Brockden Brown to Hawthorne "introduce the marvelous into their novels and tales"; *American Gothic*, p. 9.

114. See, for instance, Poe's "The Domain of Arnheim" and "Landor's Cottage"; Melville's *Pierre; or, The Ambiguities,* especially the early chapters; Cooper's *The Spy;* Paulding's *The Dutchman's Fireside;* Bryant's poem "The Catterskill," as well as *Picturesque America,* which he edited; Joseph Rodman Drake's poem "The Culprit Fay"; and N. P. Willis's *Rural Letters.*

115. It did not hurt either that Charles Pryer, the author of *Reminiscences of an Old Westchester Homestead,* had been director of Putnam's tellingly named Knickerbocker Press; "Charles Pryer Dies in New York City," New Rochelle *Paragraph,* June 9, 1916, biographical vertical files, WCHS.

116. At the turn of the twentieth century, ghost stories and tales of the supernatural occupied at least some of the attention of major American writers, including Edith Wharton and Henry James. A more thoroughgoing popular interest in hauntings and the supernatural can be gauged by the number and chronological dispersal of ghost story collections listed, for instance, in the card catalogue at Harvard University's Widener Library.

2. Irving's Web

Epigraph: Washington Irving, *Bracebridge Hall; or, The Humourists* (1822), ed. Herbert F. Smith (Boston: Twayne, 1977), pp. 227–228.

1. Pochmann first published these findings in "Irving's German Sources in *The Sketch Book*," *Studies in Philology* 27 (1930): 477–507. They also appear in Henry A. Pochmann, *German Culture in America: Philosophical and Literary Influences, 1600–1900* (Madison: University of Wisconsin Press, 1957), pp. 367–381.

2. "The foregoing tale," reads the note accompanying "Rip Van Winkle," "one would suspect had been suggested to Mr. Knickerbocker by a little German superstition about the emperor Frederick *der Rothbart* and the Kypphauser Mountain"; Washington Irving, *The Sketch Book of Geoffrey Crayon, Gent.* (1819–1820), ed. Haskell Springer (Boston: Twayne, 1978), p. 41. According to Walter A. Reichart, the German tale "Peter Klaus" had been named as Irving's source by comentators in 1822, 1868, and 1883, "without, however, revealing and emphasizing the full extent of such indebtedness." In 1901 German scholar R. Sprenger clearly demonstrated Irving's reliance on "Peter Klaus" and other German lore, but this investigation went generally unknown until Pochmann discovered it; Reichart, "In England," in *A Century of Commentary on the Works of Washington Irving*, ed. Andrew B. Myers (Tarrytown, N.Y.: Sleepy Hollow Restorations, 1976), pp. 294–295.

3. Ernest Ingersoll, ed., *Rand McNally and Co.'s Handy Guide to the Hudson River and Catskill Mountains*, 5th rev. ed. (Chicago, 1897), p. 192.

4. Frank H. Pierson, "The Crawbucky Tales," unpaginated manuscript, 1920, WCHS.

5. Daniel Hoffman, *Form and Fable in American Fiction* (New York: Oxford University Press, 1965), p. 84.

6. Harold W. Thompson, *Body, Boots and Britches: Folktales, Ballads, and Speech from Country New York* (New York: Dover, 1939), pp. 118–119.

7. W. V. Miller, "Folklore of the Hudson River: Ghostly Teutonic Phantoms Haunt Old Burial Grounds," *Chatham Courier*, February 20, 1958, Folklore file, CCHS. Another regional historian suggests that Irving may have heard German tales during a stay at Clermont (Dutchess County), where he was "surrounded by the German-descended tenants of the Livingstons"; Alf Evers, *The Catskills: From Wilderness to Woodstock* (Garden City, N.Y.: Doubleday, 1972), p. 322.

8. "Where Are You, Ichabod Crane?" *Asheville Citizen Times,* October 31, 1982, p. D1, Folklore file, CCHS. A 1953 *Yankee* magazine article similarly probes what it calls the "Kinderhook-Tarrytown 'Sleepy Hollow controversy'"; "Yankee Visits Sleepy Hollow," *Yankee,* July 1953, p. 36.

9. See Irving, "Rip Van Winkle," in *The Sketch Book,* p. 41. Regarding Irving's German reference, see Pochmann, *German Culture,* p. 370. Pochmann implies that the misdirection was deliberate. Reichart suggests that it might have been based on the placement of tales within commonly used German collections available to Irving; Reichart, "In England," pp. 296–297.

10. Irving, "The Legend of Sleepy Hollow," in *The Sketch Book,* p. 296.

11. Washington Irving, "Sleepy Hollow," sketch in *The Knickerbocker,* May 1839, p. 408.

12. Washington Irving, *Tales of a Traveller* (1824), ed. Judith Giblin Haig (Boston: Twayne, 1987), p. 4.

13. Irving, *Bracebridge Hall,* p. 247; idem, *Tales of a Traveller,* p. 4. In *Bracebridge Hall* Irving explains: "In a note which follows ['Rip Van Winkle'] I had alluded to the superstition on which it was founded, and I thought a mere allusion was sufficient. . . . In fact, I had considered popular traditions of the kind as fair foundations for authors of fiction to build upon" (p. 247).

14. Irving, *Bracebridge Hall,* p. 4.

15. In "The Custom-House," in *The Scarlet Letter* (1850), Hawthorne writes of "a neutral territory, somewhere between the real world and fairyland, where the Actual and the Imaginary may meet, and each imbue itself with the nature of the other"; Nathaniel Hawthorne, *Novels,* ed. Millicent Bell (New York: Library of America, 1983), p. 149. William Hedges argues that "the romantic awareness that [Irving] gradually developed came in large part as the natural consequence of the tensions, personal, intellectual, and literary, in which he was immersed"; William L. Hedges, *Washington Irving: An American Study, 1802–1832* (Baltimore: Johns Hopkins Press, 1965), p. 15.

16. Sources for biographical information include Stanley T. Williams, *The Life of Washington Irving,* 2 vols. (New York: Oxford University Press, 1935); Pierre M. Irving, *Life and Letters of Washington Irving,* 3 vols., rev. ed. (New York: G. P. Putnam and Sons, 1869); Hedges, *Washington Irving;* Jeffrey Rubin-Dorsky, *Adrift in the Old World: The Psychological Pilgrimage of Washington Irving* (Chicago: University of Chicago Press, 1988); and

Irving's journals, notes, and letters, collected in various volumes of *The Complete Works of Washington Irving*, published by the University of Wisconsin Press and Twayne Publishers, Boston.

17. For a discussion of Irving's "crisis of identity" and how it relates to cultural anxieties of the United States more broadly, see Rubin-Dorsky, *Adrift in the Old World*.

18. Irving, *Bracebridge Hall*, p. 3.

19. P. Irving, *Life and Letters*, 1: 16, 22–23.

20. Irving's travels along the river also included visits to Peekskill, Newburgh, Haverstraw, and Highland Grange, and to country estate of Cadwallader Colden in Orange County, the home of Matilda Hoffman's mother. For details about Irving's visits in the Hudson Valley, see Washington Irving, *Journals and Notebooks*, vol. 2: *1807–1822*, ed. Walter A. Reichart and Lillian Schlissel (Boston: Twayne. 1981), p. x; and Williams, *The Life of Washington Irving*, 1: 88.

21. Irving, "Sleepy Hollow" (*Knickerbocker* sketch), pp. 405–406.

22. Washington Irving, "The Catskill Mountains," in *The Home Book of the Picturesque* (New York: G. P. Putnam, 1852), p. 75.

23. For discussions of Irving's neoclassicism versus his romanticism, see essays in Stanley Brodwin, ed., *The Old and New World Romanticism of Washington Irving* (New York: Greenwood Press, 1986).

24. Washington Irving, *A History of New York* (1809), in *Washington Irving: History, Tales, and Sketches*, ed. James W. Tuttleton (New York: Library of America, 1983), p. 624.

25. All quotations are from Irving, *Journals and Notebooks*, 2: 31.

26. Ibid., p. 36. Such statements forecast discourses on superstition by Crayon in *Bracebridge Hall*.

27. See Irving, *Journals and Notebooks*, 2: 35. The dream of the Indian seems to be a fragment for a sketch set in the Highlands.

28. When Knickerbocker begins to refer, for instance, to legends of evil spirits in the Highlands and demons at the Duyvil's Dans-kammer, he stops himself: "But no! Diedrich Knickerbocker—it becomes thee not to idle thus in thy historic wayfaring"; Irving, *A History of New York*, p. 627. For Irving's treatment of supernatural tales in his early works, see Donald A. Ringe, *American Gothic: Imagination and Reason in Nineteenth-Century Fiction* (Lexington: University of Kentucky Press, 1982), pp. 81–82.

29. Irving, *Bracebridge Hall*, p. 4.

30. Irving, "The Author's Account of Himself," in *The Sketch Book*, p. 9.

31. Hoffman, *Form and Fable*, p. 83.

32. Williams, *The Life of Washington Irving*, 1: 156, 159–163.

33. Walter Scott, "Introduction," in Thomas of Erceldonne, *Sir Tristrem: A Metrical Romance of the Thirteenth Century*, 2d ed. (Edinburgh: Archibald Constable, 1806), p. xxvi. See also Hedges, *Washington Irving*, p. 113.

34. See Williams, *The Life of Washington Irving*, 1: 163, 154; and Reichart, "In England," pp. 280–318.

35. Irving's style of ghost-story writing tends toward what has been variously called the "sportive" or "ambiguous" mode, in which, through narratorial play, the author suggests rational explanation but, unlike in what has been called the "explained" gothic mode, does not entirely disregard the possibility of supernatural agency. See G. R. Thompson, "Washington Irving and the American Ghost Story," in *The Haunted Dusk: American Supernatural Fiction, 1820–1920*, ed. John W. Crowley, Charles Crow, and Howard Kerr (Athens: University of Georgia Press, 1983). Regarding Irving's theoretical grasp, Ralph Aderman writes: "Although Irving reflected many of the romantic tendencies of the early nineteenth century, there is little evidence that he was much concerned about the theoretical aspects of romanticism"; Ralph Aderman, "Washington Irving as a Purveyor of Old and New World Romanticism," in Brodwin, *Romanticism of Irving*, p. 14.

36. That Irving took popular taste into account is indicated by the fact that *The Sketch Book* was published in segments in the United States, and that Irving wrote and shifted selections in reaction to correspondence with friends and family members at home. "The Legend of Sleepy Hollow," which would be included in the penultimate installment of *The Sketch Book*, was composed after Irving was aware of positive responses to "Rip Van Winkle," which had appeared in the first installment. He wrote in a letter accompanying the manuscript: "There is a Knickerbocker story which may please from its representation of American scenes"; Washington Irving to Ebenezer Irving, December 29, 1819, quoted in P. Irving, *Life and Letters*, 1: 346.

37. See particularly Rubin-Dorsky, *Adrift in the Old World*, on the ideas of home and homelessness in Irving.

38. "Notes, 1815–1821," in Irving, *Journals and Notebooks*, 2: 65. Also noteworthy is a letter Irving wrote to Henry Brevoort in August 1820: "What I would not give for a few days among the Highlands of the Hudson, with

the little knot that was once assembled there! But I shall return home and find all changed, and shall be made sensible how much I have changed myself. It is this idea which continually comes across my mind, when I think of home"; quoted in P. Irving, *Life and Letters*, 1: 360–361.

39. Williams, *The Life of Washington Irving*, 1: 168–169. Williams cites as the source Elihu Burritt, "Birthplace of Rip Van Winkle," *Packard's Monthly*, November 1869, pp. 333–334. He also gives evidence for the authenticity of the anecdote, noting that nothing regarding "Rip Van Winkle" appears in Irving's notes for the preparation of *The Sketch Book* before the sudden appearance of the draft. In contrast, the creation and amendment of other tales can be traced in the notebooks (p. 166).

40. From the opening of *A History of New York*, Knickerbocker highlights the obscurity of New York history: "I treat of times long past over which the twilight of uncertainty had already thrown its shadows" (Irving, *History of New York*, p. 377). Knickerbocker himself is aware of the capacities for invention this allows the "historian": "I might have availed myself of the obscurity that hangs about the infant years of our city, to introduce a thousand pleasing fictions" (p. 379). Although he goes on to say, "But I have scrupulously discarded many a pithy tale and marvelous adventure," the historical obscurity Knickerbocker delineates provides Irving opportunities for comic effects, mythmaking, and political satire.

41. Washington Irving, *A Book of the Hudson* (New York: G. P. Putnam, 1849), p. 11.

42. Irving, "The Haunted House," in *Bracebridge Hall*, p. 248. Further references, cited parenthetically in the text, are to this edition.

43. Irving, "The Legend of Sleepy Hollow," p. 272. This and further references, cited parenthetically in the text, are to Springer's 1978 edition of *The Sketch Book*.

44. For historical discussion of the post-Revolutionary influx of New Englanders into New York, see Dixon Ryan Fox, *Yankees and Yorkers* (New York: New York University Press, 1940). From 1800 to 1820 the population of Connecticut grew only 10 percent while that of New York leapt 130 percent, largely as a result of migrations from New England; Fox, *Yankees and Yorkers*, p. 192. Thus, Fox writes, "in the New York Constitutional Convention of 1821 the majority of the one hundred and twenty-seven delegates were born in Connecticut or were sons of fathers who were born there" (p. 221).

45. Irving, *Bracebridge Hall*, pp. 232, 82, 83–84.

46. See Thompson, "Irving and American Ghost Story," pp. 13–34; Ringe's chapter on Irving in *American Gothic;* and John Clendenning, "Irving and the Gothic Tradition," *Bucknell Review* 12 (1964): 90–98.

47. Washington Irving, "Conspiracy of the Cocked Hats," *The Knicker-bocker,* October 1839, p. 305.

48. Although Diedrich Knickerbocker is purportedly the narrator of "The Legend of Sleepy Hollow," he says in a postscript: "The preceding tale is given, almost in the precise words in which I heard it related at a corporation meeting of the ancient city of Manhattoes. . . . The narrator was a pleasant, shabby, gentlemanly old fellow, in pepper and salt clothes, with a sadly humourous face." Irving also introduces the tale in such a way as to make it possible that someone other than Knickerbocker is narrating. That the tale is "Found among the Papers of the late Diedrich Knickerbocker" seems to indicate that Knickerbocker recorded it. But a later note stating that the postscript specifically was "Found in the Handwriting of Mr. Knickerbocker" could imply that the tale itself was in someone else's handwriting. See Irving, "The Legend of Sleepy Hollow," pp. 272, 296.

49. Irving, "Rip Van Winkle," in *The Sketch Book,* p. 39. This scene clearly echoes in the letter Irving wrote to Henry Brevoort in August 1820: "I shall return home and find all changed, and shall be made sensible how much I have changed myself"; quoted in P. Irving, *Life and Letters,* 1: 361.

50. Rubin-Dorsky, *Adrift in the Old World,* p. xviii.

51. Ibid., pp. 65, xv. A count of editions listed in Stanley T. Williams and Mary Allen Edge, comps., *A Bibliography of the Writings of Washington Irving* (Folcroft, Pa.: Folcroft Press; New York: Oxford University Press, 1936), shows that by 1900 approximately 130 editions of *The Sketch Book* had been printed, along with more than 50 independent editions of "The Legend of Sleepy Hollow" and almost 100 of "Rip Van Winkle."

52. William Cullen Bryant, "A Discourse on the Life, Character, and Genius of Washington Irving" (1860), in Myers, *A Century of Commentary,* p. 15.

53. Henry W. Boynton, *Washington Irving* (Boston, 1901), quoted in Myers, *A Century of Commentary,* p. 73.

54. For a discussion of products and productions associated with Irving's tales, see Evers, *The Catskills,* chaps. 44 and 45. For visual materials, see also *Visions of Irving: Selected Works from the Collection of Historic Hudson*

Valley (Tarrytown, N.Y.: Historic Hudson Valley Press, 1991); and Kathleen Eagen Johnson, *Irving Illustrated: Graphic Design and Literary Art in the Collection of Historic Hudson Valley* (Tarrytown, N.Y.: Historic Hudson Valley, 1999).

55. "The most fashionable fellow of the day" was how English publisher John Miller described Irving after the publication of *The Sketch Book;* quoted in Williams, *The Life of Washington Irving*, 1: 192; Myers, "Introduction," in *A Century of Commentary*, p. xxvii.

56. "A Visit to the Catskills," in *The Atlantic Souvenir*, 1828, quoted in Evers, *The Catskills*, p. 748, n. 8.

57. Raymond J. O'Brien, *American Sublime: Landscape and Scenery of the Lower Hudson Valley* (New York: Columbia University Press, 1981), p. 121.

58. *Sketches of the North River* (New York: Wm. H. Colyer, 1838), pp. 1, 72–73.

59. Daniel Wise, *Summer Days on the Hudson: The Story of a Pleasure Tour from Sandy Hook to the Saranac Lakes* (New York: Nelson and Phillips, 1876), p. 123. In a similar episode, one of the party steals off to read "The Legend of Sleepy Hollow" while in Tarrytown, "because I thought it would be nice to read about [Icahbod Crane] near the valley which was the scene of his fright and flight" (pp. 67–68).

60. A. E. P. Searing, *When Granny Was a Little Girl* (Garden City, N.Y.: Doubleday, Page, 1926), pp. 144–145.

61. Ibid., pp. 151, 149–150.

62. *Pine Hill Sentinel,* January 6, 1886, and June 5, 1897, quoted in Evers, *The Catskills,* pp. 520–521.

63. Beatrice Hasbrouck Wadlin, *Times and Tales of Town of Lloyd* (Highland, N.Y.: privately published, 1974), p. 127.

64. "Yankee Visits Sleepy Hollow," *Yankee,* July 1953, p. 36. This article reveals a varying level of knowledge and appreciation of Irving's tales. Although the response at the firehouse at Catskill is less than enthusiastic, a farmer nearby plays along, saying that he's heard the ghost crew's bowling. In Kinderhook, the reporters are surprised to find that the proprietor of the general store has never heard of "The Legend of Sleepy Hollow," but, as it is required reading at the local high school, the younger generation is quite familiar with the story, which they are taught was set in their town.

65. Wallace Bruce, *The Hudson: Three Centuries of History, Romance and Invention* (New York: Bryant Union, 1907), p. 65.

66. Wallace Bruce, *The Hudson* (Boston: Houghton Mifflin, 1881).

Bruce wrote a series of guidebooks from the 1870s into the twentieth century.

67. *Legends and Poetry of the Hudson* (1868; reprint, Astoria, N.Y.: J. C. and A. L. Fawcett, n.d.), p. 85.

68. Bruce, *The Hudson: Three Centuries*, p. 65.

69. C. G. Hine, *The New York and Albany Post Road* (New York: privately published, 1905), pp. 17, 20; idem, *The West Bank of the Hudson River: Albany to Tappan* (1906; reprint, Astoria, N.Y.: J. C. and A. L. Fawcett, n.d.), p. 21.

70. Paul Wilstach, *Hudson River Landings* (Indianapolis: Bobbs-Merrill, 1933), pp. 239, 222.

71. Jeff Canning and Wally Buxton, *History of the Tarrytowns from Ancient Times to the Present* (Harrison, N.Y.: Harbor Hill, 1975), pp. 60–61.

72. *Legends and Poetry of the Hudson*, pp. 15–16, 52.

73. Charles M. Skinner, *Myths and Legends of Our Own Land*, vol. 1 (Philadelphia: J. B. Lippincott, 1896), pp. 5, 17, 47. Skinner's first section, "The Hudson and Its Hills," has more than twenty-five tales, but I have excluded from my count tales set in places not in the Hudson Valley. (Skinner includes in this section places as far away as Niagara Falls.)

74. Evers, *The Catskills*, p. 520.

75. A. E. P. Searing, *The Land of Rip Van Winkle: A Tour through the Romantic Parts of the Catskills, Its Legends and Traditions* (New York: G. P. Putnam's Sons, Knickerbocker Press, 1884), p. 91. See also Evers, *The Catskills*, p. 522, for acts of "Legend Piracy" by hotel proprietors in the Catskills.

76. T. Morris Longstreth, *The Catskills* (New York: Century, 1918), pp. 96, 99.

77. See Jim Haviland, "Searchers Comb Catskills for Rip Van Winkle, $100,000 Prize," *Poughkeepsie Journal*, October 10, 1989, Hudson River file, Newburgh Free Library, Local History Collection, Newburgh, N.Y.

78. Irving, "Sleepy Hollow" (*Knickerbocker* sketch), p. 404.

79. Irving, *Tales of a Traveller*, p. 255.

80. Irving, "The Storm-Ship," in *Bracebridge Hall*, p. 283.

81. Washington Irving, "A Chronicle of Wolfert's Roost," *The Knickerbocker*, April 1839, p. 312.

82. Washington Irving, "The Crayon Papers," *The Knickerbocker*, March 1839, pp. 207, 208; and "Sleepy Hollow" (*Knickerbocker* sketch), pp. 404, 409.

83. Irving, *A Book of the Hudson,* p. viii.

84. See especially Thompson, "Irving and American Ghost Story," pp. 13–36.

85. Irving, "Dolph Heyliger," in *Bracebridge Hall,* p. 300.

86. Ringe, *American Gothic,* p. 87.

87. Quoted in Evers, *The Catskills,* p. 324. In a letter to his brother Peter, dated July 9, 1832, Irving–who was then visiting the Catskills for the first time–reported spending a day "visiting the waterfall, glen, etc. that are pointed out as the veritable haunts of Rip Van Winkle." His brother replied: "I have little doubt but some curious travellers will yet find some of the bones of the dog if they can but hit on the veritable spot of his long sleep"; quoted in "Old Ulster and Washington Irving," *Olde Ulster: An Historical and Genealogical Magazine* 1 (January 1905): 8–9.

88. Edgar Mayhew Bacon, *Chronicles of Tarrytown and Sleepy Hollow* (New York: G. P. Putnam's Sons, 1897), p. 115.

3. The Colorful Career of a Ghost from Leeds

Epigraph: Ella Rush Murray, letter to the editor, *Catskill Daily Mail,* quoted in JFA, entry 127C; Charles Rockwell, *The Catskill Mountains and the Region Around* (New York: Taintor Brothers, 1867), p. 151; C. G. Hine, *The West Bank of the Hudson River: Albany to Tappan* (1906; reprint, Astoria, N.Y.: J. C. and A. L. Fawcett, n.d.), p. 41.

1. For the women in white and black, see Hine, *West Bank of the Hudson,* pp. 20–21, 42–43. For the woman in gray, see Charles F. Wilde, "Ghost Legends of the Hudson Valley" (Master's thesis, New York State College for Teachers, 1937), p. 43. A number of ghost stories in the vicinity seem to relate to violence against women. For instance, the ghost of an Indian woman, killed by a jealous Indian man for marrying a white trapper, is said to streak by on horseback in Coxsackie, bound to her murderer; see Charles M. Skinner, *Myths and Legends of Our Own Land,* 2 vols. (Philadelphia: J. B. Lippincott, 1896), 1: 42–45. In a tale from Cornwallville, a young woman is killed when she refuses a suitor who accosts her as she is riding home through the woods one night. Although she does not appear as a ghost, the horse and attacker do; Claude Haton, "Hallowe'en Tale: The Haunted Horse of Merchant's Wood," Catskill *Daily Mail,* October 31, 1981, p. 14.

2. See JFA, entries 108 and 123, for both identifications.

3. Town names, as well as town and county boundaries, shifted quite a

bit in the late eighteenth and early nineteenth centuries. The village now called Leeds was originally called Catskill (sometimes spelled Katskill or Kaatskill), then was known for a while as Old Catskill, when the village on the river, four miles away, which was previously known as "The Landing," was incorporated as the village of Catskill in 1806. Both villages were and are part of the Town of Catskill (established 1788). Old Catskill came to be part of what is now the village of Leeds in 1827 (having been called Madison in between). The town that would be Leeds was originally in Albany County, was made part of Ulster County in 1798, and finally was included in the newly created Greene County in 1800.

4. Versions of this story have received attention in regional historical and folkloric studies, most notably Charles Huguenin, "Condemned to the Noose," *New York Folklore Quarterly* 16 (autumn 1960): 187–196. However, these efforts have primarily rested at the level of cataloging or narrating the various details of different versions. (Huguenin's article, for instance, largely rehashes Miriam Coles Harris's 1862 novel, *The Sutherlands*.) Few accounts have been written with an awareness of, or attention to, the original incident, or with sufficient attention to what appears to be the earliest printed version of the story (that written by William Leete Stone, probably in 1824). Moreover, none has significantly attempted to situate the details of the tales with regard to historical contexts.

5. That the bill of indictment may not have been in county records is evidenced by the late-nineteenth-century claims of Dr. Claudius Van Deusen, a Leeds native. In an entry for R. Lionel DeLisser's *Picturesque Catskills* (Northampton, Mass.: Picturesque Publishing, 1894), he states that the case never went beyond an inquest: "if other proceedings had been taken, and an indictment found it would be on record in the County Clerk's office in Albany, then the place of record; but after a diligent search, no indictment can be found against the party in question, though there are those against other persons" (p. 21). The statement is somewhat ambiguous (i.e., he might be indicating the bill of indictment when he speaks of the inquest), but it has been taken as meaning there was no evidence of a case. (See, for instance, Huguenin, "Condemned to the Noose," p. 195.) The historical rediscovery of the bill of indictment seems to have been made by Jesse Van Vechten Vedder, who says that a "document" then at the Catskill Public Library "proves that the indictment was quashed"; Jesse Van Vechten Vedder, *History of Greene County*, vol. 1: *1651–1800* (1927; reprint, Cornwallville, N.Y.: Hope Farm Press, 1985), p. 37. Vedder, how-

ever, does not comment further on why the document was at the public library instead of in Albany County records.

6. "Salisbury, William, Indictment for Murder," 1762, manuscript vertical file, GCHS. My transcription of this document is aided by a typed transcript accompanying it in the files, although I read the spelling of the foreman's name as "Douw," whereas the transcript has it as "Doew." I have also added commas in order to facilitate reading. "Ignoramus" as a legal term used by grand juries means "we take not notice of [bill or indictment]."

7. Salisbury had a partner in the purchase and patent, a wealthy Dutch man named Martin Gerritse Van Bergen. Information about the Catskill Patent, the early history of Catskill, and the Salisbury family is derived primarily from *The History of Greene County* (New York: J. B. Beers, 1884); genealogical data compiled by Edward Salisbury in 1994, on file at GCHS; and the Leeds–Salisbury–Newkirk manuscript files, GCHS. Silvester (sometimes spelled Sylvester) Salisbury, who first came over as part of the British takeover from the Dutch in 1664, was a man of some prominence in the region. He numbered among his close friends the royal governor, Edmund Andros, who approved the patent.

8. *The History of Greene County* (1884), p. 25.

9. Ibid., p. 98.

10. See Florence Christoph, *Upstate New York in the 1760s: Tax Lists and Selected Militia Rolls of Old Albany County, 1760–1768* (Camden, Maine: Picton Press, 1992). On the 1766 tax list, William Salisbury is assessed at 69 pounds, the highest of the 136 who paid taxes in the town in Catskill, and among the top 40 in the entire county, in which over 5,000 taxpayers were listed. (What was then Albany County is now fourteen counties.) Stephen Van Rensselaer, the patroon of the massive manor of Rensselaerwyck, was assessed at 270 pounds. Most contemporaneous assessments in the town of Catskill were less than 10 pounds. The property William had inherited from his father (who died in 1756) included the fertile plain known as the Potick, which contained part of Catskill Creek, and a second stone house that his father had built in 1730. William also acquired patents to other local lands over time (*The History of Greene County* [1884], pp. 236–237 and 243). At his death in 1801 he left substantial parcels of land for his wife, his eight surviving children, and the children of two deceased sons; William Salisbury's Will, Greene County Surrogate Court, Will Book A, pp. 136–140, GCHS.

11. Searle, quoted in Rockwell, *The Catskill Mountains*, p. 153. Searle was pastor of the Reformed Dutch Church of Leeds in the mid-nineteenth century.

12. No one with a name spelled "Swarts" appears in Berthold Fernow, *Calendar of Wills on File and Recorded in the Offices of the Clerk of the Court of Appeals of the County Clerk at Albany* (New York: Knickerbocker Press, 1896); in eighteenth-century tax lists listed in Christoph's *Upstate New York in the 1760s;* or in all of New York State in the 1790 federal census (although there are three heads of households listed in New York State in the 1790 census with the names Swartz, and a few people with the name Swart in Fernow's *Calendar of Wills* for Albany County). The absence of the name from records of wills and taxes might simply indicate that Anna Dorothea Swarts came from a poor family. In 1769 a Benjamin Swarts from Kingston was ordered to bind out his children because he lacked the means to support his family (Thomas S. Wermuth, *Rip Van Winkle's Neighbors: The Transformation of Rural Society in the Hudson River Valley, 1720–1850* [Albany: State University of New York Press, 2001], p. 42). But I do not know of any connection between them.

13. Samuel McKee, *Labor in Colonial New York, 1664–1776* (New York: Columbia University Press, 1935), p. 63.

14. William Salisbury's Will, Greene County Surrogate Court, Will Book A, pp. 136–140, GCHS.

15. There was a settlement of several hundred Palatinate German immigrants nearby at West Camp (now in Ulster County), brought there in 1710 to work for Robert Livingston. However, according to *The History of Greene County* (1884), many of these immigrants left to settle on lands in the Mohawk and Schoharie Valleys, and "in less than ten years it is said nearly the whole colony had gone away" (p. 24).

16. For a sense of the variety of explanations see Hine, *West Bank of the Hudson*, pp. 40–42; and Rockwell, *The Catskill Mountains*, pp. 148–155.

17. The death occurred in 1755 (the twenty-eighth year of the reign of George II, noted in the bill of indictment), but the bill of indictment is dated 1762 and refers to the *late* king.

18. Douglas Greenberg, *Crime and Law Enforcement in the Colony of New York, 1691–1776* (Ithaca, N.Y.: Cornell University Press, 1974), pp. 189–195. Between 1691 and 1776, 36 percent of all criminal cases appearing in New York court records were never resolved. In Albany (and what became Charlotte County in 1772), 58.8 percent were never resolved (p. 190). Re-

cords for Albany County in the 1750s are missing. According to Greenberg, "law enforcement was more precarious and difficult in Albany than elsewhere. The area of the local sessions court's jurisdiction was simply too wide" (p. 88).

19. The average case in Albany County during this period took 3.7 months; ibid., p. 190.

20. See McKee, *Labor in Colonial New York*, p. 101 and elsewhere, regarding such laws.

21. The first federal census of 1790 gives the population of Catskill as 1,980 people, with 279 "heads of household" and 305 slaves. For Albany and Ulster Counties, see Edgar J. McManus, *A History of Negro Slavery in New York* (Syracuse: Syracuse University Press, 1966), pp. 197–198. Though these statistics are for "Negro" rather than specifically "slave" populations, McManus writes that the terms were used interchangeably on census forms, and data from 1790 suggest that most if not all of those counted as Negroes in the eighteenth century would have been slaves (p. 200).

22. See McKee, *Labor in Colonial New York*, pp. 99–100, 75. In the case of apprentices, McKee states: "Disobedience, unruliness, laziness or any form of misconduct could be punished by scolding, deprivation, or whipping, except that the punishment must not be immoderately cruel or such as would permanently disfigure or maim the apprentice" (p. 75). See also Greenberg, *Crime and Law Enforcement*, pp. 108–109.

23. Henry Brace, "Old Catskill," in *The History of Greene County* (1884), p. 95. Brace writes of this as "an indistinct tradition," but an Indian Camp Ground is marked on the map of the town of Cairo, just adjacent to Catskill, in F. W. Beers, *The Atlas of Greene County* (New York: Beers, Ellis & Soule, 1867). The Indian footpath appears on maps of Athens in the Beers's *Atlas* and in Hine, *West Bank of the Hudson*.

24. For more detailed discussions of the tenant uprisings of the eighteenth century, see Sung Bok Kim, *Landlord and Tenant in Colonial New York: Manorial Society, 1664–1775* (Chapel Hill: University of North Carolina Press for the Institute of Early American History and Culture, 1978); and Patricia U. Bonomi, *A Factious People: Politics and Society in Colonial New York* (New York: Columbia University Press, 1971), pp. 179–228.

25. Greenberg, *Crime and Law Enforcement*, pp. 56, 95. According to Greenberg, "That almost 80% of the prosecutions took place in the counties [rather than the city] and that more than 30% of all prosecutions in

the counties were for riots, breaches of the peace, and the like seems especially remarkable" (p. 56).

26. Christoph, *Upstate New York in the 1760s*, p. 31.

27. Records for the Albany County Court of Sessions from 1763 to 1781 are at the Albany County Hall of Records, Albany, N.Y. The surviving records for the Albany County courts contain major gaps, among them the years 1724-1762. An assessment of ninety pounds appears on the 1766 tax list for "Renselaer Nicolls and son"; Christoph, *Upstate New York in the 1760s*, p. 51. Nichols (sometimes spelled Nicolls, Nicholls, or Nicoll) was the son of Anna Van Rensselaer and William Nichols.

28. *The History of Greene County* (1884), pp. 205-206. Barker had emigrated from England with his wife, a descendant of the Tudors, bringing along tenant families to settle the land; one of Salisbury's sons married Barker's daughter. This statement regarding Barker is an enigma, not only in that it says he served as a defense lawyer in a case that did not go to trial, but also in that it calls the case "celebrated" and indicates that the victim was a "slave." That nothing else seems to survive from the period of the original incident to support any of these assertions means either that the history was drawing upon sources now unavailable, and provides special insight into the case, or that it was influenced by the profusion of nineteenth-century legends about the case. Still, as no involvement by Barker or any other lawyer appears in any of the stories I have seen, the reference may have some historical substance.

29. *The New Shorter Oxford English Dictionary* (1993 ed.).

30. *The History of Greene County* (1884), p. 437. Though of British ancestry, the Salisburys heavily intermarried with families of Dutch descent. William's wife was Teuntje (called Eunice) Staats.

31. The Catskill Mountain House was set on a ledge on the northeast side of South Mountain, in the town of Catskill, about eight miles southwest of the village of Leeds.

32. The narrative implies that Stone heard this story when he visited in 1824. However, other possibilities exist. First, Stone may have heard something of the case or ghost story during his tenures at newspapers in the nearby towns of Hudson (1814-1816) and Albany (1816-17). Another possibility is that Stone heard the tale from Thurlow Weed, who was born in the town of Cairo and had lived in the village of Catskill until 1811. Weed worked as a journeyman under Stone at the *Herkimer American,* which

Stone managed and then owned from 1812 to 1814. Thus, it is possible that Stone is interpolating the story into his travel narrative, having heard it earlier. Another mystery that also needs to be addressed is when Stone's version of this story actually appeared in the *Commercial Advertiser*. The passages are cited by John Barber and Henry Howe in *Historical Collections of the State of New York* (New York: S. Tuttle, 1842) as having appeared in that newspaper, and the story is also cited by Charles Rockwell in *The Catskill Mountains* in 1867 as having come from that paper. Catskill-area historian Alf Evers specifies that the passage appeared in the September 3, 1824, edition. There is a gap in the general microfilm record of this newspaper from 1821 to 1825. However, hard copies may be found in a few places, including the New-York Historical Society. Yet although the September 3, 1824, edition included a segment of Stone's "Ten Days in the Country," and although the places mentioned in that segment match those of the ghost story, the actual passage—two long paragraphs—does not appear in the September 3, 1824, evening edition I saw or in the surrounding issues or segments of "Ten Days in the Country." Perhaps a different edition contained the passage. A slight hint that the passage might have been edited out appears in the September 3 article: just at the point one would expect the ghost story to appear, the article cuts off, saying: "But we shall not dwell too long upon single objects." This may correspond in some way to the statement in the excerpted ghost story: "We linger longer at this spot than our wonted manner." The best that can be said seems to be that Stone probably wrote the story up in 1824, and that it appeared in the *Commercial Advertiser* sometime between 1824 and 1842 (when it was excerpted by Barber and Howe).

33. All quotations of this passage are from the excerpt in Barber and Howe, *Historical Collections*, pp. 187–188. The house to which Stone alludes here is Francis Salisbury's (Stone mentions that the house bears the date 1705), not William's, built in 1730. At the time Stone visited, the town was called Madison.

34. Details about the turnpike are taken from *The History of Greene County* (1884), p. 44. No month and day are given for William's death in standard genealogical sources, but his grandson, General William Salisbury, is quoted as remembering that his grandfather died in the autumn of 1801; Rockwell, *The Catskill Mountains*, p. 155.

35. Brown quoted in Vedder, *History of Greene County*, pp. 38–39.

36. Spafford's *Gazetteer* of 1813, quoted in Frank A. Gallt, *Dear Old Greene County* (Catskill, N.Y.: n.p., 1915), p. 221. The population of Catskill (town) was 1,980 in 1790 and 4,245 in 1810. The figures for 1790 are from the federal census; the figures for 1810 are taken from Gallt, p. 60, because the federal census for that year is not broken down by town in New York. Rev. Clark Brown estimated Catskill's population in 1803 at 5,000 to 6,000 (Vedder, *History of Greene County*, p. 38). The population of Greene County, as recorded in the federal censuses of 1800 and 1820, rose from 12,584 to 22,996. The growth of population in the Catskill area significantly slowed after 1820.

37. [William Leete Stone], "Ten Days in the Country, no. III," New York *Commercial Advertiser*, August 31, 1824, p. 2.

38. Alan Taylor, *William Cooper's Town: Power and Persuasion on the Frontier of the Early American Republic* (New York: Vintage/Random House, 1995), p. 4. The state's population went from 340,120 in 1790 to 1,372,812 in 1820.

39. See Barber and Howe, *Historical Collections;* and Rockwell, *The Catskill Mountains.*

40. For related material on developing sentiments toward murder, especially murders of young women, in the area, see Alan Taylor, "'The Unhappy Stephen Arnold': An Episode of Murder and Penitence in the Early Republic," in *Through a Glass Darkly: Reflections on Personal Identity in Early America*, ed. Ronald Hoffman, Mechal Sobel, and Fredrika J. Teute (Chapel Hill: University of North Carolina Press for the Omohundro Institute of Early American History and Culture, 1997). For a broader discussion of a shift from eighteenth- to nineteenth-century conceptions of murder, see Karen Halttunen, *Murder Most Foul: The Killer and the American Gothic Imagination* (Cambridge, Mass.: Harvard University Press, 1998).

41. The original article is in the Hudson *Northern Whig*, August 31, 1813, p. 3. It is quoted (with the wrong date) in Barber and Howe, *Historical Collections*, pp. 181–182, with their added perspective on the trials and gravestone (p. 183). Their introduction to the passage—"the following account of the murder of Miss Hamilton"—indicates an expectation of readers' recollection of the case.

42. Stone, "Ten Days in the Country," New-York *Commercial Advertiser*, August 31, 1824, p. 2.

43. See Roland Van Zandt, *The Catskill Mountain House* (New Bruns-

wick, N.J.: Rutgers University Press, 1966); John F. Sears, *Sacred Places: American Tourist Attractions in the Nineteenth Century* (New York: Oxford University Press, 1989); and Kenneth Myers, *The Catskills: Painters, Writers, and Tourists in the Mountains, 1820–1895* (Yonkers, N.Y.: Hudson River Museum of Westchester; Hanover, N.H.: University Press of New England, 1987), for discussions of the Catskills in art and tourism.

44. *The History of Greene County* (1884), p. 206. The 1820 federal census records 134 slaves in Greene County. New York was the second-to-last state to pass a law abolishing slavery (New Jersey being the last). For details see McManus, *Negro Slavery in New York*.

45. See Stith Thompson, *Motif-Index of Folk Literature*, rev. ed. (Bloomington: Indiana University Press, 1966; CD-ROM, InteLex Corp., 1993). Thompson's cataloging of ghost cows, dogs, and horses (generally under E423 and E521) points mainly to sources in Northern European, British, Irish, and American folktales and myths, although in some cases variations from other areas are indicated, and Thompson by no means claims to present an exhaustive catalogue of occurrences. A specifically white horse is a type that has been noted in England and the United States; see Ernest Wallace Baughman, *Type and Motif Index of the Folktales of England and North America*, Indiana University Folklore Series, no. 2 (The Hague: Mouton, 1966). The female figure with flames for fingertips may derive from a motif that Thompson catalogues as "Fingers of Saints (Angels) give light or fire" (F552.1.2), which appears in Christian myth. The image may also relate to what is called the "Hand of Glory"—a candle made from a criminal's hand, which is supposed to lead to hidden treasure; but the former connection seems more plausible. She may also relate to the banshee in Irish and Scottish lore.

46. The Jones Folklore Archives contain a folder dedicated to stories of animal ghosts collected in New York. One story from Wittenberg, Ulster County, tells of a white ghost cow near a bridge there (entry 170). Ghost dogs seem primarily to appear in two capacities: first, to protect treasure or property; second, to indicate a place that is generally haunted by something else. The ghost dogs that appear in the Jones Archives are usually described as black, if a color is indicated. See JFA, entries 61.52 and 166, for examples.

47. Biographical information on William Leete Stone (1792–1844) is derived primarily from William L. Stone, Jr., "The Life and Times of Wil-

liam Leete Stone," a biography written by his son and attached to the 1866 printing of William L. Stone, *The Life and Times of Sa-Go-Ye-Wat-Ha, or Red Jacket* (Albany: J. Munsell, 1866), pp. 2–101. Stone's father, a Revolutionary War veteran and Congregationalist minister from Connecticut, having temporarily settled at the time of Stone's birth in New Paltz (Ulster County), soon thereafter moved on to frontier territory along the Susquehanna. Stone began his newspaper career at the age of seventeen in Cooperstown, moving on from there to Herkimer (1811–1814), Hudson (1814–1816), Albany (1816–17), and Hartford, Connecticut (1817–1821), before his long tenure as editor of the New-York *Commercial Advertiser* beginning in 1821.

48. Stone quoted in Dixon Ryan Fox, *The Decline of Aristocracy in the Politics of New York*, ed. Robert V. Remini (New York: Harper Torchbooks, 1965), p. 429. Stone writes of Shays' Rebellion in "The Mysterious Bridal," a tale appearing in his *Tales and Sketches, Such as They Are*, vol. 2 (New York: Harper and Brothers, 1834), p. 95. Shays' Rebellion (1786–87) was a series of uprisings by farmers primarily in Massachusetts in protest against foreclosure laws and high taxes. Stone was also against women's rights.

49. Among the literary groups and journals Stone founded was one in Hartford called the "Knights of the Round Table." In addition to his two-volume *Tales and Sketches, Such as They Are* (1834), Stone produced several biographies of Iroquois figures and a history of border incidents of the American Revolution and created the New York State Historical Agency (for transcribing documents related to New York history that were in European archives). The bibliography of his publications reveals that he was also interested in such topics as animal magnetism and religious delusion. *Tales and Sketches* is replete with tales of witches and ghosts.

50. See the New York *Commercial Advertiser*, July through October, 1824 (or the New York *Spectator and Semiweekly Commercial Advertiser*, which contains the same articles). Stone's "Ten Days in the Country" ran in sixteen installments, at irregular intervals, from August 26 to October 23, 1824. The review of *Tales of a Traveller* appears in the August 31, 1824, *Commercial Advertiser*, p. 2.

51. See David D. Hall, *Worlds of Wonder, Days of Judgment: Popular Religious Beliefs in Early New England* (Cambridge, Mass.: Harvard University Press, 1989), pp. 205, 295, n. 129.

52. "A Recipe for Modern Romance," originally in the Philadelphia

Weekly Magazine, June 1798, quoted in Sister Mary Mauritia Redden, *The Gothic Fiction in the American Magazines, 1765–1800* (Washington, D.C.: Catholic University of America Press, 1939), p. 165.

53. The woman in white features in "The Adventure of My Uncle," the first story told at the hunting dinner in *Tales of A Traveller.*

54. Stone, *Tales and Sketches, Such as They Are,* 1: 231, 233.

55. Barber and Howe, *Historical Collections,* p. 187.

56. Skinner, *Myths and Legends of Our Own Land,* 1: 6.

57. [Miriam Coles Harris], *The Sutherlands* (New York: Carleton, 1862), p. 472. In the novel, Sutherland's murder of the girl sets off a chain of events that result in the deaths of Sutherland's only son, his son's intended bride, and his own wife; the last two also come back as ghosts (p. 472). Harris (1834–1925) was born in Long Island, descended from Winthrop Fleet Puritans. She was educated at exclusive New York City schools and was married in 1864 to a New York City lawyer. She published at least seventeen books, beginning with a novel titled *Rutledge* (1860). *The Sutherlands* was her second novel. According to the *Dictionary of American Biography,* her novels "were considerably read during the late 19th century"; Sarah G. Bowerman, "Miriam Coles Harris," in *The Dictionary of American Biography,* ed. Dumas Malone, vol. 8 (New York: Charles Scribner's Sons, 1932), pp. 317–318.

58. Harris, *The Sutherlands* (1st ed.), p. 389.

59. [Miriam Coles Harris], *The Sutherlands,* 11th ed. (New York: Charles Scribner, 1871), p. 474.

60. Rockwell, *The Catskill Mountains,* p. 151.

61. An 1847 map in the Leeds–Salisbury–Newkirk manuscript files, GCHS, shows part of this land as belonging to Josiah Sutherland. The name (spelled "Southerland") also appears on the property in the 1867 Beers's *Atlas of Greene County.*

62. In Albany-area Dutch usage, the syllable *-tje* is a diminutive suffix for a name. The name Annatje would be the equivalent of "Annie" in English. See Charlotte Wilcoxen, *Seventeenth Century Albany: A Dutch Profile,* rev. ed. (Albany: Education Department of the Albany Institute of History and Art, 1984), p. 129.

63. Harris, *The Sutherlands* (1st ed.), p. 9. The opening occurs in England, but the point holds.

64. Ibid., pp. 369, 389.

65. Douglas received 3,537 votes, Lincoln 3,137. The vote on the Fif-

teenth Amendment was more definitive: 548 for, and 4,530 against; *The History of Greene County* (1884), p. 53.

66. Harris, *The Sutherlands* (1st ed.), pp. 45, 393.

67. Conflict between Native Americans and white settlers comes up in several instances in the novel. For instance, before Nattee runs away, Harris writes that there had been a band of Indians in the neighborhood who had made off with one of Sutherland's cows. When Nattee runs away, she thinks of going to join her father's people, who have been driven out of the area. Harris is not entirely consistent, nor consistently "liberal" in her attitudes toward African and Native Americans. Stereotypical adjectives—"stealthy" Indians, "cunning" and grinning" blacks—crop up. In addition, the locus of blame is somewhat muddied, both by the exceptional perversity attributed to Ralph Sutherland and by wavering internal logic. If Nattee was a runaway slave, and if Sutherland killed her accidentally while retrieving her (as is suggested in Harris's account), certainly this would not be considered murder. In sticking to the details of the received ghost story (that he is convicted of murder), Harris risks attenuating a deeper perception of inherent injustice or inevitable tragedy in a slaveholding society that would have been achieved if there had been no conviction. Nonetheless, the novel clearly leans toward a critique of slavery and suggests a critique of Indian dispossession as well.

68. Renée L. Bergland, *The National Uncanny: Indian Ghosts and American Subjects* (Hanover, N.H.: Dartmouth College, University Press of New England, 2000), p. 7.

69. Werner Sollors points to Stowe's Uncle Tom as an example of mid-nineteenth-century "romantic racialism"; Sollors, *Beyond Ethnicity: Consent and Descent in American Culture* (New York: Oxford University Press, 1986), p. 29.

70. Skinner, *Myths and Legends of Our Own Land*, 1: 27.

71. Ibid., p. 25.

72. Rockwell, *The Catskill Mountains*, pp. 154, 155.

73. See, for instance, Skinner's adaptation of "Rip Van Winkle" in *Myths And Legends of Our Own Land*, 1: 17–21. Skinner generally follows the substance and plot of Irving's tales, but he works to obscure Irving's authorship and adds and subtracts details. In the New England section of the book, Skinner also presents a tale titled "Father Moody's Black Veil," which conflates Hawthorne's "The Minister's Black Veil" with an instance Hawthorne refers to in a note to that tale.

74. Johnson Rossiter, ed., *The 20th Century Biographical Dictionary of Notable Americans*, vol. 9 (Boston: Biographical Society, 1904), unpaginated. Skinner was born in western New York, descended from Massachusetts Bay colonists, and lived his early life in New England. He joined the editorial staff of the *Brooklyn Daily Eagle* in 1884 and syndicated a series of articles on labor conditions, the army, prisons, and American communities, among other topics. In addition to *Myths and Legends of Our Own Land*, Skinner wrote *Myths and Legends beyond Our Borders* (1898), *Myths and Legends of Our New Possessions* (1899); a play, *Villon the Vagabond* (1898); and several other books.

75. Skinner, *Myths and Legends of Our Own Land*, 1: 5.

76. Turner downplays slavery, the Civil War, and the Native American presence and assumes Anglo-Saxon underpinnings as he emphasizes an inevitable, progressive process of Americanization occurring at westward-moving frontiers; and, as Alan Trachtenberg points out, African Americans were neither invited nor permitted to exhibit in the 1893 Exposition's central space, the "White City," while "Indians found themselves included among the exhibition of the ethnology department"; Trachtenberg, *The Incorporation of America: Culture and Society in the Gilded Age* (New York: Hill and Wang, 1982), p. 220.

77. See Joel Williamson, *A Rage for Order: Black-White Relations in the American South Since Emancipation* (New York: Oxford University Press, 1986), pp. 171–181.

78. Skinner, *Myths and Legends of Our Own Land*, 1: 119, 24. In the first case, Skinner to some extent cannot help but include the black character, as the tale "The Party of Gibbet Island" is based on an Irving story.

79. Ibid., p. 6.

80. Ibid., 2: 71.

81. These efforts culminated in the National Origins Act of 1924, which set quotas that heavily favored immigration from northern European countries. For discussions of anti-immigration movements and legislation, see John Higham, *Strangers in the Land: Patterns of American Nativism, 1860–1925* (New Brunswick, N.J.: Rutgers University Press, 1992).

82. Rockwell, *The Catskill Mountains*, p. 155; Hine, *West Bank of the Hudson*, p. 41.

83. On interest in folk cultures in the 1930s, see Richard H. Pells, *Radical Visions and American Dreams: Culture and Social Thought in the Depression Years* (Middletown, Conn.: Wesleyan University Press, 1973), p. 101.

84. Ella Rush Murray, letter to the editor, *Catskill Daily Mail,* August 7, 1942, pp. 3, 8; quoted in JFA, entry 127C.

85. For instance, the fact that a student from Greene County uses Rockwell's *Catskill Mountains* in her submission suggests that the book was available locally, and thus could lend to the selective resurrection any of the four different versions of the story it contained, including Stone's and Harris's (JFA, entry 127D). Another entry quotes a version of the story that appeared in *Harper's New Monthly Magazine* in 1883 (JFA, entry 127.53).

86. Other accounts make similarly assumptive references to Spooky Hollow; for instance, county historian Jesse Van Vechten Vedder uses it without explanation, saying that her closest childhood neighbors lived just beyond "Spooky Hollow . . . where my footsteps always quickened unless supported by numbers"; Vedder, *Historic Catskill* (1922; reprint, Astoria, N.Y.: J. C. and A. L. Fawcett, n.d.), p. 56. Murray's references to the scenes associated with the legend both reflect and participate in a long-running inscription of the story in the landscape. Murray's reference, for instance, to the "Giant's Bowling Alley" echoes and updates similar mappings in earlier accounts. Searle identified the place where the girl was killed as "on the old Coxsackie road, half a mile northwest of the church, between the house of Mr. William Newkirk and the foundry of Mr. Milton Fowks," while General Salisbury in the nineteenth century locates the house of a "low family" the girl had been said to visit "in the fields where the Jacksons reside"; both quoted in Rockwell, *The Catskill Mountains,* pp. 154–155. Vedder, writing in the twentieth century, locates this house "at the foot or second turn of what is now known as Phelan's Hill, on lands of Newkirk (now Schaefer's)"; *Historic Catskill,* pp. 5–6.

87. Beatrice George, "'Haunting' Spooky Hollow," Catskill *Daily Examiner,* October 16, 1935, p. 8.

88. Hine, *West Bank of the Hudson,* p. 38.

89. See Van Deusen's account in DeLisser's *Picturesque Catskills* (p. 22), along with the Salisbury genealogy assembled by Edward Salisbury in 1994, GCHS.

90. Hine, *West Bank of the Hudson,* p. 41.

91. The account here is a composite of Claudius Van Deusen, "Old Happenings in Leeds," in DeLisser, *Picturesque Catskills,* pp. 20–22; and the version given in Hine, *West Bank of the Hudson,* pp. 40–42. The quotations are from Delisser, p. 21; and Hine, p. 42.

92. Van Deusen, "Old Happenings in Leeds," p. 22.

93. Gallt names as the early residents of the Catskill Patent "the Bronks, Van Bergens, Van Deusens, Salisburys, Vedders, Van Vechtens, and Whitbecks"; *Dear Old Greene County,* p. 119. Vedder (1859–1952) was the first county historian (the position was established in the early 1920s), and she had a long tenure. She was also a founding member of the local chapter of the Daughters of the American Revolution and of the Greene County Historical Society, and was instrumental in local historical preservation projects. Although Vedder was descended from one of the old families of the area and appears to have had something of a privileged childhood, it seems that either she herself was not a wealthy woman or she had financial difficulties in later years. Biographical information on Vedder can be gleaned from the foreword to the reprint edition of her *History of Greene County* and from biographical materials at GCHS.

94. In *Historic Catskill,* Vedder writes: "Opposite the entrance to the Newkirk farm, before the state road was built, was a large boulder known as 'spook rock,' and here at midnight on the anniversaries of her death a huge gray horse with rider and girl appear to superstitious townfolks" (p. 6).

95. Undated handwritten draft of a letter by Vedder, transcribed in 1978 by Raymond Beecher, librarian at the Vedder Memorial Library of the GCHS (Legends–Greene County file). The draft is undated, and no addressee is given. Beecher suggests that it was probably written in the 1930s.

96. Vedder, *Historic Catskill,* p. 6.

97. Vedder letter, Legends–Greene County file, GCHS.

98. See Van Zandt, *The Catskill Mountain House,* p. 308.

99. Letter to Louis Jones, October 15, 1956, Supernatural–Ghosts–Murders file, JFA. The writer of the letter, who apparently lived in Tuxedo, in Orange County, also asks Jones about the possibility of getting a historical marker placed near the site of the 1705 house, where the Salisbury graveyard still stood. Jones's *Spooks of the Valley: Ghost Stories for Boys and Girls* (Boston: Houghton Mifflin, 1948) casts Anna Dorothea Schwartz as German, and has her ghost speak to an onlooking William Salisbury: "ve are vaitink for you to rite mit us" (p. 44).

100. Diane Galusha, "Historic Home with a 'Ghost' Opening as an Antique Shop," Catskill *Daily Mail,* 1975, Leeds–Historic Sites file, GCHS.

101. For the ghostly hitchhiker, see Jan Harold Brunvand, *The Vanishing Hitchhiker: American Urban Legends and Their Meanings* (New York: W. W. Norton, 1981).

102. Kathleen Brogan, *Cultural Haunting: Ghosts and Ethnicity in Recent*

American Literature (Charlottesville: University Press of Virginia, 1998), p. 9. Renée Bergland similarly writes: "From repressions, Freud teaches us, come ghosts"; *The National Uncanny*, p. 11.

103. Avery F. Gordon, *Ghostly Matters: Haunting and the Sociological Imagination* (Minneapolis: University of Minnesota Press, 1997), p. 196.

104. For a concise discussion of the economic and legal marginality of women in the eighteenth century, see Deborah A. Rosen, *Courts and Commerce: Gender, Law, and the Market Economy in Colonial New York* (Columbus: Ohio State University Press, 1997). Explaining coverture, William Blackstone wrote in 1765: "By marriage, the husband and wife are one person in law: that is, the very being or legal existence of the woman is suspended during the marriage, or at least is incorporated and consolidated into that of the husband: under whose wing, protection, and cover, she performs everything"; quoted in Rosen, *Courts and Commerce*, p. 112.

105. In *The National Uncanny*, Bergland writes of a "ghosting" of white women in the nineteenth century, which paralleled the ghosting of Native Americans and slaves. See especially her chapter on Lydia Maria Child's *Hobomok* (pp. 69–82).

106. I have yet to find a version asserting specifically that the girl was Dutch—a remarkable omission, as Dutch ghosts are predominant in regional ghostlore. However, as later chapters will demonstrate, Dutch ghosts are usually portrayed as ancestral. The sense of conflict or lowliness suggested in the case of Anna Dorothea Swarts is perhaps not suited to the images of Dutchness that resonate in regional ghost stories.

107. David Lowenthal, *The Past is a Foreign Country* (Cambridge: Cambridge University Press, 1985).

108. Brogan, *Cultural Haunting*, p. 6.

109. Hine, *West Bank of the Hudson*, p. 41.

110. A. E. P. Searing, *The Land of Rip Van Winkle: A Tour through the Romantic Parts of the Catskills, Its Legends and Traditions* (New York: G. P. Putnam's Sons, Knickerbocker Press, 1884), p. 27.

4. Local Characters

Epigraph: Legends and Poetry of the Hudson (New York: P. S. Wynkoop & Sons, 1868), p. 22.

1. Michael Kammen, *Mystic Chords of Memory: The Transformation of Tradition in American Culture* (New York: Alfred A. Knopf, 1991), p. 93. See

Kammen for an extensive discussion of concepts of tradition in this and other periods in the United States.

2. Scully quoted in ibid., p. 146.

3. Charles Pryer, *Reminiscences of an Old Westchester Homestead* (New York: G. P. Putnam's Sons, Knickerbocker Press, 1897), pp. 166, 167, 171.

4. Ibid., p. 173.

5. Philip H. Smith, *Legends of the Shawangunk (Shon-Gum) and Its Environs* (1887; reprint, Syracuse: Syracuse University Press, 1965) p. ix. The Shawangunks are mountains occupying Orange, Ulster, and Sullivan Counties.

6. Charles M. Skinner, *Myths and Legends of Our Own Land*, vol. 1 (Philadelphia : J. B. Lippincott, 1896). I count the first twenty-one because after this Skinner moves beyond the Hudson Valley into central and western New York. He does come back at the end of that section to a handful of tales from Westchester.

7. *Legends and Poetry of the Hudson*, pp. 28–30. Describing the "gigantic outlines of a recumbent Indian" that were said to be traceable in the Catskills, A. E. P. Searing expresses a more encompassing sense of Indian hauntedness: "Of course he had his story; what hill, or valley, or appearance in nature, had not its reason for being in the misty shadow-land of the Indian's past?"; *The Land of Rip Van Winkle: A Tour through the Romantic Parts of the Catskills, Its Legends and Traditions* (New York: G. P. Putnam's Sons, Knickerbocker Press, 1884), p. 28.

8. *Legends and Poetry of the Hudson*, p. 28. The "Indian lovers' leap" motif generally has the daughter of a chief falling in love with someone of whom her father disapproves, and killing herself by leaping from a high rock or cliff to avoid living without her chosen lover, to escape an arranged marriage, or to mourn a lost lover. Sollors notes that this motif is common throughout the United States, and that variations "have appeared in print at least since William Byrd's *Histories of the Dividing Line* [1728]. Perhaps derived from European legends, these stories were generally of white American origin and merely projected upon the American Indians"; Werner Sollors, *Beyond Ethnicity: Consent and Descent in American Culture* (New York: Oxford University Press, 1986), pp. 114–115. See Ernest Wallace Baughman, *Type and Motif Index of the Folktales of England and North America*, Indiana University Folklore Series, no. 2 (The Hague: Mouton, 1966), for additional sources and variations.

9. Searing, *The Land of Rip Van Winkle,* p. 60. On Tarrytown, see Edgar Mayhew Bacon, *Chronicles of Tarrytown and Sleepy Hollow* (New York: G. P. Putnam's Sons, Knickerbocker Press, 1897), p. 113. The tale about Mahopac appears in Skinner, *Myths and Legends of Our Own Land,* pp. 58–60. Different versions of the tale of Spook Rock in Claverack are given in Roland B. Miller, "Columbia County Legends: A Continuity: Felona, or Spook Rock," *Hudson Daily Star,* [January] 1926, Folklore file, CCHS; and Charles F. Wilde, "Ghost Legends of the Hudson Valley" (Master's thesis, New York State College for Teachers, 1937), pp. 27–28. The legend as applied to Gypsy Rock in Hudson is recorded in JFA, entry 78C. On the Catskills, see Terry James Gordon, "The Legend of Utsayantha," *The Catskills,* winter 1973–1974, pp. 19–20.

10. "Hearing Took on Historical Aspect: Dull Hearing before Commission Brightened by History of Verplanck Property: The Spook Field," *Poughkeepsie Daily Eagle,* February 14, 1913, p. 6. See C. G. Hine, *The New York and Albany Post Road* (New York: privately printed, 1905), p. 31; and Skinner, *Myths and Legends of Our Own Land,* pp. 57–8.

11. For a discussion of Indian hauntings in American literature, see Renée Bergland, *The National Uncanny: Indian Ghosts and American Subjects* (Hanover, N.H.: Dartmouth College, University Press of New England, 2000).

12. *Legends and Poetry of the Hudson,* p. 33.

13. See, for instances, *Legends and Poetry of the Hudson;* Skinner, *Myths and Legends of Our Own Land;* Bacon, *Chronicles of Tarrytown and Sleepy Hollow;* and Daniel Wise, *Summer Days on the Hudson: The Story of a Pleasure Tour from Sandy Hook to the Saranac Lakes* (New York: Nelson and Phillips, 1876). The Dobbs Ferry story appears in *Legends and Poetry of the Hudson,* pp. 56–62.

14. Skinner, *Myths and Legends of Our Own Land,* p. 37. Some tales simply tripped over themselves with exaggerated Dutchness. Here, for example, is the opening of Skinner's version of "The Baker's Dozen": "BAAS [BOSS] VOLCKERT JAN PIETERSEN VAN AMSTERDAM kept a bake-shop in Albany"; and here is how Baas speaks: "Vell, den, if you vant anodder, go to de duyvil and ged it"; ibid., pp. 29, 30.

15. See, for instance, *Legends and Poetry of the Hudson,* pp. 54–55; Searing, *The Land of Rip Van Winkle,* p. 91; and Bacon, *Chronicles of Tarrytown and Sleepy Hollow,* p. 106.

16. Searing, *The Land of Rip Van Winkle*, p. 111. Searing spells the town's name "Caatsbaan." See also JFA, entry 32, in which a man from Coxsackie tries speaking to a ghost in Dutch before trying English.

17. C. G. Hine, *The Old Mine Road* (1908; reprint, New Brunswick, N.J.: Rutgers University Press, 1963), p. 24. See ibid., pp. 24–26, regarding stories about this church involving a ghostly painter and a hobgoblin (related to an Irving story about the Heer of the Dunderberg). On Kingston's Old Dutch Church, see also JFA, entry 32.88, which involves a haunting by old Dutch townsmen. Charles Pryer also reveals a penchant in local imagination for old Dutch houses. See "The Mystery of a Pelham Farmhouse," in *Reminiscences of an Old Westchester Homestead*. Stories involving Dutch manor houses appear in Hine, *The Old Mine Road*, p. 31; in Wilde, "Ghost Legends of the Hudson Valley," pp. 18, 29, and 44; and in JFA, entry 97.33. Several accounts of ghosts at Van Cortlandt Manor are in the Westchester County, N.Y.–Folklore file, WCHS.

18. Regarding the history and persistence of Hudson Valley Dutch culture and language, see Elisabeth Paling Funk, "Washington Irving and His Dutch American Heritage" (Ph.D. diss., Fordham University, 1986); and Van Cleaf Bachman, Alice P. Kenney, and Lawrence G. Van Loon, "Het Poelmeisie: An Introduction to the Hudson Valley Dutch Dialect," *New York History* 61 (April 1980): 161–185.

19. L. Maria Child, *Letters from New-York* (New York: Charles S. Francis; Boston: John Munroe, 1843), pp. 18, 164, 162. For a similar depiction of Dutch antiqueness, see Washington Irving, "Communipaw," *The Knickerbocker*, September 1839, pp. 257–262.

20. Hal Redington, "Up the Hudson," *Rockland County Journal*, October 27, 1877, p. 1.

21. Searing, *The Land of Rip Van Winkle*, p. 91. Compare the phraseology, for instance, with that of Wallace Bruce in *The Hudson River by Daylight* (New York: John Featherstone, 1873), where he says that Pollipel's Island was "supposed by the Indians to be a supernatural spot" (p. 47).

22. Searing, *The Land of Rip Van Winkle*, p. 113.

23. Skinner, *Myths and Legends of Our Own Land*, pp. 21–22. Skinner continues: "and thus it was that Rip Van Winkle found [the crew] on the eve of his famous sleep" (p. 22).

24. "Hearing Took on Historical Aspect," p. 6. For other stories that link Indian and Dutch elements, see Miller, "Columbia County Legends," in which a rock associated with an Indian tragedy is supposed to move

when the bells of the Dutch church ring; and Henry D. B. Bailey, *Local Tales and Historical Sketches* (Fishkill Landing, N.Y.: John W. Spaight, Fishkill Standard Office, 1874), p. 87, in which an Indian maiden dies of heartbreak after being abandoned by her Dutch sailor lover.

25. F. Shonnard and W. W. Spooner, *History of Westchester County: From Its Earliest Settlement to the Year 1900* (1900; reprint, Harrison, N.Y.: Harbor Hill, 1974), p. 101.

26. Pryer, *Reminiscences of an Old Westchester Homestead*, pp. 14, 16. "States-General" refers to the Dutch legislative assembly.

27. Ibid., p. 18. The names are drawn from real names of prominent Hudson Valley Dutch families, but they are also puns—Tenbroeck for "ten breeches," indicating a Dutch habit of layering clothing (a pun used by Irving in *A History of New York*), and Beakman, indicating a "long beak," or nose.

28. Ibid., p. 16.

29. *The History of Greene County* (New York: J. B. Beers, 1884), p. 19. To explain the Indians' disappearance, the author refers to a legend that comes from "a descendant of the old Dutch settlers" (p. 20).

30. Alice P. Kenney, *Stubborn for Liberty: The Dutch in New York* (Syracuse: Syracuse University Press, 1975), p. 235. For efforts to recover colonial Dutch history, and obstacles to this recovery, see ibid., pp. 235–254.

31. See Bachman, Kenney, and Van Loon, "Het Poelmeisie," for a discussion of the attitudes of Dutch-speaking enclaves toward outsiders in the late nineteenth and early twentieth centuries.

32. Bergland, *The National Uncanny*, p. 3.

33. Skinner, *Myths and Legends of Our Own Land*, p. 57; Frank H. Pierson, "The Crawbucky Tales", unpaginated manuscript, 1920, WCHS.

34. Pryer, *Reminiscences of an Old Westchester Homestead*, pp. 17–18. Pryer employs this territorial language throughout the tale: "the domain of the spirits" (p. 16). For fears about trespassing on Indian burial grounds, see also Wise, *Summer Days on the Hudson*, p. 56.

35. Sollors, *Beyond Ethnicity*, p. 123.

36. Writing of the town of Caatsbaan (or Katsbaan), which was well stocked with Dutch houses, Searing's "Miss Rutherford" says: "altogether the place has an old-world haunted look, and even its ghosts would seem foreign fancy"; Searing, *The Land of Rip Van Winkle*, p. 111.

37. Arthur Abbott, *The Hudson River Today and Yesterday* (New York: Historian Publishing, 1915), pp. 50, 51, 3.

38. The population of Westchester had grown from 58,263 in 1850 to 131,348 in 1870; the population numbers for Westchester dipped between 1870 and 1880 as a result of New York City's annexation of sections of the county, but starting from the 1880 census of 108,988, the population rose to 184,257 in 1900, and then to 283,055 in 1910. Between the Civil War and 1900, 200,000 acres went out of cultivation in Westchester; Stephen J. Friedman, "Industrialization, Immigration and Transportation to 1900," in *Westchester County: The Past Hundred Years, 1883–1983,* ed. Marilyn E. Wiegold (Valhalla, N.Y.: Westchester County Historical Society, 1984), p. 53.

39. Ibid., p. 69.

40. For details, see ibid. Between 1870 and 1900 the population of New Rochelle went from 3,915 to 14,720. Friedman writes that after 1893, when the New Haven Railroad began construction in the Mt. Vernon–New Rochelle region, large numbers of Italian immigrants began to arrive (p. 62), and he notes that New Rochelle was one of two cities in Westchester (the other being Yonkers) to experience conflicts between Irish and African-American laborers in this period (p. 67). New Rochelle had the highest railroad valuation in the county by 1901–$1,498,500–a massive leap from 1890, when the assessed value was $104,800 (p. 59). The two lines that joined in New Rochelle in 1873 were the New York, New Haven and Hartford, and the Harlem Railroad (p. 55). See also *New Rochelle: Portrait of a City* (New York: Abbeville Press, 1981).

41. Pryer, *Reminiscences of an Old Westchester Homestead,* pp. 2, 167. For biographical information on Pryer, see "Death Takes Charles Pryer," *New Rochelle Pioneer,* June 9, 1916; and "Charles Pryer Dies in New York City," New Rochelle *Paragraph,* June 9, 1916, both in biographical vertical files, WCHS; and *The Biographical History of Westchester County, New York,* vol. 2 (Chicago: Lewis Publishing, 1899). Pryer, a native of New Rochelle, was a financier, author, and yachtsman and had been director of the Knickerbocker Press. He was of prominent Huguenot and English descent. His ancestor Jasper Pryer had founded the family in Westchester in 1692.

42. *Legends and Poetry of the Hudson,* pp. 40–41, 15.

43. For a discussion of historical interest in and treatment of the New York–area Dutch, see Kenney, *Stubborn for Liberty,* chap. 12, "Recovering the Dutch Tradition."

44. David M. Kinnear, *Mynheer Van Schlichtenhorth and the Old Dutch*

Burghers: A Tale of Old and New Albany (Albany: privately published, 1906), unpaginated.

45. Sollors, *Beyond Ethnicity*, p. 125. Bergland, drawing from Sollors, writes that when white Americans "constructed Indians as ghosts and joyfully acquiesced [in] their own hauntedness, [they] replaced their ancestral specters with American specters"; Indian hauntings signified a "successful appropriation of the American spirit"; *The National Uncanny*, p. 19.

46. New Rochelle was settled by thirty-three Huguenot families in the 1680s, and of forty-four families living there in 1698, thirty-nine were French, three Dutch, one German, and one English. According to *New Rochelle: Portrait of a City*, "That community was distinctly French. French was spoken, and it was common practice for people in neighboring areas to send their children to New Rochelle to learn the language" (pp. 12, 14).

47. Pryer, *Reminiscences of an Old Westchester Homestead*, pp. 4–5. A. E. P. Searing, whose maternal great-grandmother was from a "Holland-Dutch family," recalls a similar scene: when her grandmother tells her about Hudson's voyage, "Anne had only to shut her eyes and, lo! she *was* Hendrik Hudson"; *When Granny Was a Little Girl* (Garden City, N.Y.: Doubleday, Page, 1926), pp. 51, 33.

48. Pryer, *Reminiscences of an Old Westchester Homestead*, p. 173. Pryer closes this and other tales with forecasts of his own death. As he was only in his forties when *Reminiscences* was published, it seems either that he was a sickly man or that was presenting himself as older than he was. He died in 1916.

49. Bergland, *The National Uncanny*, p. 4.

50. C. G. Hine, *The West Bank of the Hudson River: Albany to Tappan* (1906; reprint, Astoria, N.Y.: J. C. and A. L. Fawcett, n.d.), p. 113.

51. G. H. B., "Comboan's Vall," in "Fireside Tales," *Rockland Record* 3 (1940): 76–79, Folklore file, New City Library, Rockland Room, New City, N.Y. Another story of this type occurs at Spook Rock in Rockland County, where the ghost of a Dutch girl killed by Indians returns to curse them. Responsibility is more circular, but the end result is the same: the tribe eventually disappears; J. Fred Geist, "Ghost of Pioneer Maiden Still Haunts Spook Rock," Nyack *Journal-News*, September 26, 1940, as collected in Cornelia F. Bedell, *Now and Then and Long Ago in Rockland County, New York* (1941; reprint, New City, N.Y.: Historical Society of Rockland County, 1968), pp. 33–35.

52. The authors of *History of Westchester County* (1900) comment: "The last ghastly memorials of the slaughter have long since passed away, but local tradition preserves the recollection of many mounds under which the bones of the slain were interred"; Shonnard and Spooner, *History of Westchester County*, p. 101.

53. Ibid., p. 100. This history indicates that Underhill was central in both planning and executing the attack.

54. Bedford was settled in 1680 when twenty-two men from Stamford, Connecticut, bought 7,673 acres from the Katonah and other Indians; *A Short Historical Tour of Bedford* (Bedford, N.Y.: Bedford Historical Society, 1965), p. 4.

55. Bacon, *Chronicles of Tarrytown and Sleepy Hollow*, pp. 102–103.

56. For broader patterns of Revolutionary memory, and for issues affecting such memory in the nineteenth century, see Michael Kammen, *A Season of Youth: The American Revolution and Historical Imagination* (New York: Alfred A. Knopf, 1978); and Lewis Perry, *Boats against the Current: American Culture between Revolution and Modernity, 1820–1860* (New York: Oxford University Press, 1993). For the awakening of historical interest in the Revolution in the region, see Daniel R. Porter, "The Knickerbockers and the Historic Site in New York State," *New York History* 64 (January 1983): 35–50.

57. *Legends and Poetry of the Hudson*, p. 65.

58. Kirk Munroe, "A Canoe Camp 'mid the Hudson Highlands," *Outing and the Wheelman*, December 1884, p. 164.

59. Wallace Bruce, "The Long Drama," read at the Centennial of the Disbanding of the American Army, Newburgh, N.Y., 1883, collected in Wallace Bruce, *Old Homestead Poems* (New York: Harper and Brothers, 1888), pp. 39–46.

60. Some patriotic ghosts do appear in the Hudson Valley. According to folklore current at West Point in the 1940s, for instance, the ghosts of Generals Washington, Lafayette, and Kosciusko were all said to appear at various times, and could be approached by cadets for advice; and the sounds of the Continental Army's cannons are said to echo from the ruins of Fort Putnam there every Fourth of July. Meanwhile, the traitor Benedict Arnold is perpetually punished here, "doomed to walk for eternity" (JFA, entry 42). General "Mad" Anthony Wayne, who led the surprise night capture of Stony Point in 1779, also appears in ghost form in various places, according to several twentieth-century accounts. See, for instance, Anne

Terranova, "Legends of Rockland County," in *The Rockland County Almanac* (New City, N.Y., 1977), p. 82; and James Reynolds, *Ghosts in American Houses* (New York: Bonanza Books, 1955), pp. 84–92. In another tale from Columbia County, a ghostly Revolutionary War soldier appeared in 1942 to a gathering of people at the Van Schaaick mansion; observers believed the patriot could not sleep at a time of danger for his country (Eileen Thomas, "Tales of Old Columbia," October 25, 1946, Folklore file, CCHS). However, these patriot ghosts of the Revolution appear mainly in twentieth-century folklore—in many cases during World War II. And West Point, though the scene of much Revolutionary War activity, is a problematic, somewhat alien space in the Hudson Valley; its folklore could be considered national, more than regional or local. Also it is an institution dedicated to fostering patriotism. Moreover, even apparently patriotic ghosts can be ambivalent: the ghost of Anthony Wayne is depicted in at least one instance as a sort of demon whose horse gives off sparks and leaves an odor of brimstone; Reynolds, *Ghosts in American Houses*, p. 92.

61. Spook Field: William E. Ver Planck, *The History of Isaacse Ver Planck and His Male Descendants in America* (Fishkill Landing, N.Y.: John W. Spaight, 1892), p. 144. "Bloody Pond" (now called Hessian Lake): Munroe, "Canoe Camp 'mid the Hudson Highlands," p. 168. New Rochelle: Pryer, *Reminiscences of an Old Westchester Homestead*, p. 79. Other tales of enemy soldiers or ambivalent soldiers appear in Croton and Yorktown. See Jane Northshield, ed., *A History of Croton-on-Hudson* (Croton-on-Hudson, N.Y.: Croton-on-Hudson Historical Society, 1976), p. 148; and JFA, entry 147.2, which features a "headless Revolutionary horseman" spoken of by children in the 1880s.

62. Hine, *New York and Albany Post Road*, p. 42.

63. Charles Elmer Allison, *The History of Yonkers* (1896; reprint, Harrison, N.Y.: Harbor Hill, 1984), p. 109.

64. Pryer, *Reminiscences of an Old Westchester Homestead*, pp. 22, 107–108.

65. Of contemporary reactions, Major Benjamin Tallmadge's is typical: "[I] parted from him under the gallows, entirely overwhelmed with grief that so gallant an officer and so accomplished a gentleman should come to such an ignominious end"; quoted in William Abbatt, *The Crisis of the Revolution* (1899; reprint, Harrison, N.Y.: Harbor Hill, 1976), p. 76, n. 3. (For more such reactions, see ibid., pp. 75–76, especially the notes.) With regard to continued sympathy for André, Lydia Maria Child's response on visiting the execution site in 1842 is striking. Remembering "the

beautiful and accomplished young man" who was executed there, Child reacts thus when her guide points to Washington's nearby headquarters: "I turned my back suddenly upon it. The last place on earth where I would wish to think of Washington, is at the grave of André"; *Letters from New-York,* p. 159. See also James Fenimore Cooper, *Notions of the Americans* (1828), quoted in Kammen, *A Season of Youth,* p. 105. As Kammen delineates in *A Season of Youth,* André was one of the most commonly depicted Revolutionary figures in American art, literature, and history (p. 105).

66. Bacon writes of André: "Various sentimental efforts have been made to palliate the conduct of a man who had worked long and successfully to corrupt the military virtue of one whose reputation had before been unblemished"; *Chronicles of Tarrytown and Sleepy Hollow,* p. 84. Bacon being quite adept at irony, it is entirely possible that his reference to the ghost's being heard in recent decades pertains to renewed attention to André and debates over his case in historical magazines and local histories of the period. C. G. Hine writes that contemporary newspapers "harped on the subject" of André; *West Bank of the Hudson,* p. ii.

67. Abbatt, *Crisis of the Revolution,* p. 82.

68. These include Treason Hill, where Arnold passed papers to André; Coe's Corner, the site of a house at which André and the American soldiers guarding him stopped to eat; and Mabie's Tavern (now the Old '76 House) in Tappan, André's last place of confinement before his execution. Not all these hauntings point directly to André. According to a 1977 account, the ghosts at Coe's Corner were those of British soldiers imprisoned there (Terranova, "Legends of Rockland," p. 82). Yet it is possible that these explanations represent dilutions of earlier associations of these places with André's travails.

69. See John Shy, "The Legacy of the American Revolutionary War," in *Legacies of the American Revolution* (Logan: Utah State University, 1978), p. 52. Selections from a collection of wartime reminiscences of Westchester residents collected and transcribed by J. M. McDonald in the 1840s are featured in Bruce A. Rosenberg, *The Neutral Ground: The André Affair and the Background of Cooper's The Spy* (Westport, Conn.: Greenwood, 1994), pp. 87–93.

70. See Abbatt, *Crisis of the Revolution,* pp. 33, 53, and 83, regarding various sources.

71. William Thompson Howell, *The Hudson Highlands,* 2 vols. (New

York: Lens and Riecker for the Fresh Air Club, 1933–34), 1: 83. Howell, who was born in Newburgh, died in 1916.

72. Ibid., pp. 83, 84. Howell supports the assertions of unburied bodies' being left in the landscape by referring to Timothy Dwight's account, months after a battle, of "the bodies of soldiers burned, and of other bodies lying half buried in the waters of Bloody Pond (Highland Lake), where they had been thrown" (p. 84).

73. Ibid., pp. 85, 84, 87.

74. Kammen, *A Season of Youth*, p. 99.

75. See, for instance, Child, *Letters from New-York*, p. 158; or the 1821 account of the British consul of New York, James Buchanan, quoted in Abbatt, *Crisis of the Revolution*, p. 82.

76. On his walk up the east side of the valley, Hine notes that a field near Fishkill, "where there are probably more revolutionary dead buried than in any other spot in the State," is marked only by a single "small granite monument"; *New York and Albany Post Road*, p. 49.

77. Pryer, *Reminiscences of an Old Westchester Homestead*, pp. 79, 106.

78. Harry M. Ward, *The War for Independence and the Transformation of American Society* (London: UCL Press, 1999), p. 36.

79. The conventional estimate of 35,000 loyalists who left New York after the war derives from Alexander C. Flick, *The American Revolution in New York* (1926; reprint, Port Washington, N.Y.: Ira J. Friedman, 1967), p. 222. In *The New York Loyalists* (Knoxville: University of Tennessee Press, 1986), Philip Ranlet challenges Flick's number, estimating that perhaps 20,000 left the region after the war (app. 2).

80. See Ranlet, *The New York Loyalists*, pp. 147–149, for a more nuanced discussion of James De Lancey's loyalist cavalry and their reputation as Cowboys. Ranlet writes that James De Lancey's unpopularity caused his relatives who wished to remain in Westchester to be greatly harassed by patriots.

81. James Fenimore Cooper married Susan De Lancey, a member of this clan, and lived in the De Lancey house in Westchester from 1817–1822 while he was writing *The Spy*. Susan Cooper's father, who had fought on the British side in the war, was allowed to return to the country after 1783 by renouncing his royal commission. Her mother had been one of the women attacked in the burning of the De Lanceys' Bloomingdale in 1777. As Wayne Franklin writes in his introduction to *The Spy*, "Wherever

Cooper looked or wandered in his wife's home county, the tales of her unfortunate family richly covered the ground"; *The Spy, A Tale of the Neutral Ground* (New York: Penguin, 1997), pp. xiii–xv.

82. Dr. James Thacher, quoted in Abbatt, *Crisis of the Revolution*, p. 26. For other accounts of neutral-ground violence, see Timothy Dwight, quoted in ibid.; Rosenberg, *The Neutral Ground*, pp. 87–93; and Bacon, *Chronicles of Tarrytown and Sleepy Hollow*, pp. 71–94.

83. Pierson uses this term in "The Crawbucky Tales." In "A Chronicle of Wolfert's Roost," Irving uses the term "debatable ground," as does the Rand McNally *Hudson River Guide* (Chicago, 1923), p. 10.

84. As quoted in Abbatt, *Crisis of the Revolution*, p. 84.

85. See works by Thomas Jones, Edgar Mayhew Bacon, and William Abbatt, for varying opinions as to whether the three were patriotic militiamen, or "Skinners." Although Washington recommended the three men for rewards for their capture of André, Benjamin Tallmadge, who was involved in the events of André's capture and execution, believed them to be bandits who turned in André out of hope for reward. The three men were rewarded in part with parcels of land confiscated from loyalists.

86. This dialogue is drawn from Abbatt, *Crisis of the Revolution*, pp. 29–30. Abbatt, who bases his account on the testimonies and recollections of the captors, notes some variations.

87. For relevant discussions of *The Spy*, see Franklin's introduction to the Penguin edition of the novel; Rosenberg, *The Neutral Ground;* and Shirley Samuels, *Romances of the Republic: Women, the Family, and Violence in the Literature of the Early American Nation* (New York: Oxford University Press, 1996). "Harvey Birch" turns up in later folklore as a ghost haunting the Dutch church in Fishkill; Augusta Knapp Osborne, "The Green Fly Monster," *New York Folklore Quarterly* 11 (autumn 1955): 215.

88. Kammen, *A Season of Youth*, p. 61.

89. Edward Floyd De Lancey, preface to Thomas Jones, *History of New York during the Revolutionary War*, ed. Edward Floyd De Lancey (1879; reprint, New York: New York Times/Arno Press, 1968). De Lancey was related both to the Westchester De Lanceys and to the book's author by marriage.

90. Abbatt, *Crisis of the Revolution*, p. 36. Abbatt writes of Mabie's on pp. 57–58. On the construction of new reservoirs, a contemporary guidebook, *Little Visits to Historical Points in Westchester County: Ossining and Croton* (Mamaroneck, N.Y.: Richbell Press, 1902), states: "Since 1888 the

building of subsidiary basins and reservoirs in Westchester and Putnam Counties has been steadily prosecuted.... No less than seven of the town-ships of Westchester county [Cortlandt, Yorktown, New Castle, Bedford, Somers, Lewisboro, and North Salem] have made extensive contributions of land ... involving the extinction of several settlements" (p. 139). For a more recent historical take on the New Croton works, see Mary Josephine D'Alvia, *The History of the New Croton Dam* (N.p.: privately published, 1976).

91. Pryer, *Reminiscences of an Old Westchester Homestead*, pp. 104–105.

92. Carl Carmer, *The Hudson* (New York: Rinehart, 1939), p. 136.

93. Claude Halstead Van Tyne, *The Loyalists in the American Revolution* (1902; reprint, Gloucester, Mass.: Peter Smith, 1959), p. vii. See Lawrence H. Leder, ed., *Loyalist Historians* (New York: Harper and Row, 1971), for a dis-cussion of how historical attention to the loyalists corresponded to mo-ments of social upheaval.

94. For a discussion of Anglophilia in American culture of this period, see Kammen, *Mystic Chords of Memory*, pp. 172–175. Pryer, the raconteur of a number of ambiguous neutral-ground hauntings, was a member not only of regional historical and genealogical societies, but also of the Royal Society of Arts and the Royal Society Club of London; "Charles Pryer Dies in New York City," New Rochelle *Paragraph*, June 9, 1916, biographi-cal vertical files, WCHS. On Abbatt's "conservative outlook," see Jeff Canning, "William Abbatt and His Historical Work," in Abbatt, *Crisis of the Revolution*. Edgar Mayhew Bacon seems to have had an exceptional at-titude among contemporary Westchester writers and historians. Bacon, who was eligible for membership in the Sons of the American Revolution but never joined (biographical vertical files, WCHS), demonstrates a rela-tively laissez-faire attitude toward development in the preface to *Chronicles of Tarrytown and Sleepy Hollow:* "Houses wherein generations have lived and died, haunted with memories, disappear each year to make place for bright new bricks and mortar—that is to say, for the planting of the seeds which, in time, will yield a crop of new chronicles" (p. iii).

95. Quoted in Abbatt, *Crisis of the Revolution*, p. 84.

96. Pryer, *Reminiscences of an Old Westchester Homestead*, pp. 120–121.

97. For a discussion of scenes of locomotives interrupting pastoral mo-ments, see Leo Marx, *The Machine in the Garden: Technology and the Pastoral Ideal in America* (London: Oxford University Press, 1964). Pryer's passage echoes one from Hawthorne: "there is the whistle of the locomotive—the

long shriek, harsh, above all other harshness . . . and no wonder that it gives such a startling shriek, since it brings the noisy world into the midst of our slumbrous peace" (quoted in Marx, *Machine in the Garden*, p. 13). See also Henry David Thoreau's "Sounds" chapter in *Walden*.

98. Searing, *The Land of Rip Van Winkle*, pp. 46, 89.

99. Hine, *West Bank of the Hudson*, p. 50.

100. One early-twentieth-century New York Central advertisement depicts the Hudson Palisades as haunted by Indians, while in the clouds above are apparitions of ghostly Dutchmen and Revolutionary War soldiers; New York Central Railroad brochure, "The Valley of the Hudson River," n.d., p. 3, in "Uncatalogued collection of pamphlets and books pertaining to the Hudson River," Local History and Genealogy, New York Public Library, New York City.

101. Alexander Bolling, quoted in K. Leroy Irvis, "Negro Folktales from Eastern New York," *New York Folklore Quarterly* 11 (autumn 1955): 170.

102. JFA, entry 73. The informant in this case had been a conductor on the New York Central. The story is clearly related to tales of ghostly appearances of Lincoln's funeral train, which was said to return each April; see Louis C. Jones, "The Ghosts of New York," *Journal of American Folklore* 57 (October–December 1944): 244. But in this instance no mention is made of Lincoln.

103. JFA, entries 97.2 and 97.III.

104. For a history of ironworks in the region see Irene D. Neu, "Hudson Valley Extractive Industries before 1815," in *Business Enterprise in Early New York*, ed. Joseph R. Frese and Jacob Judd (Tarrytown, N.Y.: Sleepy Hollow Press, 1979), pp. 133–165; and James M. Ransom, *Vanishing Ironworks of the Ramapos: The Story of the Forges, Furnaces, and Mines of the New Jersey–New York Border Area* (New Brunswick, N.J.: Rutgers University Press, 1966).

105. "Frank Forester" [Henry William Herbert], *The Warwick Woodlands; or, Things as They Were Twenty Years Ago* (Philadelphia: T. B. Peterson and Brothers, 1850), p. 12.

106. E. Oakes Smith, *The Salamander; Found amongst the Papers of the Late Ernest Helfenstein*, 2d ed. (New York: G. P. Putnam, 1849), p. 17.

107. See, for instance, Munroe, "Canoe Camp 'mid the Highlands," p. 170. Along with stories about haunted Pollipel's Island and notice of Hessian ghosts at Bloody Pond, the article directed attention to the remains of the "Forest of the Dean" iron works as "one of the most pictur-

esque ruins to be seen in this country . . . its gray walls . . . mantled with ivy." That the old iron industry had achieved a romantic antiquity at the turn of the century is indicated, too, by Charles Skinner's inclusion of an adaptation of *The Salamander* in *Myths and Legends of Our Own Land;* and by C. G. Hine's 1908 book, *The Old Mine Road.*

108. For histories and examples related to the rises and declines of Hudson Valley industries, see "A Chronology of Putnam County," compiled by the Putnam County Historical Society Workshop, 1957, PCHS; Bedell, *Now and Then and Long Ago;* O'Brien, *American Sublime;* and monographs on individual industries in the region, including Ransom's *Vanishing Ironworks of the Ramapos* and DeNoyelles's *Within These Gates,* on the brickworks of Haverstraw.

109. Yonkers *Statesman,* January 11, 1872, quoted in Louis Torres, *Tuckahoe Marble: The Rise and Fall of an Industry, 1822–1930* (Harrison, N.Y.: Harbor Hill, 1976), pp. 58–59.

110. Oliver Goldsmith's poem "The Deserted Village" (1768–1770) centers on the narrator's memory of a rural English village that has been deserted as a result of the enclosure acts of the eighteenth century. He writes: "but times are altered; trade's unfeeling train / Usurp the land, and dispossess the swain / . . . . Here, as I take my solitary rounds / Amidst thy tangling walks and ruined grounds / And, many a year elapsed, return to view / Where once the cottage stood, the hawthorn grew / Here, as with doubtful pensive steps I range, / Trace every scene, and wonder at the change / . . . Even now, methinks, as pondering here I stand, / I see the rural virtues leave the land"; Martin Price, ed., *The Oxford Anthology of English Literature: The Restoration and the Eighteenth Century* (New York: Oxford University Press, 1973), pp. 691, 698.

111. Searing, *The Land of Rip Van Winkle,* p. 48.

112. Hine, *New York and Albany Post Road,* p. 55.

113. In High Falls, in Ulster County, says one account in the Jones Archives, "there is a famous (in the locality) quarry. It is a favorite place for men to commit suicide, and for murderers to throw away bodies of the murdered. Now on a moonlight night if you chance to walk past this quarry . . . you see the heads of all those people that have the quarry as their burying place" (JFA, entry 142). Another example of this sort occurs in Haverstraw: in the days before the extension of electric lighting, a section near the brickyard clay pits was believed to be haunted by a giant ghost dog who protected women on their way home from work (JFA, en-

try 175). Another claybank haunting occurs at Glasco (Ulster County) and is supposed to be that of a man killed after a saloon fight around 1915 (JFA, entry 97.96).

114. JFA, entry 32.66. Another informant remembered seeing this same railroad ghost, who "seemed to glide past us like a streak"; JFA, entry 32.65.

115. JFA, entry 97.99. It does not seem that the landslide recorded here is the infamous Haverstraw landslide of 1906, which killed nineteen people and destroyed a number of houses.

116. JFA, entry 97.97.

117. JFA, entries 175.2 and 32.72.

118. JFA, entry 175.2.

119. JFA, entry 32.72.

120. The category "preindustrial" derives from Herbert Gutman's usage in "Work, Culture, and Society in Industrializing America, 1815–1919," in *Work, Culture, and Society in Industrializing America: Essays in American Working-Class and Social History* (New York: Vintage, 1977). In *Worker and Community: Response to Industrialization in a Nineteenth-Century American City, Albany, New York, 1850–1884* (Albany: State University of New York Press, 1985), Brian Greenberg credits Gutman with driving the efforts of "new labor historians" to go beyond simple conceptions of class: to understand the "values that generated and guided workers' response to their newly acquired class position" and to "recreate workers' persistent efforts to resist the impositions of capitalist industrialization" (p. 3). However, Greenberg, among others, criticizes Gutman's bipolar counterposing of preindustrial and industrial as assuming that "industrialization involved an irreversible transition from one ideal social type, traditional society, to its mirror opposite, modernity" (p. 4). For broader discussions of how immigrant cultural backgrounds shaped working-class culture and movements, see Lizabeth Cohen, *Making a New Deal: Industrial Workers in Chicago, 1919–1939* (Cambridge: Cambridge University Press, 1990); and Roy Rosenzweig, *Eight Hours for What We Will: Workers and Leisure in an Industrial City, 1870–1920* (Cambridge: Cambridge University Press, 1983).

121. JFA, entry 97.99.

122. JFA, entry 97.97.

123. This pattern of widespread belief or currency based on slim evidence runs throughout these ghost stories and is, in essence, what gives them meaning and impact. Bolling went on to tell stories of an angry spirit

along the railroad tracks because his wife fell down; Margaret May perpetuated stories of John McGowan's ghost at Haverstraw because she heard someone say "giddap" and "hello" in the street.

124. In Chesnutt's "conjure" tales, written in the 1880s and 1890s, "Uncle Julius," an ex-slave, tells stories of ghosts and conjuring to the new, white, northern-born owner of a North Carolina plantation. In most of the instances, the owner later discovers that there may be an ulterior motive to Julius's stories. For instance, in "The Gray Wolf's Ha'nt," Julius tells the owner a ghost story that would dissuade him from clearing a certain haunted patch of land. When the owner clears the patch in spite of the story, he discovers a "bee-tree," and concludes: "I have reason to believe that. . . . Julius had been getting honey from this tree. The gray wolf's haunt had doubtless proved useful in keeping off too inquisitive people, who might have interfered with his monopoly"; Charles W. Chesnutt, *The Conjure Woman and Other Conjure Tales,* ed. Richard H. Brodhead (Durham, N.C.: Duke University Press, 1993), p. 106.

125. JFA, entry 32.83. A somewhat similar story, involving domestic servants, was told regarding Lindenwald (the Kinderhook mansion once home of Martin Van Buren) by a local businessman and lawyer, who in turn heard it from his family's "old colored servants." When new owners were going to take possession of the empty mansion, a neighbor sent one of her servants, an African-American man named Tom, to clean the kitchen. Tom expressed reluctance to do so, on the claim that the ghost of "Aunt Sarah," Van Buren's cook, maintained her rule over the kitchen in which she had served. And indeed, no sooner had he gone than he returned with this story: "The minute I took up a pan I heard a sound. I looked up and down the chimney came Aunt Sarah. She was all covered with soot, and her eyes were gleaming and blazing and the ends of her kerchief stood up on her head just like horns. So I said to myself: 'Tom, you're getting out of this cellar as fast as you can, and nobody's going to make you go back'"; JFA, entry 87.

126. JFA, entry 32.72.

127. *Legends and Poetry of the Hudson,* p. 22; Skinner, *Myths and Legends of Our Own Land,* p. 58.

128. Carmer, *The Hudson,* pp. 331, 337.

129. This is not to say that there are not new varieties of worker ghosts—or immigrant ghosts—to be found in subsequent regional vernacular cul-

ture, only this lore has yet to be made more widely accessible in the way that the folklore craze of the 1930s and 1940s made accessible the tales of worker ghosts from preceding decades.

5. Possessing High Tor Mountain

Epigraph: Maxwell Anderson, *High Tor: A Play in Three Acts* (Washington, D.C.: Anderson House, 1937), p. 77.

1. Anderson, *High Tor,* p. 24. Maxwell Anderson (1888–1959), a prolific and well-noted playwright, wrote nearly forty plays, almost thirty of which appeared on Broadway, including *What Price Glory* (1924); *Both Your Houses* (1933), which won the Pulitzer Prize; *Valley Forge* (1934); *Winterset* (1935) and *High Tor* (1937), both of which won New York Drama Critics Circle Awards; *Key Largo* (1939); and *Knickerbocker Holiday,* a musical with Kurt Weill (1938). He also wrote screenplays, including *All Quiet on the Western Front;* radio plays; poetry; a novel; and two collections of essays on theater. For biographical information see primarily Alfred Shivers, *Maxwell Anderson* (Boston: Twayne, 1976) and *The Life of Maxwell Anderson* (New York: Stein and Day, 1983). Other information can be gleaned from Barbara Lee Horn, *Maxwell Anderson: A Research and Production Sourcebook* (Westport, Conn.: Greenwood, 1996); Laurence G. Avery, ed., *Dramatist in America: Letters of Maxwell Anderson, 1912–1958* (Chapel Hill: University of North Carolina Press, 1977); and several short pieces written by Anderson's son, Alan Haskett Anderson, especially "The Rockland Years: Maxwell Anderson on South Mountain Road," *South of the Mountain* 32 (July–September 1988): 3–9; and "Maxwell Who?" in *Maxwell Anderson and the New York Stage,* ed. Kenneth Krauss and Nancy H. Doran Hazelton (Monroe, N.Y.: Library Research Associates, 1991).

2. From the citation accompanying the Drama Critics Circle Award, quoted in Avery, *Dramatist in America,* p. 295.

3. Shivers, *Maxwell Anderson,* p. 114.

4. Legends of buried treasures guarded by ghosts or supernatural beings abound in the lore of the Hudson Valley, many of them based on the fact that the pirate William Kidd was known to frequent the region. For examples see Patricia Edwards Clyne, *Hudson Valley Tales and Trails* (Woodstock, N.Y.: Overlook, 1990), pp. 249–254; Washington Irving, "The Money Diggers," in *Tales of a Traveller* (1824), ed. Judith Giblin Haig (Boston: Twayne, 1987); Charles Pryer, "The Treasure Hunters," in *Reminis-*

cences of an Old Westchester Homestead (New York: G. P. Putnam's Sons, Knickerbocker Press, 1897); Frank H. Pierson, "The Treasure Hunters," in "The Crawbucky Tales," manuscript, 1920, WCHS; and Kirk Munroe, "A Canoe Camp 'mid the Hudson Highlands," *Outing and the Wheelman*, December 1884, pp. 167–168. For a discussion of treasure-hunting tales in the Northeast, see Alan Taylor, "The Early Republic's Supernatural Economy: Treasure Seeking in the American Northeast, 1780–1830," *American Quarterly* 38 (spring 1986): 6–34.

5. To present only a handful of related examples: Charles Pryer writes that the tenant of a haunted Pelham farmhouse "thoroughly resolved to give the spirits full possession of the house on the following day [and although] this happened fifty years ago, the house has been empty ever since"; *Reminiscences of an Old Westchester Homestead*, pp. 11–12. The Jones collection reveals a great number of hauntings that arise from property disputes, and of places whose abandonments are explained by hauntings, including houses in Waterford (JFA, entries 61.63 and 61.71), Amenia (entry 45), Crescent (entry 50), and Warwick (entry 61.53), as well as a hayfield in Rhinebeck (entry 32.4).

6. Opinion of Justice Rubin of the New York State Supreme Court, Appellate Division, in *Stambovsky v. Ackley*, cited in Jesse Dukeminier and James E. Krier, *Property*, 3d ed. (Boston: Little, Brown, 1993), pp. 605–609. Other cases of ghosts taking official dimensions occur. The 1830s assessment rolls of Poughkeepsie, for instance, register a "haunted house"; Helen Myers, "Countian Recalls Tales of Restless Ghosts That Haunted Famous East Fishkill Tavern," *Poughkeepsie Sunday New Yorker*, July 11, 1954, p. C1.

7. Born in rural Pennsylvania, the son of a Baptist preacher, Anderson graduated from the University of North Dakota, his family having come to settle there after eleven moves in nineteen years. After receiving a master's in English at Stanford in 1914, he taught at high schools and at Whittier College before moving to New York City in 1918 to write for the *New Republic*, and then for the *Globe* and the *New York World*. In 1921 he bought thirty acres and a farmhouse on South Mountain Road in New City, in Rockland County, and moved his family there in 1922. He lived there for thirty years before moving with his third wife to Stamford, Connecticut, in 1955.

8. Among Anderson's neighbors were artist Henry Varnum Poor; composer Kurt Weill and his wife, actress Lotte Lenya; actors Rollo Peters and

Burgess Meredith; artist and woodcarver Carroll French; landscape architect Mary Mowbray-Clarke; and poet Amy Murray. Henry Varnum Poor's paintings of the mountain include *Gray Day* (1933) and *Lotte Lenya's House and High Tor* (1932). Amy Murray's "Looking East at Sunrise," which depicts wispy ghosts in the mountain's shadows, appeared in her 1940 collection *November Hereabout,* for which Anderson wrote the foreword.

9. Alan Haskett Anderson, "The Rockland Years," p. 7.

10. In the play Anderson remarks negatively about the road and the factory, comparing the latter with Sing Sing prison.

11. According to Alan Anderson, "Dad was disturbed about the traprock company tearing down the mountain for road material"; quoted in Nancy Cacioppo, "High Tor Remembered," Rockland County *Journal-News,* November 12, 1984, p. D1. According to a 1942 article, 600,000 to 1 million cubic yards of traprock were being quarried from Middle Mountain each year; Isabelle K. Savell, "High Tor on the Hudson Being Sought for a Park," *New York Times,* November 15, 1942, sec. II, p. 6.

12. Traprock quarrying was also being done at Mount Taurus and Little Stony Point to the north. See Francis F. Dunwell, *The Hudson River Highlands* (New York: Columbia University Press, 1991), pp. 186–201. Dunwell writes that in 1931 "the Hudson River Stone Corporation bought 1000 acres on Mt. Taurus . . . and began quarrying at a speed never previously witnessed" (p. 186).

13. Shivers, *Maxwell Anderson,* p. 115.

14. "Mounting High Tor," *New York Times,* February 14, 1937, sec. X, p. 2. Meredith played the lead in *High Tor.*

15. Savell, "High Tor Being Sought for Park."

16. Raymond O'Brien, *American Sublime: Landscape and Scenery of the Lower Hudson Valley* (New York: Columbia University Press, 1981), pp. 55, 59–60.

17. Shivers, *Maxwell Anderson,* p. 115. Elmer Van Orden held that George Washington had once drunk from the spring behind his house; "High Tor Owner Sees Play: Elmer Van Orden Objects to Stage Rocks and Burgess Meredith Selling Out," New York *Sun,* March 18, 1937, p. 35. Another source claimed that Washington had used High Tor as a lookout and planning point; Danton Walker, *Spooks Deluxe: Some Excursions into the Supernatural* (New York: Franklin Watts, 1956), p. 165.

18. O'Brien, *American Sublime,* pp. 95, 93. For local industrial history see Cornelia F. Bedell, *Now and Then and Long Ago in Rockland County,*

New York (1941; reprint, New City, N.Y.: Historical Society of Rockland County, 1968); and Daniel DeNoyelles, *Within These Gates* (Thiells, N.Y.: privately published, 1982).

19. Anderson describes the brickyard lagoons in *High Tor*, p. 112. See also Charles Holbrook, "Running through History from Haverstraw to Upper Nyack," *South of the Mountain* 37 (October–December 1993): 13–16.

20. Clyne, *Hudson Valley Tales and Trails*, p. 218. This legend is also associated with other mountains along the river.

21. Dirck St. Remy, *Stories of the Hudson*, 3d ed. (New York: G. P. Putnam and Sons, 1871), pp. 164–173. For a less convoluted synopsis see Paul Wilstach, *Hudson River Landings* (Indianapolis: Bobbs-Merrill, 1933), p. 26; or Patricia Edwards Clyne, "Legendary High Tor," *Hudson Valley*, June 1986, p. 34.

22. Charles M. Skinner, *Myths and Legends of Our Own Land* (Philadelphia: J. B. Lippincott, 1896), pp. 53–56. This story is obviously related to the 1848 novel *The Salamander*, by E. Oakes Smith, which incorporates High Tor. Versions of this legend can be found in Clyne, "Legendary High Tor," p. 34; and Jane McDill Anderson, *Rocklandia: A Collection of Facts and Fancies, Legends and Ghost Stories of Rockland County Life* (N.p.: Morgan and Morgan, 1977), p. 19, where it is tied specifically to a band of ironworkers from the Harz Mountains in Germany who came to work in the Hassenclever Mines in 1740.

23. Daniel DeNoyelles, "Camping on High Tor," *South of the Mountain* 21 (January–March 1977): 21.

24. According to Isabelle Savell, "To Save a Mountain—High Tor," *South of the Mountain* 32 (July–September 1988): 16, Van Orden "always insisted there were ghosts on the craggy peak. 'Sometimes come right down to my strawberry patch,' he would say." A 1937 New York *Sun* article reports: "Some folks may think the scenes of the play dealing with the ghosts . . . are sort of fantastic, but Mr. Van Orden doesn't think so. 'I've seen 'em,' he announces solemnly'"; "High Tor Owner Sees Play." The story of Van Orden's fiancée appears in several sources, including New York newspaper columnist Danton Walker's 1956 book *Spooks Deluxe*, in which Walker writes that a neighbor told him of a ghost who haunted her eighteenth-century farmhouse along the mountain. This neighbor said that Van Orden identified the ghost; *Spooks Deluxe*, pp. 166–167. See also Cathy Carroll, "Farmhouse's Demolition Prompts an Outcry," Rockland County *Journal-News*, March 30, 1990, p. A1: "The ghost of a young

woman whom Van Orden had loved was said to have visited Van Orden . . . at the house."

25. These stories appear in a number of sources, including Skinner, *Myths and Legends of Our Own* Land, pp. 46–47 (for Rambout Van Dam) and 49–50 (for the Storm Ship).

26. Walker, *Spooks Deluxe*, p. 165; Shivers, *Maxwell Anderson*, p. 115. The belief that Treason Hill in West Haverstraw was haunted is part of local folklore that I knew growing up in the area.

27. See Bedell, *Now and Then and Long Ago*, pp. 42–45.

28. On Ossining, see Pierson, "The Crawbucky Tales." The headless horseman, of course, is from Irving; the horseman loses his bridge in Edgar Mayhew Bacon, *Chronicles of Tarrytown and Sleepy Hollow* (New York: G. P. Putnam's Sons, Knickerbocker Press, 1897), p. 116.

29. Danton Walker contends in *Spooks Deluxe* that Anderson never met Van Orden before the play (p. 166), but Patricia Edwards Clyne writes that Anderson met Van Orden "shortly after he moved to New City" ("Legendary High Tor," p. 34); and Alan Anderson says that his father had been up to see Van Orden on the mountain (Shivers, *Maxwell Anderson*, p. 119).

30. See Bedell, *Now and Then and Long Ago*, p. 45: "the field worker who got this information [about the Guardian of Hook Mountain] spoke of it to Mrs. Mary Mowbray-Clarke, who mentioned it to Maxwell Anderson, the playwright, who incorporated it as part of a play and book he calls 'High Tor.'"

31. "Mounting High Tor." Alfred Shivers attaches some authority to this article: "The reporter or publicity agent to whom we are indebted for this information recorded the details from—in all likelihood—Anderson's own lips"; *Maxwell Anderson*, p. 118.

32. Maxwell Anderson to the New York Newspaper and Magazine Theater Critics, September 15, 1946, in Avery, *Dramatist in America*, p. 210.

33. Anderson, *High Tor*, pp. 102–103.

34. For production details, see Horn, *Maxwell Anderson*, pp. 36–38.

35. Anderson's ship, the *Onrust*, is a fictional addition to Hudson's enterprise. Hudson's *Half Moon* was unaccompanied.

36. Anderson, *High Tor*, pp. 78–79, 31–32, 23–24.

37. Ibid., p. 110.

38. Ibid., pp. 112–113. Van is associated with the ghosts throughout the play: "Sometimes I stand here at night and look out over the river when a

fog covers the lights. Then if its dark enough and I can't see my hands . . . I'm damned if I know who I am, staring out into that black. Maybe I'm cloud and maybe I'm dust. I might be old as time" (p. 58); "God knows where ghosts leave off and we begin" (p. 111). "The Indian," Anderson wrote in a 1939 letter, was "more symbolic than realistic"; Avery, *Dramatist in America*, p. 84.

39. Anderson, *High Tor*, pp. 111, 127–128, 142.

40. See Nelson Greene, *History of the Valley of the Hudson, River of Destiny, 1609–1930*, vol. 1 (Chicago: S. J. Clarke, 1931), p. 198.

41. For instance: "wraithlike, half-effaced, the print we make upon the air [a] thin tracery, permeable, a web of wind" (Anderson, *High Tor*, p. 31); "meaningless, picked clean of meaning" (p. 34); "stamped forever on the moving air . . . fading out like an old writing" (p. 103). Anderson also uses rhetorical strategies that underline the associations between ghostliness, historical vagueness, evasive narrative, and usable possibility: "Van: 'They say the crew climbed up . . . Maybe the Indians got them. Anyway, on dark nights . . . they say, you sometimes see them.' Judith: 'Have you seen them?' Van: '. . . Maybe I have. You can't be sure" (p. 13).

42. This potential for industrial hauntedness does come to a sort of fruition. An article in *South of the Mountain* (the journal of the Historical Society of Rockland County) presents the industrial ruins at High Tor's base—including disused stone crushers—as incitements to imagination and memory; Holbrook, "Running through History," p. 15.

43. An article dated January 19, 1937, titled "The Story of High Tor, Put Into a Play—It's a Peak Up the Hudson and Long, Long Ago Had Its History Written Down," shows that the New York press rapidly picked up on and helped promote the story behind *High Tor*, which had opened less than two weeks before ("High Tor" file, HSRC). This article, however, which is obviously meant to help urbanites place the mountain, seems to have the wrong mountain in mind or to be making false claims to heighten the peak's importance—confusing High Tor with Stony Point in Revolutionary history. Other articles included "Mounting High Tor" and "High Tor Owner Sees Play."

44. "The Savior of High Tor," *New York Times*, June 17, 1939, sec. I, p. 14; and "Neighbors Honor Owner of High Tor," ibid., June 16, 1939, sec. I, p. 25.

45. The chairmanship was apparently honorary, but Alan Anderson re-

members his father as heading the opposition, and Clyne says that he and the cast of *High Tor* were in the forefront of the fundraising; *Hudson Valley Tales and Trails,* p. 220.

46. Maxwell Anderson to Archer Milton Huntington, August 10, 1942, in Avery, *Dramatist in America,* p. 126. Huntington donated his land at the base of High Tor, and $1,000 to the campaign; Savell, "To Save a Mountain," p. 16.

47. See, for instance, Savell, "High Tor Being Sought for Park": "The Hudson River people know too well what happens when their foothills fall onto the open market. They saw their Palisades chiseled down from Hoboken almost to Englewood; they have seen great raw gashes driven into the foothills beyond the Palisades."

48. Ruth Morgan to Mrs. Maurice Heaton, November 5, 1942, High Tor file, HSRC. High Tor is the highest point in the Palisades, not the Highlands.

49. Quoted in Savell, "To Save a Mountain," p. 15.

50. Ibid., p. 16 (author's note). Receipts, lists of donors, and letters on file at the Historical Society of Rockland County reveal support from people outside the county, including a number of Manhattanites. The Hudson River Conservation Society had its offices in New York City.

51. Amy Murray, "High Tor Sitting for Its Portrait, Offers Many Pictures," Rockland County *Journal-News,* January 13, 1943, p. 5.

52. Savell, "To Save a Mountain," p. 16.

53. "High Tor Lands Purchased by West Nyacker," 1952, High Tor file, HSRC. Danton Walker also credits Anderson with giving the mountain the necessary romance to motivate the conservation campaign; see *Spooks Deluxe,* p. 166; and Walker, "The Ghost on High Tor," *American Weekly,* December 20, 1953, p. 9. A 1942 letter from the Rockland County Conservation Association's Committee to Save High Tor posited ironically that if the mountain were allowed to be sold to the quarry, at least "we shall be able to say to [our children], 'They are going to revive Maxwell Anderson's great play, "High Tor" this year, and you will see what the mountain once meant to us'"; High Tor file, HSRC.

54. Jeffrey Borak, "'High Tor' Created from Anderson's Infatuation with a Rocky Pinnacle," *Poughkeepsie Journal,* February 29, 1980, Entertainment sec., p. 2; James Fair, "High Tor, Ancient and Forever," manuscript, 1992, King's Daughters Public Library, Haverstraw, N.Y.

55. Anderson, *High Tor,* p. 126.

56. Floyd D. Frost, "Why Fuss about High Tor?" letter to the editor, Rockland County *Journal-News*, December 10, 1942, p. 4.

57. See O'Brien, *American Sublime*, for a discussion of how quarrying motivated conservation movements. The Palisades Interstate Park Commission came into being largely to protect against quarrying, and the Hudson River Conservation Society was formed in direct response to quarrying at Mount Taurus.

58. See Bacon, *Chronicles of Tarrytown and Sleepy Hollow*, pp. iv–v. Quoting an earlier commentator on the lack of preservationism in that area in the nineteenth century, Bacon admonishes that such demolitions of tourist-drawing sites are "money out of your pockets" (p. v).

59. Hilton Kramer, "The New Discovery of America," *New York Times Book Review*, January 20, 1974, p. 4; quoted in Michael Kammen, *Mystic Chords of Memory: The Transformation of Tradition in American Culture* (New York: Alfred A. Knopf, 1991), p. 435. See Jane S. Becker, *Selling Tradition: Appalachia and the Construction of an American Folk, 1930–1940* (Chapel Hill: University of North Carolina Press, 1998), for a discussion of the folk phenomenon of the Depression era.

60. Kammen, *Mystic Chords of Memory*, pp. 468–469, 479.

61. For a discussion of Depression-era theater, see Richard H. Pells, *Radical Visions and American Dreams: Culture and Thought in the Depression Years* (Middletown, Conn.: Wesleyan University Press, 1973), pp. 252–263. On the rise of American folklore studies in New York, see Kammen, *Mystic Chords of Memory*, p. 432; and Louis C. Jones, *Three Eyes on the Past: Exploring New York Folk Life* (Syracuse: Syracuse University Press, 1982), pp. xi–xxxvi.

62. Another manifestation of this renaissance of haunting in the Hudson Valley and its attachment to contemporary contexts is Anya Seton's 1944 novel, *Dragonwyck*, a gothic novel about a haunted Hudson Valley manor set in the 1840s, which was distributed to American troops abroad during World War II.

63. O'Brien writes: "After a sleepy hiatus of sorts between 1909 and the coming of the New Deal, a second national wave of conservation consciousness . . . found fertile ground along the Hudson. . . . In the 1930s defenders of the Palisade and highland regions also became alarmed with what were seen as the dire changes caused by the construction of the George Washington Bridge and the long-envisioned Palisades Parkway. Since the opening of the Bear Mountain Bridge and Storm King Highway

in 1923–4, 5 million recreationists per year were pouring into the highlands. They also feared that a prime suburban real estate zone would be developed atop the Palisades"; *American Sublime*, p. 23.

64. Historian Robert McElvaine writes of FDR's interest in conservation: "It was an area that one would expect to be of concern to a Hudson estate owner. At Hyde Park, FDR had overseen the planting of tens of thousands of trees . . . As governor of New York he had put up to 10,000 unemployed men to work on a reforestation program"; Robert S. McElvaine, *The Great Depression: America, 1929–41* (New York: Times Books, 1984), p. 154. According to Kammen, FDR had "personally intervened to ensure that federal post offices in the area near Hyde Park would be built in the colonial style"; *Mystic Chords of Memory*, p. 462. Roosevelt also wrote prefaces for two books on Hudson Valley Dutch colonial houses: Helen Wilkinson Reynolds's *Dutch Houses in the Hudson Valley before 1776* (1929) and Rosalie Fellows Bailey's *Pre-Revolutionary Dutch Houses in Northern New Jersey and Southern New York* (1936).

65. See Kammen, *Mystic Chords of Memory*, p. 371 and elsewhere. Rockefeller had been the motive force behind the restoration of Colonial Williamsburg, beginning in the mid-1920s. In the Hudson Valley, he had made contributions toward preserving Washington's White Plains headquarters in 1917, and in the 1940s became involved in the effort to preserve Philipse Castle—a 1643 Dutch manor house in North Tarrytown, near the Rockefellers' principal home—and Irving's Sunnyside. In the 1950s Rockefeller again stepped in to save Van Cortlandt Manor in Croton. In his regional preservation activities, Rockefeller was not without precedent or company: in 1897 J. P. Morgan, then vice-president of the New York–based American Scenic and Historical Preservation Society, had helped secure state funds for making Stony Point battlefield a park, and had bought land along the Palisades to stop destructive quarrying in 1900; John D. Rockefeller Sr. had also been instrumental in the preservation of the Palisades; see O'Brien, *American Sublime*, pp. 22, 23.

66. The Newburgh site had been Washington's headquarters. See Daniel R. Porter, "The Knickerbockers and the Historic Site in New York State," *New York History* 64 (January 1983): 35. See O'Brien, *American Sublime*, pp. 247–280, regarding the Palisades Interstate Park Commission. After its creation in 1900 the PIPC—which was signed into existence by then governor Teddy Roosevelt—acquired 75 percent of the land along the Palisades from Fort Lee to the state line by 1905. In 1906 its jurisdiction was ex-

tended as far north as Stony Point, and it acquired Hook Mountain and Rockland Lake (1911–1915), Tallman Mountain in 1928 (under threat of quarrying), and then High Tor in 1943. By 1909 the commission had also acquired land in the Highlands—the basis of what is now Harriman State Park—including a 10,000-acre gift from the Harriman family.

67. Letter from Ruth Morgan (RCCA president), November 5, 1942; O'Brien, *American Sublime*, p. 24.

68. See Dunwell, *The Hudson River Highlands*, chap. 11, for details on the activation of private and governmental conservation and preservation sentiments during the 1930s.

69. See Avery's introduction to *Dramatist in America* for a delineation of Anderson's political shift from socialism to a more conservative emphasis on individualism through the 1930s, to anticommunism after World War II. James A. Farley, Roosevelt's campaign manager and postmaster general, and a Rockland County native, comes under attack in the play; Anderson, *High Tor*, p. 8.

70. See Dunwell, *The Hudson River Highlands*, pp. 202–230. Con Edison unveiled the plan in 1962, sparking nearly two decades of protests and legal battles. For power plant controversies, see also Robert H. Boyle, *The Hudson River: A Natural and Unnatural History* (New York: W. W. Norton, 1969), especially chap. 8.

71. For details, see Clyne, *Hudson Valley Tales and Trails*, p. 55; O'Brien, *American Sublime*, pp. 247–280; and *Palisades Interstate Park, 1900–1960* (Bear Mountain, N.Y.: Palisades Interstate Park Commission, 1960).

72. O'Brien, *American Sublime*, p. 28; Kammen, *Mystic Chords*, p. 613.

73. Lewis C. Rubenstein, *Historic Resources of the Hudson: A Preliminary Inventory* ([Tarrytown, N.Y.]: Hudson River Valley Commission, 1969), p. 5.

74. O'Brien, *American Sublime*, p. 14.

75. Jack Focht, quoted in Leslie Boyd, "Lost Towns of Palisades Park: Two Passionate Men Are Trying to Save the Memories," *Rockland Journal-News*, March 7, 1993, p. C12.

76. Frost, "Why Fuss about High Tor?"

77. Ruth Morgan, "For High Tor Conservation," letter to the editor, Rockland County *Journal-News*, December 16, 1942, p. 4.

78. In the landmark case of Storm King, for instance, the people of Cornwall, where the mountain is located, had voted 425 to 25 in favor of Consolidated Edison's plan to built a pumped storage hydroelectric plant

into the side of the mountain. But the plan was challenged by environmental groups that drew support not only from up and down the river valley but also, as Dunwell writes, from "nearly all American states and several foreign countries" (*The Hudson River Highlands*, p. 203). In 1980 the plan was abandoned, and the company donated the 500-acre site for park use. See Dunwell, chap. 12.

79. Alan Haskett Anderson, "The Rockland Years," p. 3.

80. Maxwell Anderson to the University of North Dakota, November 3, 1958, in Avery, *Dramatist in America*, p. 289.

81. Anderson, *High Tor*, p. 111.

82. Kent C. Ryden, *Mapping the Invisible Landscape: Folklore, Writing, and the Sense of Place* (Iowa City: University of Iowa Press, 1993), p. 8.

83. In general, the legends about Hudson Valley hauntings are relocated with striking frequency. The legend regarding High Tor as the place where evil spirits were kept by Manitou, for example, is also found in the folklore of several mountains in the Hudson Highlands, as are tales of thunder-causing imps.

84. New York newspaper columnist Danton Walker commented on Anderson's decisions to incorporate ghosts into the play: "Though keenly aware of the dramatic potentialities of Elmer's long fight with the traprock concern, Anderson also knew that it would have to be embellished for a stage plot. A romance was indeed indicated"; *Spooks Deluxe*, p. 166.

85. Alan Haskett Anderson, "The Rockland Years," p. 7.

86. Shivers, *Maxwell Anderson*, p. 115.

87. Quoted in "High Tor Owner Sees Play." When Burgess Meredith, doing publicity shots on the mountain, mentioned the play to Van Orden, his response—"I'd like to see that goddam show"—seemed less than supportive of the venture; "Mounting High Tor."

88. This view has a factual basis. The number of farms in Rockland County had declined from 1,000 to 355 between 1920 and 1941; Bedell, *Now and Then and Long Ago*, p. 238.

89. William Thompson Howell, *The Hudson Highlands*, 2 vols. (New York: Lens and Riecker for the Fresh Air Club, 1933–34), 1: 115.

90. See Becker, *Selling Tradition*, pp. 1–10.

91. Anderson, *High Tor*, p. 113.

92. "High Tor Owner Sees Play."

93. Croswell Bowen, *Great River of the Mountains: The Hudson* (New York: Hastings House, 1941), p. 8. Carl Carmer offers a similar depiction

of superstitious mountain people in his "Witches Make Star Tracks" chapter of *The Hudson* (New York: Rinehart, 1939).

94. Many of the historic house and site museums in the region have had, at some time, reputations for ghosts. Certainly, some of these museums embrace their ghostlore. Yet some, even as they operate from an idea of historical imagination and restoration that is similar to haunting, have chosen to deemphasize their ghost stories. In the case of Van Cortlandt Manor, for instance—a site that has had at least seven ghosts in its lore over the nineteenth and twentieth centuries, ghosts that the family itself spoke of and that were reported in national publications—Historic Hudson Valley prefers not to emphasize hauntings in its interpretation of the site (as the organization told me several years ago when I called to ask about the house's ghost stories). Local historian Patricia Edwards Clyne writes regarding Van Cortlandt Manor: "Now a museum-house open to the public ... [it] gives not a hint of the six different ghosts that legend has placed in its walls" (Clyne, "Haunting Tales of Westchester Past," *Westchester Magazine*, October 1981, p. 45). Of Cherry Hill near Albany (the site of a famous murder in 1827), she similarly notes: "Now [it is] an impressive housemuseum whose operators would—understandably—rather talk about the building's architecture and artifacts than apparitions" (Clyne, *Hudson Valley Tales and Trails*, p. 281). Another article says: "employees at Sunnyside ... or the Old Dutch Church laugh at the notion of hauntings"; Melanie Eversley, "From Small Source Flow Tall Tales, Great Diversity," *Poughkeepsie Journal*, October 10, 1989, pp. C16–17.

95. Boyd, "Lost Towns of Palisades Park," p. C1.

96. Leslie Boyd, "Return to Doodletown: 25 Years Ago a Ghost Town Was Born in a Dark Valley," Rockland County *Journal-News*, August 17, 1989, p. C1. For more on Doodletown, including a list of articles in local papers, see Elizabeth Stalter, *Doodletown: Hiking through History in a Vanished Hamlet on the Hudson* (Bear Mountain, N.Y.: Palisades Interstate Park Commission, 1996).

97. Boyd, "Lost Towns of Palisades Park," pp. C12, C1.

98. Smith quoted in ibid., p. C12.

99. Jon Livingston, quoted in Boyd, "Return to Doodletown," p. C2.

100. Focht quoted in Boyd, "Lost Towns of Palisades Park," p. C12.

101. Ibid., p. C1.

102. Joseph Berger, "Passions Stir in 'Sleepy Hollow': Debate on Name Change for Prestige and Profit," *New York Times*, October 20, 1996, sec. I,

p. 33. In a vote on December 10, 1996, the measure passed. See other articles on the renaming of North Tarrytown in the *New York Times,* December 11, 1996, p. B2; January 5, 1997, sec. IX, p. 7; and April 20, 1997, sec. XIII–WC, p. 1. Similar contests and questions, of course, rattle in other places. See, for example, Philip G. Terrie, *Contested Terrain: A New History of Nature and People in the Adirondacks* ([Syracuse]: Adirondack Museum/Syracuse University Press, 1997).

103. Kammen, *Mystic Chords of Memory,* p. 10.

Epilogue

Epigraph: T. Coraghessan Boyle, *World's End* (New York: Viking Penguin, 1987), p. 17.

1. See Boyle, *World's End,* chap. 1. Boyle does not here identify the apparition as the Dunderberg Imp, but only describes him. The identification is made by inference through other references to the Imp in the novel.

2. Boyle describes the book as a "historical fugue" on the copyright page. Boyle was born in Peekskill in 1948 and grew up there, leaving to study at the State University of New York, Potsdam. He later joined the University of Iowa Writers' Workshop and received a Ph.D. in English literature. He currently teaches at the University of Southern California. *World's End,* for which he received the PEN/Faulkner Award, was his third novel.

3. Walter's grandmother tells him an Indian legend in which a Mohawk warrior partially devoured the daughter of a Kitchawank chief (Boyle, *World's End,* pp. 4–5). The legend holds that this occurred on the spot where the Van Brunts soon thereafter took up their tenancy, and where the patriarch Van Brunt became afflicted with a mysterious illness that caused him to devour all of the family's winter food stock (pp. 21–24). This idea of a devouring force recurs throughout the novel as characters lose limbs and appendages or are afflicted by moments of insatiable hunger. The dwarf, whom Boyle describes as embodying "the malicious forces of the supernatural" (p. 171), shows up not only in legends and Walter's ghostly visions, but also in apparent flesh in both the seventeenth and twentieth centuries. Although Boyle implies that the imp figure is the incarnation of the preexisting devouring curse on the land (see Harmanus Van Brunt's repetition of the word *pie* in chapter 2), the dwarf's name suggests that he is linked to the Dutch colonization, related to the fictional

Jan Pieterse and to the real Dutchmen Pieter Stuyvesant and Pieter Minuit (the purchaser of Manhattan), both of whom are referenced in the novel as well. Notably, Depeyster Van Wart dresses up as Stuyvesant each Halloween, and his costume is described in the same terms used to describe the Imp, suggesting it is the Van Warts who haunt and destroy the Van Brunts (see ibid., pp. 3, 6, and 363).

4. The riot, which also has overt anti-Semitic and racist aspects, is based on a real incident in Peekskill, which centered on a Paul Robeson concert organized in part by Jewish socialists living nearby. See Michael Kammen, "T. Coraghessan Boyle and *World's End*," in *Novel History: Historians and Novelists Confront the Past (and Each Other)*, ed. Mark C. Carnes (New York: Simon and Schuster, 2001), p. 253.

5. The man with "a head like a pumpkin" (*World's End*, p. 9) is Walter's father, who, like Brom Bones in "The Legend of Sleepy Hollow," is a Van Brunt. Boyle's omniscient third-person narrator allows us to see the bits of folklore various characters carry with them, including *pukwidjinnies* from Native American lore (p. 27); the *loup-garou*, a creature prominent in French-based Louisiana folklore, which makes its way into the novel via African-American characters (p. 65); and Knecht Ruprecht (a trickster figure associated with Saint Nicholas), from Dutch lore (p. 28).

6. Boyle, *World's End*, pp. 115, 14, 6. Jeremias Van Brunt loses his foot on p. 29. The reference to the Kitchawank totem occurs on p. 197, in a scene in which Walter's father has a piece of his ear bitten off by Jeremy Mohonk. The name Jeremy Mohonk also appears on the marker that Walter crashes into.

7. Ibid., pp. 124, 16. The historical marker commemorates the 1693 hanging of a Cadwallader Crane and a Jeremy Mohonk for inciting a riot against the Van Warts. Walter finally learns through his father that one of his ancestors, Wouter (the Dutch equivalent of Walter), was responsible for the act that led to the hanging of the two young men (one of whom—Mohonk—was his "half-breed" cousin), and that Wouter had betrayed them to save his own life. The revelation brings no enlightenment to Walter, although his father sees it as the key to Walter's (and his own) character and fate.

8. For instance, Boyle provides a fictional explanation and identity for what becomes in legend the Wailing Woman, by showing us how in the seventeenth century Katrinchee Van Brunt, daughter of the first Van

Brunt, went mad, and died after wandering out into the snow (ibid., pp. 199–206).

9. For instances and variations, see ibid., pp. 150, 62–63, 66.

10. T. C. Boyle, "History on Two Wheels," in Carnes, *Novel History*, p. 259. Boyle is here affirming a point made by Michael Kammen in an accompanying article.

11. As quoted in Charles Trueheart, "Boyle and His Prized Pursuit," *Washington Post*, April 20, 1988, p. C6. In a *New York Times Book Review* interview, Boyle says of *World's End:* "I wanted to re-invent history; to use it as a point of departure for a meditation on what my life has been, where I came from, what my antecedents and the antecedents of the region I grew up in were"; quoted in Michael Freitag, "Growing Up a Pampered Punk," *New York Times Book Review*, September 27, 1987, p. 53.

12. See Brogan, *Cultural Haunting*, for a discussion of haunting and ethnicity in recent American literature. As Brogan argues, "cultural hauntings" are a major theme in American literature from the 1970s to the 1990s, appearing in works by Toni Morrison, Maxine Hong Kingston, Leslie Marmon Silko, William Kennedy, Bharati Mukherjee, Richard Rodriguez, Oscar Hijuelos, Amy Tan, and many others (see pp. 1–4). See also Theo D'Haen, "The Return of History and the Minorization of New York: T. Coraghessan Boyle and Richard Russo," *Revue française d'études americaines*, no. 62 (November 1994): 393–403.

13. Actually, since Jeremy Mohonk is descended from Van Brunts as well as Kitchawanks, the birth promises both a race-based recovery and a class-based takeover of the Van Wart property.

14. Boyle himself implies this extension by having Walter go to find his father in the "Last American Frontier"–the farthest reach of Alaska–where Walter's father dwells among Eskimos who hate him; *World's End*, pp. 385–396.

15. Ibid., p. 83.